D1555419

Test Policy and Test Performance: Education, Language, and Culture

Evaluation in Education and Human Services

Editors:

George F. Madaus, Boston College, Chestnut
   Hill, MA, U.S.A.
Daniel L. Stufflebeam, Western Michigan
   University, Kalamazoo, MI, U.S.A.

**National Commission on Testing
and Public Policy**

Gifford, B.; *Test Policy and the Politics of
   Opportunity Allocation: The Workplace and
   the Law*

Gifford, B.; *Test Policy and Test Performance:
   Education, Language, and Culture*

Test Policy and Test Performance: Education, Language, and Culture

edited by

Bernard R. Gifford

Graduate School of Education
University of California, Berkeley

Kluwer Academic Publishers
Boston   Dordrecht   London

Distributors for North America:
Kluwer Academic Publishers
101 Philip Drive
Assinippi Park
Norwell, Massachusetts 02061 USA

Distributors for all other countries:
Kluwer Academic Publishers Group
Distribution Centre
Post Office Box 322
3300 AH Dordrecht, THE NETHERLANDS

Library of Congress Cataloging-in-Publication Data

Test policy and test performance : education, language, and culture /
    edited by Bernard R. Gifford.
        p.   cm. — (Evaluation in education and human services series)
      Papers prepared for presentation at a conference which was held at
    the University of California at Berkeley, Dec. 11-13, 1986.
      Includes index.
      ISBN 0–7923–9014–8
      1. Educational tests and measurements—United States—Congresses.
    2. Education and state—United States—Congresses.   3. Test bias—
    United States—Congresses.   4. Educational evaluation—United
    States—Congresses.   I. Gifford, Bernard R.   II. Series.
    LB3051.T42   1989
    371.2′6—dc19   89-2382
                                                                      CIP

Printed in the United States of America

Contents

Contributing Authors

Eva L. Baker, Professor, Director, Center for the Study of Evaluation, Co-director, Center for Research on Evaluation, Standards, and Student Testing, University of California, Los Angeles

Edward Haertel, Associate Professor, School of Education, Stanford University, Stanford, California

Walter M. Haney, Professor, Department of Education, Boston College, Chestnut Hill, Massachusetts

George Hanford, President Emeritus, The College Board, New York, New York

Christopher Jencks, Professor, Center for Urban Affairs and Policy Research, Northwestern University, Evanston, Illinois

Thomas Kochman, Professor, Department of Communication and Theater, University of Illinois at Chicago Circle, Chicago, Illinois

George F. Madaus, Professor and Director, The Center for the Study of Testing, Evaluation, and Educational Policy, Department of Education, Boston College, Chestnut Hill, Massachusetts

William A. Mehrens, Professor, Department of Counseling, Educational Psychology, and Special Education, Michigan State University, East Lansing, Michigan

Elsie G. J. Moore, Associate Professor, Department of Counselor Education, Arizona State University, Tempe, Arizona

Mary Catherine O'Connor, Postdoctoral Research Linguist, National Commission on Testing and Public Policy, University of California, Berkeley

Chui Lim Tsang, Executive Director, Career Resources Development Center, Inc., San Francisco, California

Guadalupe Valdés, Professor, Graduate School of Education, University of California, Berkeley

Introduction

Bernard R. Gifford

In the United States, the standardized test has become one of the major sources of information for reducing uncertainty in the determination of individual merit and in the allocation of merit-based educational, training, and employment opportunities. Most major institutions of higher education require applicants to supplement their records of academic achievements with scores on standardized tests. Similarly, in the workplace, as a condition of employment or assignment to training programs, more and more employers are requiring prospective employees to sit for standardized tests. In short, with increasing frequency and intensity, individual members of the political economy are required to transmit to the opportunity marketplace scores on standardized examinations that purport to be objective measures of their abilities, talents, and potential. In many instances, these test scores are the only signals about their skills that job applicants are permitted to send to prospective employers.

THE NATIONAL COMMISSION ON TESTING AND PUBLIC POLICY

In view of the importance of these issues to our current national agenda, it was proposed that the Human Rights and Governance and the Education and Culture Programs of the Ford Foundation support the establishment of a "blue ribbon" National Commission on Testing and Public Policy to investigate some of the major problems, as well as the untapped opportunities, created by recent trends in the use of standardized tests, particularly in the workplace and in schools. The commission's charter is to conduct a systematic, *policy-oriented analysis* of these issues, particularly the role that standardized tests — as measures of individual merit and as predictors of future classroom and workplace performance—play in the allocation of educational, training, and employment opportunities.

The three primary objectives of the National Commission on Testing and Public Policy are:

1. To conduct a comprehensive survey of the array of policy- relevant issues and problems resulting from the growing use of standardized paper-and-pencil tests in the allocation of educational, training, and employment opportunities in the United States today, identifying and explicating a critical subset of these issues that can reasonably be expected to yield to a thorough, interdisciplinary policy analysis;

2. To commission and coordinate the work of experts from a variety of disciplines in the analysis of select issues isolated in the first phase, particularly

those that promise to yield suggestions for eliminating some of the more problematic aspects of testing; and to issue policy-sensitive recommendations that might inform and influence future directions in testing research, practice, and policy; and

3. To prepare and disseminate materials resulting from the first and second phases, designing them for and directing them to audiences with a strong interest in the proper use of tests to allocate educational, training, and employment opportunities. This dissemination objective is particularly important because to make changes in current test policies and practices requires effective communication and collaboration within and between different groups of discipline-based testing experts; non-expert test users; policymakers in education, training, and employment; and representatives of interest groups that have traditionally been excluded from technical and policy debates about the uses and consequences of testing.

In accomplishing these objectives, the commission will focus on a set of five main issues chosen because they call for consideration both of the functional role of testing within employment, training, and educational institutions, and of the social consequences of testing in the society as a whole.

1. The political, social, and economic logics of testing in opportunity allocation: What kinds of political, social, and economic assumptions, objectives, and constraints influence test makers and test users in the construction and administration of tests and in the interpretation and use of test scores?

2. The role of law and regulation in resolving testing conflicts: What are the possibilities and limitations of preventing and/or ameliorating testing conflicts through regulation and litigation?

3. Language, culture, and standardized tests: What is the current state of testing research and development with respect to a) the improved design of tests administered to individuals from language minority backgrounds; b) more informed interpretation of the scores of examinees from language minority backgrounds on existing standardized tests; and c) increasing understanding of the differential performance of majority and minority populations on standardized tests?

4. General versus specific functions and methods of testing and assessment: What are the problems and opportunities associated with the use of general ability tests, compared to the advantages and disadvantages of assessing specific skills in specific contexts using devices such as subject matter achievement tests, essays, biodata questionnaires, assessment centers, work samples, and the like?

5. Future directions in testing and assessment: How will factors such as recent advances in cognitive science, technological developments, and the growing linguistic and cultural diversity of the population affect the instruments and the methods by which educators and employers identify

talent and find the best fit between students and educational opportunities, and between workers and training and job opportunities?

CONTENTS OF THIS VOLUME

This is the second volume in a two-volume set that is the first in a series of works to appear under the aegis of the National Commission on Testing and Public Policy. The papers were prepared for presentation at a conference to plan the commission, which took place at the University of California at Berkeley on December 11-13, 1986. Experts in a number of fields relevant to testing policy contributed significantly to the shaping of the commission's aims. Each section is composed of papers focusing on a particular area of interest; in addition to the formal papers, several sections contain written versions of informal remarks presented at the conference.

The papers in the first section, "Tests as Tools of Educational Policy: Theory, Attribution, and Belief," directly address the complex configuration of federal, state, and local policy objectives; special interest goals; and testing practices that have emerged over the last decade in the United States. All the authors are significant participants in the field of educational testing and policy, and most share the opinions that a) test use is increasing due to a growing desire to gain political control of educational practice and have easily accessible indicators of accountability; b) much of this policy-driven test use, although instituted in the cause of educational reform, is not based upon a real understanding of the strengths and limitations of testing and may lead to undesired consequences; and c) professional standards for test use are not sufficient barriers to illegitimate uses of educational testing.

In the second section, "Tests in Educational Decision Making: Psychometric and Political Boundary Conditions," we find three papers that have different but complementary views of tests, and how decisions are made using test data. From the measurement perspective, we learn first how test-based decisions should be made—in the ideal setting, there is an acceptable fit between the function of the test, the model of decision making, and the inferences that may be drawn from the test scores. Next we are presented with a sociological perspective on the societal risks of using alternatives to standardized testing in educational decision making. Finally, informal remarks from the perspective of a leader of a major test-using organization point us toward a number of problematic issues in test-related decision making, issues that have persisted over many years and that have yet to be resolved.

The last section of this volume, "Language, Culture, Ethnicity, and Testing," contains papers on issues that have provoked some of the most stringent criticisms of the institution of standardized testing. Each paper approaches the issues of language, culture, race, ethnicity, and testing from a different angle. We are first given a review of previous research on the *sources* of differential test performance between minorities and others, along with suggestions for new avenues of research. Next is a study of the *outcomes* of standardized test performance among a national sample of American youth, and the possible career consequences for the minority groups in the study. The third paper in this section describes a case study of the successful collaboration of scholars and public sector agencies on the development of language proficiency tests for specialized occupations that require bilingual competencies. Finally, two papers consider the communicative and behavioral style differences between Anglos and, respectively, Asian Americans and African Americans. In informal assessments, these style differences can become crucial.

ACKNOWLEDGEMENTS

There are a number of people who contributed to the efforts that culminated in this volume. Lynn Walker, Deputy Director of the Human Rights and Governance Program of the Ford Foundation, committed the funds for the planning and execution of the conference on which this volume is based. Linda C. Wing organized the conference program and played a major role in coordinating the editing and production of this volume. Catherine O'Connor assisted in the review and substantive editing of the papers. Suzanne Chun and Mary Lou Sumberg served as able copy editors. Word processing and technical assistance were efficiently provided by Mandy Rasmussen, Alissa Shethar, Nancy Vasquez, and Darren Wong.

I

TESTS AS TOOLS OF EDUCATIONAL POLICY: THEORY, ATTRIBUTION, AND BELIEF

Mandated Tests: Educational Reform or Quality Indicator?

Eva L. Baker

INTRODUCTION

The thesis of this chapter is that achievement tests no longer function primarily as indicators of educational accomplishments. In addition, they have become instruments of educational policy and are regarded as effective means to alter educational achievement and productivity. I will explore this assertion by using examples of research and development from state and national testing activities. I will also consider how these alternative functions affect system behavior, legitimate policy inferences, technical requirements of tests, and ultimately our understanding of educational quality.

BACKGROUND

Educational testing has long been with us, but recently has demanded new attention as states and the federal government have increased both their investment in and their attention to the problem of measuring educational achievement. The function of tests used to be straightforward: to find out what some person knew or could do. We all took tests of this sort in school. These tests were most often idiosyncratic in design, made up by one or more teachers. Such tests might have seemed formal or even frightening to students, but their creation was informal; teachers determined their content and the standards used for their scoring. Even bureaucratically entrenched and successful tests, such as the New York State Regents Examinations, were reasonably flexible in that they were developed by teams of teachers and test writers and changed annually to reflect transitions and modifications in the curriculum.

The intellectual roots of standardized testing have been well documented (Coleman, Cronbach, and Suppes 1987). Driven by pressing national needs to make personnel decisions during wartime, the mechanics of test design, administration, and analysis became more refined, more esoteric, and in turn, more credible to a technologically oriented society.

For example, test-based selection for admission to colleges and universities using the Scholastic Aptitude Test (SAT), has been a regular part of students' experience for the last forty years. Yet, many regard the SAT as an end rather than as a tool. When SAT scores declined (see Harnischfeger and Wiley 1975, and Wirtz 1977 for analyses), inferences were drawn about school effectiveness, even though the SAT was never designed to measure whether educational programs were meeting their goals. The concurrent rise in the minimum competency test movement, where students need to pass examinations on certain basic skills for graduation from high school or even for grade-to-grade promotion, moved testing squarely into the mainstream of American policy options (Jaeger and Tittle 1980). In minimum competency programs, in the 1970s in particular, the test triggered a variety of policies that dramatically changed the rules (Lazarus 1981). The goal became appropriate test performance by almost any means necessary, and, at first, at almost any cost, including long-term effects on children (Cohen and Haney 1980; Kennedy 1980). The most recent phase of testing involves a conceptual extension of the idea of minimum competency to content and skills purportedly demonstrating higher levels of subject matter competence (see the positions of Hirsch 1987, and Finn and Ravitch 1987), extending the notion of competency from minimal to optimal—but more about this topic later.

THE POLICY ATTRACTIVENESS OF TESTING

Even though the testing of students and teachers remains controversial and is occasionally the subject of litigation and judicial review, many policymakers in school districts, state houses, and at the federal level continue to see higher standards as the cornerstone of educational reform efforts, and tests as their operational implementation. Why? Even as the phrase "There are no quick fixes" grows more popular in our rhetoric, we still continue our search for the chimera. Testing is assumed to be a relatively expedient remedy and continues to attract policy proponents, who are in turn supported by a well-connected commercial testing industry.

What is it that testing seems to offer? I believe that testing suggests a wealth of metaphors, the strongest one based on the image of good management. Testing provides a "We mean business" lever on the efficiency and effectiveness of educational organizations and provides a mechanism that promises to demonstrate how schools can be made more efficient (see, for example, Kirst 1981, 61). In the simplest terms, testing sends the message that schools (and the funds that support them) can be managed. Thus, testing offers a convenient way to communicate that is backed by sanctions. The contents of a test say, "This is important! Pay attention!" Societal ascriptions of test importance stem from how tests are interpreted by policymakers and the public. The stability of this perceived importance may turn out to be independent of how effective tests actually are in improving educational quality.

Tests cost money, but their costs are relatively small compared to options such as adding teachers or investing heavily in staff development to update teachers' content knowledge and pedagogical skills. Tests may not, in fact, be a quick fix; but they may be a cheaper option than grass-roots restructuring and reform. And they are tangible. Educational reform often deals in ideas and concepts whose distinctions are not well understood by the public. Recall, for instance, the public furor over "New Math." Tests almost magically avoid such confusion. Everyone knows what a test is. Furthermore, tests may be one of the few options that can be imposed top-down (from the state house, for instance) and that appear to have an effect on our diverse educational settings. And as tests become policy instruments, with public political investments behind them, it is not too surprising that their findings take on more importance to those who require them.

TESTS AS INDICATORS

When tests are seen as one component of a system of outcome measures or indicators, rather than as the creators of effects, how we attend to them differs dramatically. In some ways, the differences are paradoxical, and depend upon the conditions under which the test results are actually used.

For example, if a test is seen as a policy device ("Teach this because it is important"), then that which does not appear on the test loses credibility and currency in the school environment. If tests do not include science, then science (or art, or music, or history) may not be taught seriously.[1] If tests are seen, however, as one of many indicators of data that bear on educational quality *but do not define it*, then our teaching and curriculum do not hinge as precariously on what those tests indicate. The arguments for test-driven education (Popham 1974) are persuasive, but I believe they can ultimately decrease the long-range stability of an educational system designed to improve performance of all students. For when tests are intended not only to measure the effects of particular reforms, but are the reforms themselves, the interpretation of positive and negative patterns of growth are extremely problematic. Interpretations of increases or decreases in performance are confusing. (Note, however, that increases in performance are not studied too diligently; they are usually accepted and attributed to the most recent set of reforms.) Was the test successful in communicating new standards? Were the programs and instruction inferior? Are there any data conditions under which the policy of testing is itself questioned? Another difficulty results from the logical interest in looking at tests over time, to infer trends of various sorts for policy action. Such trend analyses place content constraints and technical requirements on measurement that limit the real match between what are or could be important educational goals and what we, some years earlier, made a

---

[1] The Center for Research on Evaluation, Standards, and Student Testing (CRESST) is currently conducting research to assess the impact of teaching.

commitment to measure. Unless these concerns are explicitly accounted for, they can only impede our understanding of educational quality.

I believe that we are now in a phase in which tests are changing from indicators to policy instruments. This transformation is caused partly by the staunch belief of many decisionmakers in the validity or "hardness" of measurement data, and partly by the insidious proposition submerged in the notion of testing as policy: If it isn't tested, it isn't important. When a system explicitly attempts to measure all the important areas of schooling—a task at which it can never succeed—the requirement for inclusiveness damages the entire educational enterprise and unbalances schooling. Part of the damage is caused because tests as policy instruments are almost always indirect. Teachers are tested because the quality of their selection and the preparation they receive at colleges and professional schools of education is doubted, or because a way is sought to influence them. Children are tested because we are not sure teachers know how to teach them. Tests run downhill from the issue that we really wish to influence and often onto the people who are the recipients rather than the instigators of the suspect policies.

MAPS OF STATE TESTING

In this section, I propose to shift from a general position statement on test functions to a relatively detailed description of the topography of state testing. I will report on state testing activities at a particular point in time, and attempt to provide a snapshot of some of the intense activities in testing at the state level. The purpose of this description is to show what is being tested where, what investments are being made, and to set the stage for a following section that demonstrates how our educational system responds to such mandates.

The impetus for state-level testing was multiple, but can undoubtedly be attributed to the changes in funding for education derived from the *Serrano v. Priest* decision. This case considered the state's responsibility to "equalize" educational expenditures across districts with different property-tax bases, and preempted responsibility on matters of accountability from local agencies. Moreover, the retreat from programmatic federal action in education that began with the Reagan administration lodged additional power and initiative at the state level. Testing programs, already in place in California, Florida, and New York, became the focus of much new state activity.

How widespread was this activity? Let's start with a time period following the release of *A Nation At Risk* (National Commission on Excellence in Education 1983), the U.S. Department of Education report that undoubtedly stimulated much state-level reform. At the end of 1984, thirty-nine states were operating at least one statewide testing program. Thirty-five states were conducting "assessment programs" to monitor the overall effects of educational services in the state in terms of student achievement. Thirty-six states were operating minimum competency testing (MCT) programs. Twenty-two states had both assessment and MCT programs. These data were developed as part of a major study conducted by researchers at the University of California at Los Angeles on the feasibility of using existing state achievement data to provide a picture of national student achievement (Burstein, Baker, Aschbacher, and Keesling 1985). This study clearly demonstrated that a major investment had been made in testing. The rest of this section will draw upon this study as its primary source of information.

Who Gets Tested?

Who were the students tested? What were state testing programs like? Testing in states focused on eighth grade, with a total of thirty-two programs testing at this level. Other frequently tested grades were three, four, six, ten, and eleven. Least frequently tested were grades one, two, seven, and twelve. At the time of the report, twenty-four of the states were testing all students at the target grade level(s)—census testing—and as one would expect, all competency programs tested every eligible student. Most states with testing programs tested children in more than one grade.

What other information was collected about the students? The most frequently obtained data were about students' sex and ethnicity, although about one-third of the reporting states did not require such information. Language status and program participation, for example, Chapter 1, were information items collected by a relatively few states. Peculiarly, student age and years in school were of interest to only one or two states.

What Is on the Tests?

What content was tested? In almost every case, reading and mathematics were tested. Fewer than half the states giving tests conducted writing assessments, using student essays as the data. But more than half tested in at least one additional content area, such as social studies, science, or language arts. This research also reports a detailed set of analyses that focused on test content. These analyses were developed by carefully categorizing the items on actual copies of these tests, or, in some cases where test security was an issue, by inspecting the test specifications and sample test items. The research team first developed a model to guide our analyses, consisting of a relatively flat hierarchy of major skills and subskills (see figure 1). Based on this kind of analysis, major skill categories were developed for reading, mathematics, and writing (see figure 2).

FIGURE 1

Relations Among Content Areas,
Major Skill Areas, and Subskills

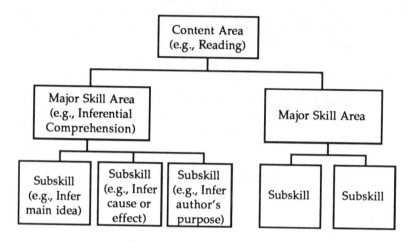

FIGURE 2

Major Skill Areas Exhibited in State Testing Items

Reading	Mathematics	Writing
Inferential Comprehension	Numbers and Numeration	Grammar
Literal Comprehension	Measurement	Word Usage
Vocabulary	Variables	Organization
Word Attack Sample	Geometry	Writing

Leigh Burstein recently created a graphic display of this distribution and a quick review of figure 3 will give a good picture of the distribution of skills by content area and grade level tested.

FIGURE 3
Distribution of State Tested Skills by Content,
Skill Level, Grade Tested, and State

	Reading				Math				Writing			
State	1-3	4-6	7-9	10-12	1-3	4-6	7-9	10-12	1-3	4-6	7-9	10-12
AL												
AK												
AZ												
AR												
CA												
CO												
CT												
DE												
FL												
GA												
HI												
ID												
IL												
IN												
IA												
KS												
KY												
LA												
ME												
MD												
MA												
MI												
MN												
MS												
MO												

Legend:

Inferential Comprehension — Numbers & Numeration — Word Usage

Literal Comprehension — Measure — Grammar

Vocabulary — Variables — Organization

Word Attack — Geometry — Writing Sample

None of the Above — None of the Above — None of the Above

No Data

FIGURE 3, (continued)
Distribution of State Tested Skills by Content,
Skill Level, Grade Tested, and State

The team's analysis was more intensive.[2] Analysis of the skill areas was decomposed into an additional level, consisting of subskills, and examples of the type of items measuring such subskills were provided. In Appendix 1 an example of the inferential comprehension tasks in reading is presented.

Using this analytical framework, the distribution of state efforts was categorized according to the range of topics covered, the "spread" of items across subskills, the depth of coverage within subskills, or how many items, and the distribution of items on subskills classified as higher-order skills, or skills with cognitive demands of inference, application, or problem solving as opposed to mere information retrieval by students. Eleven states were found to have relatively broad subskill coverage. In depth of coverage, only California had many items for each subskill area, a phenomenon directly related to California's matrix sampling approach. (Many items for many skill areas on a census test would create a time and fatigue burden for students.) In other states, depth was a function of topic and grade level tested. About one-third of the states included higher-order test items in their testing programs. This analysis was used to help identify the commonality of tested skills and was, in fact, conducted as part of a feasibility study to examine aggregation of state tests to serve as a national indicator of school achievement.

In 1987, the Office of Technology Assessment (OTA) provided an update on the grade, general content area, and ancillary data collected in state assessments. Because their data collection was within six months of the UCLA study, no major changes emerged. The OTA report did include some snapshots of state testing policy history and plans from a sample of eight states. What is striking is that in almost every case, the move is toward more testing—in more grade levels, for more subject matters, for more students.

California cites plans for consolidation of local and state measures to meet this state goal (Bennett and Carlson 1986). In addition, the institution of the Golden State Examinations aims to provide individual incentives for students to achieve higher standards, standards that will be demonstrated by taking appropriate tests. Successful students will receive special recognition on their diploma. California also uses a cash incentive program to encourage schools to raise scores on their twelfth-grade California Assessment Program (CAP) scores. The policy investment in this approach is high:

> Standardized tests are expected to focus the attention of educators and policymakers at all levels on the knowledge, skills, concepts, and processes which are essential for success in the more demanding high-tech job market of the future, for responsible citizenship, and for personal fulfillment. The core of content and skills to be spotlighted represents a rigorous

---

[2] This work was primarily conducted by Pamela Aschbacher.

curriculum in the humanities, natural sciences, and math, and emphasizes higher-order skills such as those required to analyze complex relationships, draw inferences, and reason deductively. Although it is assumed that in practice, the scope and pace of the curriculum will reflect differences in aptitude and intelligence . . . it is also assumed that the majority of students are not working up to their potential, and that it is the responsibility of the schools to challenge them to do so—both for their own good and for the good of the society. (Bennett and Carlson 1986, 169)

The Colorado state testing summary shows what happens when a test without a history of large-scale assessment is used (Martin 1987). Colorado's approach is still at a very general level compared to recent efforts in California, Illinois, or in the southeastern states. Nonetheless, during Colorado policymakers' deliberation, the tendency to use such tests as an omnibus solution to all problems arose. We specifically talked with policymakers on the costs and benefits of using such measures as indicators of teaching performance. We also have been observing other state efforts that attempt to generalize the use of student-testing measures to teacher assessment, that is, to see student scores as indicators of teacher competency, an approach that is clearly a bad idea on conceptual and technical grounds.

SYSTEMIC RESPONSES TO TESTS AS THE CONVEYORS OF STANDARDS

In this section, I wish to recount briefly the findings of some of my colleagues at the Center for Research on Evaluation, Standards, and Student Testing (CRESST). One of our three research programs is studying the impact of testing on educational quality. We wanted to find out if having such standards and tests (as created by recent state and local reform efforts) helps or hurts the educational system. One question was whether tests such as those required for high school graduation have positive or negative effects. James Catterall (1987) has reported on a study of those ten states with four or more years of a high school graduation test requirement. Interviews with educators were obtained that described their analysis of the function of such tests. Catterall went on to select two states with the highest and two with the lowest graduation rates. A survey was administered to 736 students sampled from within three representative districts in each state. On the basis of his survey, Catterall predicts that dropping out is significantly related to failure on such competency tests, and finds an interaction for Hispanic students. Socioeconomic class as well as "track" in school are also strong predictors. Furthermore, such relationships were "invisible" in his terms to the school personnel interviewed. If his findings are confirmed, then the role of tests as the conveyors of standards may need some review. Clearly, we can improve overall performance by driving out poorly performing students. But such a function is diametric to our intentions.

The second study, on the Texas Examination of Current Administrators and Teachers (TECAT), was conducted by Lorrie Shepard, a CRESST researcher from the University of Colorado. Shepard, Krietzer, and Graue (1987) looked extensively at the TECAT from its policy inception to the results and remedies that resulted from its administration. The TECAT was designed to identify teachers and administrators not qualified to serve in educational roles.

Shepard and her team cast the impetus for the TECAT in the context of the need to revitalize the state economy. Shepard traces the roles of the newly elected governor, as well as the head of the state task force on schooling, H. Ross Perot, a successful technologist. The timing of the *Nation at Risk* report was also critical. Shepard points out the TECAT was a literacy test measuring precollege abilities and writing skills, with "harsh consequences" (Shepard, Kreitzer, and Graue 1987, 87), since failing the test twice resulted in loss of job. The process of preparing for this test was reported by Shepard and seemed to focus on succeeding at the particular test items included, and not on reducing the kinds of grammatical errors ("he don't") that partly instigated public support in the first place. The TECAT had a passing rate of 99 percent. Because the standards were set so low, teachers could make a few flagrant errors and still pass. Moreover, the people the test "identified" may have been "real losses" to the system, such as those who worked with the mentally retarded, shop teachers who had not been certified through the usual means, and minority teachers. The test actually failed "1,199 teachers with some of the worst grammar skills. It may also have forced out another 1,000 to 2,000 teachers who considered themselves at risk on the test" (Shepard, Kreitzer, and Graue 1987, 89). The authors conclude that the TECAT harmed public opinion about education and involved a set of:

> . . . unforeseen consequences: enormous cost, frenetic preparation and worrying about the test, demoralized teachers, and a public disillusioned by the high pass rate. Although these outcomes were not intended, they may be inevitable features of a reform that hangs so much importance on a test pitched to the lowest level of performance on the lowest of teaching skills. (p. 91).

The work of Shepard and her associates suggests that intentions are insufficient to assure positive use and interpretation of test results. Rudner (1987) reports on the status of teacher testing in forty-four states. His analyses suggest that the "impact of such tests on minorities has been severe" (p. 5). In a paper by Algina and Legg (1987), the validity and technical decision process is criticized. Given the demonstrable negative effects and potential validity problems, teacher tests as approaches to reform should be more carefully scrutinized.

Finally, Ellwein and Glass (1986), in a study conducted for CRESST, presented a series of case studies of standard-setting using tests. In a shorter version of this study (Glass and Ellwein 1986), the authors briefly summarize the six case studies, which investigated four states and two local districts. By analyzing the intentions of such programs, in contrast to their operations and effects, the authors generate a devastating set of summary observations:

1. When standards on tests are raised, safety nets are strung up (in the form of exemptions, repeated trials, softening cut-scores, tutoring for retests, and the like) to catch those who fail. If 100 incompetent persons enter the arena, 99 will ultimately survive. The one who doesn't was probably no less able than many, but lost heart and quit.

2. Both the courts and professional educators honor the principle that students should be warned of impending standards and remediated when they fail.

3. Even the most orthodox and doctrinaire justification of cut-scores in terms of skills and competence is moderated in the end by consideration of pass-fail rates. Norm referencing drives out criterion referencing. Pre-criterion referencing exists only in textbooks and scholarly journals; it is not found in the world of practice.

4. People focus on first-test failure rates and are less interested in ultimate failure rates.

5. In raising educational standards, the more technical-looking approach packs more political muscle. The language of arbitrary authority is despised. The language of technical rationality is widely honored.

6. Cut-score determination methods require the added authority of political symbols for their credibility (titles, political composition of groups of judges, technical authority such as Educational Testing Service)—these symbols are invoked to lend authority to what is actually a quite arbitrary procedure.

7. Managers of the educational system will act to soften the hard edges of technology and reclaim political discretion that has been appropriated by zealous technologists (in this case, technologists who would turn over the responsibility for determining who graduates from high school or is licensed to teach to a test and a statistical standard).

8. Universities are raising standards, in part as an attempt to get out of the business of remedial instruction. But in a showdown, excellence comes in second to economics; competence loses out to enrollments.

9. In the end, standards are determined by consideration of politically and economically acceptable pass rates, symbolic messages and appearances, and scarcely influenced by a behavioral analysis of necessary skills and competencies. The latter are relied on to the exclusion of the former to the extent that passing or failing the test has no lasting consequences in the lives of either students or teachers. (Glass and Ellwein 1986, 4)

Glass and Ellwein distinguish between instrumental and symbolic acts, and place testing and standard reform squarely in the symbolic category. As testing has shifted from something integral to instruction to a "policy" imposed from outside, it appears to have lost much of its assumed power. The authors conclude with a set of questions about standards and testing:

1. What purposes and political interests are served by raised standards? Whatever they are, we suspect they have little to do with the accomplishments and chances for "life success" of the pupils in whose name the reforms are undertaken.

2. What effect is the movement having on schools, teachers, and the way pupils learn? Schools may be winning renewed public confidence. Teachers are bearing the brunt of both the blame for the crisis that brought about the reforms and the busy work that the reforms have engendered. Pupils take what is dished out and move on. (Glass and Ellwein 1986, 5–6)

THE NATIONAL TESTING SCENE

The questions above and the analyses by Catterall, Shepard et al., and Glass and Ellwein have growing salience in light of a series of interesting policy deliberations related to the federal role in testing. The National Assessment of Educational Progress (NAEP) was created as an indicator system (Tyler 1966). However, the attempt by the Department of Education to create a national picture of educational performance with its infamous "wall chart" has begun to transform NAEP from an indicator to a reform instrument. The wall chart used college entrance examinations such as the SAT to rank states on outcomes from best to worse without regard for socioeconomics, mobility, or student ethnicity. Chief state school officers attempted to argue for more valid measures (instead of against the entire enterprise). In fact, there was a short-term benefit from the rankings because they permitted arguing for greater resources from state legislatures, for reforms, and so forth. Subsequently, a broadly composed group of scholars and practitioners reviewed NAEP (Alexander and James 1986). Part of their deliberations involved the redesign of NAEP to extend its sampling, reporting, and interpretation to the fifty states. Thus, rankings or other measures of relative state performance would be possible. A series of discussions, planning activities, and now proposed legislation are moving this process along. While such a system would undoubtedly be an improvement over the SAT score base for state comparisons, the use of NAEP for such a function raises serious issues of the sort raised earlier in this chapter and by my colleagues cited above.

State-by-state reporting would change NAEP from an indicator to a policy instrument because states would undoubtedly attempt to increase their relative standing. The existence of such a salient national measure has other implications as well. First, the fifty states would have to agree on the content and skills tested. Clearly, to avoid making inappropriate inferences, states would want NAEP to conform as closely as possible to their historical testing programs. If accurate, such a desire would drop content to the lowest common denominator. Second, the desire for trend data would tend to hinder the addition of new approaches to testing or to the addition or substitution of content areas. Third, the creation of such a test would result in a *de facto* national test and curriculum. While some claim that a national curriculum created by the test publishing companies is already in place, the federalizing of standards through testing raises an alternative set of questions.

Further, a consequence of the adoption of NAEP (with supplemental state funding) as a proxy state educational outcome measure would be to reduce existing state assessment programs, since they will compete for some of the same funds. Thus, diversity will diminish. Under these conditions, a number of the concerns articulated by Shepard and Glass and Ellwein come into play.

Another set of concerns involves national policy. A large investment in NAEP may reduce the actual support for other indicators of national achievement, such as the studies of comparative U.S. performance conducted through the International Education Association (IEA) and supported by both government and private foundations. If NAEP becomes the measure of performance, then it will be used to assess the effectiveness of a range of educational policies. The danger of using a single measure is that it can produce anomalous results, as has been demonstrated in the recent difficulty in the 1986 NAEP reading scores (Rothman 1988).

Without doubt, the functions of tests will continue to evolve. We can hope that continued, parallel research analysis of their actual functions will be a regular part of the implementation or strong modification of any of the major testing programs. Tests as metaphors, signs, and symbols are important, but no less important are their actual effects on educational quality and on the people who participate in our educational system.

APPENDIX 1

Decomposition into Subskills and Items for the Inferential
Comprehension Skill Area in Reading

1. DETAILS, SUPPORT STATEMENTS

(Given passage)
Which statement best supports James Lee's claim that the late bus would benefit students?
a. The school board should find a way to resume the services of the late bus
b. Extracurricular activities provide students with valuable learning experiences
c. Some students can get rides from their parents
d. Some working parents cannot take their children home from school

2. MAIN IDEA, SUMMARY, TITLE

(Given passage, infer best title, summary statement, title)
The main idea of these rules is that:
a. both adults and children enjoy the swimming pool
b. there is a snack bar at the swimming pool
c. safety is extremely important at the swimming pool
d. the swimming pool is open every day

3. MISSING/ IRRELEVANT INFORMATION

(Given passage, infer missing information or identify important information to include or exclude)
Which of the following would be most important for the editors to include in this editorial?
a. The school has never given the band any money for its uniforms
b. Helmets and padding protect football players from injury
c. Members of the marching band perform indoor concerts too
d. The football team has longer practices than the marching band

4. MISSING WORDS   (Given reading passage with several words
                      omitted, identify best word to fit in blank
                      from context)
                      (Note: New York's entire reading test was like this.)

5. SEQUENCE   (Given a passage, infer order of events or
                      logic)
                      What indicates that Minnie was the first in her
                      neighborhood to have a sewing machine?
                      a. The neighbor women all came to see it
                      b. She had to make everyone's clothes
                      c. Fred bought it
                      d. She didn't know how to operate it at first

6. CAUSE/EFFECT   (Given passage, infer cause or effect)
                      A major reason Paramount Studio moved to
                      California was to:
                      a. allow the Army to use the Astoria plant
                      b. avoid the destruction of the studio by
                          vandals
                      c. enable the Astoria plant to become a
                          museum
                      d. be able to make movies less expensively

7. CONCLUSIONS   (Given passage, chart, etc., draw conclusions)
                      Based on the information in this chart, it may
                      be concluded that:
                      a. cross-ventilation helps to warm a room
                      b. gas heat is more expensive than electric
                          heat
                      c. fans use very little electricity
                      d. insulating walls conserve energy all year
                          round

8. PREDICTIONS   (Given a passage, predict probable outcome)
                      What probably happened next in this story?
                      a. The girl became angry and went home
                      b. Marina and the girl told each other their
                          names
                      c. The girl made fun of Marina
                      d. Marina became embarrassed and stopped
                          talking

9. FACT/OPINION

(Given passage or statement, distinguish fact from opinion)
Which of the following is an example of an opinion?
a. "In 1860, a midwestern stagecoach company let people know about an exciting new plan."
b. "The mail must go through."
c. "The route cut directly across from Missouri to Sacramento."
d. "Each rider rode nonstop for about 100 miles."

10. PURPOSE, ATTITUDE

(Given passage, infer author's purpose or attitude)
The author's attitude toward the Pony Express riders can best be described as one of
a. confusion
b. amusement
c. worship
d. admiration

11. CHARACTER

(Given passage, identify character traits, identify motivations, draw conclusions about character's feelings)
The beasts and birds can best be described as
a. proud and closed-minded
b. understanding and wise
c. sleepy and lazy
d. thrifty, hard-working

12. FIGURATIVE LANGUAGE

(Given passage, identify meaning of metaphor, simile, idiom, or other image or figure of speech used)

The author's choice of words "sets up business" and "cleaning station" are used to show that

a. the wrasse's means of getting food is almost like a business service
b. wrasse fishing is big business
c. all fish set up stations
d. the wrasse enjoys cleaning itself in the water

13. TONE

(Given passage, recognize mood)

At the beginning of the story, the mood is one of

a. disappointment and sorrow
b. curiosity and excitement
c. fear and suspense
d. thankfulness and joy

14. COMPARE/ CONTRAST

(Given passage, infer similarities, differences)

Compared to American managers, Japanese baseball managers are

a. better advisors
b. better paid
c. more knowledgeable
d. more powerful

15. ORGANIZATION

(Given passage, select portion to complete outline or organizer based on organization of passage)

The following outline is based upon the last paragraph of the passage. Which topic below is needed to complete it?

I.

   A. Federalists
   B. Republicans
      a. Competing parties
      b. Jefferson's rivals
      c. Election pay-offs
      d. Strong governments

16. SETTING,
    PLOT DIALOGUE

(Given passage, identify and interpret time, place of story or event)
You can tell that his story took place
a. in a city park
b. at a zoo
c. in a forest
d. near a boot factory

17. TYPE OF
    LITERATURE

(Given passage, recognize example of fiction, nonfiction, biography, autobiography, similes, metaphors, etc.)
The reading selection appears to be an example of
a. an autobiographical account
b. historical fiction
c. a biographical sketch
d. ancient mythology

REFERENCES

Alexander, L., and H. T. James. 1987. *The nation's report card: Improving the assessment of student achievement.* Cambridge, MA: National Academy of Education.

Algina, J., and S. M. Legg. 1987. Technical issues. In *What's happening in teacher testing: An analysis of state teacher testing practices,* ed. L. M. Rudner. Washington, DC: Office of Educational Research and Improvement.

Bennett, S. M., and D. Carlson. 1986. A brief history of state testing policies in California. In *State educational testing practices.* Office of Technology Assessment. Washington, DC: Office of Technology Assessment.

Burstein, L. 1986. *Educational quality indicators in the United States: Latest developments* (Draft deliverable, OERI Grant G-86-0003). Los Angeles: UCLA Center for the Study of Evaluation.

Burstein, L., E. L. Baker, P. Aschbacher, and J. W. Keesling. 1985. *Using state test data for national indicators of education quality: A feasibility study* (Final report, NIE Grant G-83-001). Los Angeles: UCLA Center for the Study of Evaluation.

Burstein, L., E. L. Baker, R. Linn, and P. Aschbacher. 1987. *Study group on pre-collegiate education quality indicators* (Final report, OERI grant G-86-0003). Los Angeles: UCLA Center for the Study of Evaluation.

Catterall, J. S. 1987. *Competency tests and school dropouts: Results of national study* (Draft deliverable, OERI grant G-86-0003). Los Angeles: UCLA Center for the Study of Evaluation.

Cohen, D. K., and W. Haney. 1980. Minimums, competency testing, and social policy. In *Minimum competency achievement testing: Motives, models, measures, and consequences,* ed. R. M. Jaeger and C. K. Tittle. Berkeley, CA: McCutchan Publishing Corporation.

Coleman, S., L. J. Cronbach, and P. Suppes. 1987. *Research for tomorrow's schools: A disciplined inquiry for education.* New York: MacMillan.

Ellwein, M. C., and G. V. Glass. 1986. *Standards of competence: A multi-site case study of school reform* (CSE Report No. 263). Los Angeles: UCLA Center for the Study of Evaluation.

Glass, G. V., and M. C. Ellwein. 1986. Reform by raising test standards. *Evaluation Comment* (December): 1–6.

Harnischfeger, A., and D. E. Wiley. 1975. *Achievement test score decline: Do we need to worry?* Chicago: ML-Group for Policy Studies in Education.

Hirsch, E. D. 1987. *Cultural literacy: What every American needs to know.* Boston: Houghton Mifflin.

Jaeger, R. M., and C. K. Tittle, eds. 1980. *Minimum competency achievement testing: Motives, models, measures, and consequences.* Berkeley, CA: McCutchan Publishing Corporation.

Kennedy, M. M. 1980. Test scores and individual rights. In *Minimum competency achievement testing: Motives, models, measures, and consequences,* ed. R. M. Jaeger and C. K. Tittle. Berkeley, CA: McCutchan Publishing Corporation.

Kirst, M. W. 1981. Loss of support for public secondary schools: Some causes and solutions. *Daedalus* 110 (3): 45-68.

Lazarus, M. 1981. *Goodbye to excellence: A critical look at minimum competency testing.* Boulder, CO: Westview Press.

Martin, W. 1987. A brief history of state testing policies in Colorado. In *State educational testing practices.* Office of Technology Assessment. Washington, DC: Office of Technology Assessment.

National Commission on Excellence in Education. 1983. *A nation at risk: The imperative for educational reform.* Washington, DC: United States Department of Education.

Office of Technology Assessment. 1987. *State educational testing practices.* Washington, DC: Author.

Popham, W. J. 1974. *An approaching peril: Cloud-referenced tests.* Los Angeles: UCLA Graduate School of Education.

Ravitch, D., and C. R. Finn. 1987. *What do our 17-year-olds know? The first national assessment of what American students know about history and literature.* New York: Harper and Row.

Rothman, R. 1988. Drop in scores on reading test baffles experts. *Education Week* (January 20): 1, 27.

Rudner, L. M. 1987. *What's happening in teacher testing: An analysis of state teacher testing practices.* Washington, DC: Office of Educational Research and Improvement.

Shepard, L. A., A. E. Kreitzer, and M. E. Graue. 1987. *A case study of the Texas Teacher Test: Technical report* (Draft deliverable, OERI grant G008690003). Los Angeles: UCLA Center for the Study of Evaluation.

Tyler, R. W. 1966. Development of instruments for assessing educational progress. In *Proceedings of the 1965 Invitational Conference on Testing Problems.* Princeton, NJ: Educational Testing Service.

U.S. Congress. Congressional Budget Office. 1987. *Educational achievement: Explanations and implications of recent trends.* Washington, DC: Author.

U.S. Congress. Congressional Budget Office. 1986. *Trends in educational achievement.* Washington, DC: Author.

Wirtz, W. 1977. *On further examination: Report of the Advisory Panel on the Scholastic Aptitude Test score decline.* New York: The College Board.

Student Achievement Tests as Tools of Educational Policy: Practices and Consequences

Edward Haertel

I. INTRODUCTION

From the time students enter the school system, they confront a barrage of objective achievement tests. Some of these are chosen or created by their classroom teachers, but many are imposed from outside the classroom. These *externally mandated* tests are the focus of this chapter. They are administered by various agencies for different policy purposes. The data they yield are used to describe and compare not only individual students, but their teachers, schools, districts, states, and even the nation as a whole. Each of these tests has some justification, and is of some value. Often, however, the negative consequences of all this testing go unrecognized, and the potential benefits go unrealized because test data are used in thoughtless or inappropriate ways. This chapter examines achievement tests as policy tools. Although the discussion is in general terms, the focus is on the way different tests have actually been used, and on the actual consequences of their use. Examples could be cited of every misuse described.

This chapter begins with definitions of some terms and distinctions. Externally mandated tests are described and criterion-referenced versus norm-referenced test interpretations are distinguished. The remainder of the introduction presents four different ways of using tests to influence curriculum and instruction. The rest of the chapter reviews each of these four mechanisms of policy influence, raising issues and then offering some recommendations. The chapter concludes with a brief summary.

Externally Mandated Tests

I use the term "externally mandated tests" somewhat more broadly than other authors (for example, Madaus 1988) to include not only tests administered from outside the school district, but also tests imposed on classroom teachers by the school district, typically the standardized achievement test batteries used in districtwide assessment programs. In some schools, students may take additional tests throughout the year to assess their mastery of prescribed behavioral objectives, especially in reading and mathematics. These tests, provided by the curriculum developer, are externally mandated if their use is required by the district. This kind of instructional management system is addressed below in the section on "Measurement-Driven Curriculum and Instruction."

Externally mandated tests include minimum competency tests (MCTs), which must be passed to earn a high school diploma; standardized achievement tests; and even some tests that students take at their own initiative, especially the Scholastic Aptitude Test (SAT) and the American College Testing Program (ACT) examinations. They include the Advanced Placement (AP) tests set by the College Entrance Examination Board (CEEB), through which students successfully completing high school AP courses may earn college credits; and, in some states, tests like the New York Regents examinations, which may entitle students to a more distinguished diploma. Externally mandated tests also include the California Assessment Program (CAP) and other state testing and assessment programs used for school or district-level comparisons and sometimes used to track state-level achievement trends over time.

These and other externally mandated tests influence what is taught and how it is taught in ways that are beyond the control of classroom teachers. Almost all are multiple-choice objective tests, although some include brief, structured student writing samples or other item formats.

Modes of Interpretation

Test interpretations are traditionally discussed as criterion-referenced and norm-referenced, and tests intended primarily for one form of interpretation or the other are referred to as criterion-referenced tests (CRTs) and norm-referenced tests (NRTs). Criterion-referenced interpretations are "absolute." They assign meanings to particular levels of performance. On most CRTs, performance is interpreted relative to one or more cutting scores, but criterion referencing without cutting scores is also possible. A good example is the scale used to report National Assessment of Educational Progress (NAEP) reading results, with substantive interpretations provided for different scale regions, but no cutting points or passing levels. Criterion-referencing is also involved when targets are specified for school, district, or state test-score averages, either to reach a certain level or to improve by a specified number of points.

Norm-referenced interpretations are "relative," representing performance in relation to an appropriate comparison group. Performance relative to a group may be expressed using percentiles, stanines, quartiles, deciles, or grade equivalents when an individual student's achievement is reported. When test results are reported at higher levels of aggregation, norm referencing may take the form of rankings of schools, districts, or states according to average achievement scores.

Both criterion-referenced and norm-referenced comparisons are commonly used in different policy contexts. An additional basis of comparison, more akin to norm-referenced than criterion-referenced reporting, is comparison to earlier performance levels of the same individual or system. This form of comparison is illustrated by rewards to schools for annual improvement.

Mechanisms of Policy Influence

In this chapter, four broad mechanisms of policy influence are discussed. First, tests can be used to determine the allocation of rewards among individuals, schools, or districts. The highest-scoring examinee may get the scholarship, or all who pass the MCT may be eligible to receive a diploma. In California, schools with higher average scores than others in their comparison groups may receive cash bonuses; and in Texas and elsewhere, districts where student achievement falls below minimum standards may be placed under stringent controls. In all these cases, the intent of the testing is to improve whatever qualities the tests are thought to measure by encouraging people to work for higher test scores. There is an implicit assumption that if test scores improve, then the underlying qualities measured must also have improved. If the means used to raise achievement test scores do not lead to the intended student learning, then the logic of this policy mechnism fails. Higher test scores and increased learning do not always go hand in hand (Haertel 1986b).

A second mechanism is the use of tests to assure student mastery of a prescribed curriculum. Instruction is organized around a sequence of measurable learning objectives with frequent testing to assure continued satisactory progress. Often students performing poorly on one of these tests are given additional instruction and retested before being permitted to proceed to the next objective. Perhaps the best-known and most fully developed statement of this instructional model is mastery learning (Bloom 1976; Guskey 1985). This and related models have both strong adherents and strong detractors (Anderson and Burns 1987; Arlin 1984; Guskey 1987; Shoemaker 1975; Slavin 1987a, 1987b; Strike 1982).

A third mechanism is the public reporting of information about test performance—testing for public accountability. Examples include annual publication in local newspapers of achievement score averages for area schools, or the secretary of education's annual wall charts comparing test scores and other statistics across the fifty states. Such quantitative data on school performance generally attract considerable interest—test scores become the primary measure by which the public judges the success of the schools (Gallup 1985, 1986; Gallup and Clark 1987). In the past two decades, public confidence in many social institutions, including schools, has eroded. The public and their elected representatives demand assurance that education dollars are well spent, and improved test scores are a major source of that assurance. Ideally, schools would fulfill the public trust by striving toward goals valued by the community. Publication of test scores could inform the public of their schools' effectiveness, so that more realistic goals could be established or corrective actions could be taken. In fact, of course, the publication of test scores acts as a policy mechanism not by abetting public rationality, but by bringing pressure to bear on state and district personnel, school principals, and even teachers. Information about test performance may raise public concern, but the most likely responses are a retreat to slogans like "back to basics," or calls for the replacement of those suspected of malfeasance

A fourth policy mechanism is the use of tests as part of an educational indicator system to monitor student learning and to evaluate the effectiveness of programs and policies. Testing under this model would be noncoercive and nonreactive. The primary users of test data would be decisionmakers, and the information gathered would inform rational deliberation about alternative policies. Teachers may use their own classroom tests according to this model when they monitor student learning, decide how to pace instruction, or determine when to review. Using externally mandated tests for parallel purposes is much more difficult.

Diverse Requirements of Different Testing Applications

There is substantial variation within each of these four categories of policy uses, and the details of particular testing applications can be quite important. A small change in a passing score can affect the classification of thousands of students, and can have substantial fiscal implications for a district charged with providing remediation to all who fail. If minimum scores are set for each of two or three subtests as opposed to a minimum score for their total, the proportion passing may change drastically (Glass 1978b). If a high school is rewarded according to the average score of those seniors taking the SAT, then an incentive is created to discourage all but the best students from taking the examination. If the school is judged according to the ratio of seniors who earn scores above a certain level to the total number of seniors, including those who do not take the test, the incentives are changed.

It may be possible to design and implement responsible, beneficial testing programs employing any of the four mechanisms just described. Unless there is careful, intelligent deliberation about testing purposes, methods, and likely consequences, however, any benefits of testing may be overshadowed by unintended negative consequences. If testing programs are to succeed, then details matter. The particular tests selected, the setting and timing of test administrations, methods of examinee preparation, procedures for scoring, interpreting, and disseminating results, concomitant research and development, and other aspects of test use are all critical. Proper choices in one situation may be disastrous in another.

This chapter is organized around the four policy mechanisms just described. For each of these, it points out some of the pitfalls of ill-considered test use, especially for minority candidates, and then offers recommendations for improvement. Little is said about the important topics of test bias and differential validity, in part because these topics are less important in educational achievement testing than in employment testing, and in part because both topics have been ably treated elsewhere (Cole 1973, 1981; Linn 1973, 1984; Shepard, Camiilli, and Averill 1981; Shepard, Camilli, and Williams 1985). What follows should not be taken as a criticism of testing in general, but as a set of cautionary observations offered in the hope of encouraging more thoughtful and careful test use.

II. ALLOCATION OF REWARDS AND SANCTIONS

Test performance may be linked to rewards or sanctions for individuals or systems. The links may be rigid and explicit, as when legislation links MCT performance to high school graduation, or somewhat flexible, as when colleges weigh SAT or ACT scores among other factors in reaching admission decisions. An example for educational systems is the cash bonus awarded to California school districts on the basis of California Assessment Program (CAP) test scores and other indicators. A current application employing negative sanctions rather than rewards is the initiative in St. Louis linking teacher evaluations to specified student performance levels. Haertel (1986c) has offered an analysis of this type of student testing application. Rewards may occasionally be attached to poor performance, as when lowest-achieving schools or districts receive categorical funds. In some cases, bilingual funds have been allocated on this basis.

Issues

High Scores as a Goal of Schooling

Test scores are merely indicators of attainments that matter, but when the scores are rewarded, they can become ends in themselves. This substitution may interfere with deeper and more significant goals of education. It is a commonplace in psychology that when extrinsic motivators are substituted for intrinsic motivators, when a task is performed to earn some external reward rather than for its own sake, then performance of that task is less valued. The idea that a major goal of education is to earn high marks on some test appears antithetical to fostering a love of learning, or to preparing students to learn throughout their lives. The destructive effects of the Japanese leaving examination are notorious (Ogura 1987; Shimahara 1978, 1985), and in the United States, SAT or ACT test scores may assume a similarly exaggerated importance for some students. Of course, teachers have long used classroom tests not only to measure achievement but also to encourage studying (Haertel 1986a; Haertel et al. 1984). When teachers use their own tests in this way, they can determine how important each test should be, arrange other kinds of motivation to complement the marks and grades they assign, and closely monitor the effects of their testing practices. Such sensitivity is rarely possible with externally mandated tests.

High test scores may be set as a goal not only for individuals, but also for educational systems and programs. Test use may be mandated by statute or regulations for evaluation of bilingual or other categorical programs, innovative curricula, or magnet schools. Even the particular tests that must be used may be specified. Such evaluation requirements can exert a significant and not always salutary influence, creating a press for quick, measurable results and distorting the curriculum toward the improvement of test scores.

Competition within a Restricted Sphere

Tests typically foster competition rather than cooperation. Closely tied to the goal of getting high test scores is the goal of getting higher scores than other examinees. Competition and comparison are facts of life, but there are important differences between competition for high test scores and competition in the real world. Outside of school, there are multiple, complex evaluative crieria; people have some latitude in choosing the goals toward which they will strive; and a large proportion of individuals are likely to excel by at least some standards. Required tests are different. They offer only one narrow way to succeed, and that may seem unfair to those whose particular strengths are hard to demonstrate on written examinations.

Competition on the basis of tests alone might be appropriate if the tests reflected all the goals of schooling, but academic skills such as extended writing, complex reasoning, and problem solving are often underrepresented on externally mandated tests, and even on classroom tests. Schooling outcomes such as reference and study skills, good work habits, and positive attitudes toward learning are nearly impossible to test for.

One solution might be a retreat from competition among students to a focus upon improvement for each individual student. Criterion-referenced test interpretations might be emphasized, highlighting each student's attainment and progress over time, and playing down norm-referenced comparisons. This approach rings false. The problem is not with norm-referenced test interpretations, but with the range of outcomes that are recognized. A more constructive response would be to offer increased recognition for other kinds of attainments available to students, without detracting from the recognition accorded to those earning high test scores, and without detracting from the central place of academic achievement among the goals of schooling.

Discouragement of Low Achievers from Continuing Their Education

The rhetoric of testing is mostly egalitarian. It is argued that tests are not exclusionary—they foster opportunity by giving all an equal chance to demonstrate their accomplishments or their potential. MCTs, for example, are said to assure that virtually all students leave high school with certain minimum skills. It may even be argued that they most benefit those who earn low scores by identifying their weaknesses and assuring that they receive remediation. These intended benefits for low-achieving youth may not, however, be realized in practice. Almost no one is denied a diploma for failing an MCT, but some students unable to pass the test may simply leave school. Although there is as yet little empirical evidence to show that MCT graduation requirements increase dropout rates, such an effect appears plausible (Hamilton 1986; Natriello, Pallas, and McDill 1986).

Even if individual students are not required to pass a test, monitoring the *average* test performance of schools or districts may lead to an increase in the dropout rate. When schools are rewarded for high average test scores, low scorers become a liability, and incentives to keep them in school may be weakened (Fine 1986; Wehlage and Rutter 1986). The average goes up each time a weak student goes away, or, for whatever reason, misses the test.

Incentives to Shift Classroom Resources Away from Low-Achieving Students

Monitoring average test scores for classrooms may penalize low-scoring students even if they do not drop out. Within their own classrooms, teachers can best raise average scores by working most closely with students able to improve most rapidly, and these are likely to be those students who have already demonstrated high aptitudes for conventional classroom learning.

Different incentives for the allocation of instructional resources are created when mastery tests, for example, MCTs, are employed. If teachers, schools, or districts were evaluated according to the proportion of students passing, then the optimum strategy would be to work most closely with students below the cutting score, but not too far below. Still weaker students would receive less assistance under such an optimum strategy, and those judged sure to pass would receive no attention until all students had been brought up to the required level.

Recommendations

Recognize a Wider Range of Attainments in School

Without challenging the importance of the learning outcomes measured by externally mandated tests, it is important to find ways to recognize other kinds of learning outcomes. These would include not only better tests of critical thinking and other higher order skills, but also ways to recognize students' exceptional individual accomplishments, from written works or science fair projects to artistic creations. Such recognition might come with broader dissemination and discussion of the range of criteria considered by colleges for admissions, and by more serious attempts to quantify and objectify significant personal qualities and attainments not measured on written examinations.

There are also psychometric reasons for recognizing a wider range of schooling outcomes. Simplistic policies, where action is triggered by scores above or below a cutting point on a single test such as an MCT, are contrary to the consensus of professional practice in testing. The *Standards for Educational and Psychological Testing*, issued jointly by the American Psychological Association (APA), American Educational Research Association (AERA), and National Council on Measurement in Education (NCME), discourage reliance on a single test as the sole criterion in reaching any important decision, and urge the use of multiple sources of information (APA 1985). The *Standards* also call for consideration of alternative decision procedures, including the use of no test at all. Linn, Madaus, and Pedulla (1982) have noted the importance of multiple indicators in addition to MCT scores for high school graduation.

Monitor Individual Students, Not Averages

Monitoring averages for classrooms or schools may encourage a shifting of educational resources away from weak students, and could even increase the dropout rate. Rather than monitoring averages, a better strategy might be to track individual students, and to attend to the entire distribution of achievement, not just the mean. It would require almost no additional effort to report achievement levels for, say, the 25th, 50th, and 75th percentiles, in preference to reporting only averages. Far better would be to track individual students, accurately counting dropouts, and quantifying the progress of each student who remained in school. Summaries of individual student growth could then be reported to give a better picture of the effectiveness of school programs for different subgroups of learners (Rogosa 1985). Looking at the progress of individual students and then aggregating indices of individual growth is far wiser than interpreting improvements in average scores as if they reflected the progress of every individual. Better statistical methods for analyzing and reporting achievement could lead to better descriptions of student progress, and also provide a firmer basis for performance-related rewards and sanctions for teachers, schools, or districts.

III. MEASUREMENT-DRIVEN CURRICULUM AND INSTRUCTION

Measurement-driven instruction refers to the deliberate use of tests to define educational objectives and to influence what is taught. Rather than viewing the impact of testing on curriculum and instruction as a necessary evil to be minimized by careful test/curriculum match, advocates of measurement-driven instruction seek to capitalize on this impact, using tests to define and communicate educational objectives, and to assure accountability.

The idea of holding schools and teachers accountable for student learning as measured by objective tests is not new. In 1862, England adopted the Revised Code, or "Payment by Results" plan, under which schools received government grants based upon enrollment, but with a substantially larger payment per student for those passing tests in oral reading, writing from dictation, and arithmetic (Connell 1950, 203–42). Criticisms of the plan sound distinctly modern: It would lead to a narrowing of the curriculum, restrict instruction to drill and practice on the skills tested, and fail to redress the inequities that were its ostensible rationale. These were, in fact, the consequences of the plan, and by the 1890s it had been largely abandoned (Sutherland 1973; Glass 1978a).

In the United States, test-based accountability systems were given new impetus during the late 1950s and the 1960s as educators attempted to apply the principles of behaviorist psychology to instruction. Mager's influential book, *Preparing Instructional Objectives* (1962), illustrates the attempt during that time to express educational outcomes in terms of observable and quantifiable behaviors. It had become unfashionable to describe schooling outcomes using terms that referred to internal mental states like insight, understanding, or appreciation. Psychologists had defined their proper business as the investigation of connections between observable stimuli and observable responses, and educators tried to follow suit. Strike (1982, chaps. 2–4) offers a powerful philosophical critique of the behaviorist program. He examines the internal logic of this behaviorist position and finds it flawed—the concepts of stimulus and of behavior are inherently mentalistic, and meaningful learning outcomes cannot be adequately described as behavioral repertoires. Most important, our culture is founded on a conception of personal freedom and choice that is inconsistent with the passive view of learning implicit in a model that sees education as the shaping of behavior by selective reinforcement.

Today's test-driven instructional management systems and test-based accountability systems are heirs to this behaviorist psychology (Haertel and Calfee 1983; Strike 1982). Test-driven instructional management systems are integrated packages of materials for instruction and assessment, such as the Chicago Mastery Learning Reading (CMLR) system. Even though the dozens of examinations required under such systems are administered and scored by classroom teachers, their use may be required under a district-prescribed curriculum, and so they are externally mandated. Externally imposed accountability systems are established by states or school districts as tools of educational reform. Examples include competency testing programs in Maryland, Texas, and South Carolina, and in the city of Detroit, all described by Popham et al. (1985). Cuban (1984) criticized similar initiatives in California as attempts to "reform by remote control."

Implicit in measurement-driven instruction is a more or less systematic model of schooling, which has both its adherents and its detractors. Advocates of such systems include Shoemaker (1975), Popham (1981), Popham et al. (1985), and Weinstock (1984). They see measurement-driven instruction as clarifying for students and teachers what they are expected to do, establishing clear performance standards, and giving teachers latitude to attain those objectives as their professional judgment dictates. Critics view measurement-driven instruction as leading to a "factory" model of education, routinized and standardized, with testable student outcomes as its sole, dreary product. They see it as tending to minimize the scope of individual differences in aptitudes or interests, and as reducing the achievement of most students to some lowest common denominator.

Issues

The first three issues discussed in this section concern impacts of measurement-driven instructional systems on the curriculum. These include the narrowing of content covered, narrowing of the range of skills taught, and fragmentation of the material presented. The fourth and fifth issues concern impacts on instruction, namely a shift toward instructional activities that resemble testing activities, and direct classroom instruction in test-taking skills. These five points all support the sixth consequence of a measurement-based approach to schooling—success in school becomes increasingly irrelevant to success in other settings. The seventh, eighth, and ninth issues pertain to more global effects on the educational system. Local autonomy is eroded and teachers' professionalism is compromised when decisions are reached automatically on the basis of test scores, and the educational system's flexibility and adaptability are diminished.

Narrowing of Content Coverage

Despite their best intentions, teachers pressed to cover more instructional objectives than time permits are likely to focus on what will be assessed. They, like their students, may judge what is important by what is tested. The higher the stakes, the greater the rewards or sanctions for good or bad test scores, the more likely curriculum distortion becomes. Proponents of measurement-driven instruction would respond that the solution is to test a sufficiently broad range of outcomes (for example, Shoemaker 1975). In practice, however, appropriate ranges of outcomes may differ from one student to another, and the effect of testing is too often to drive the curriculum to its narrowest common denominator. Moreover, some content is harder to test, and material that is difficult to assess is likely to be slighted.

Narrowing of the Range of Skills Taught

The observation that some things are easier to test than others applies with even greater force to different kinds of skills or processes than it does to different kinds of content. The measurement of higher-order thinking skills is notoriously difficult, especially using multiple-choice or other objective tests. Higher-order skills refer here not only to Bloom et al.'s (1956) analysis, synthesis, and evaluation, but also to solving ill-structured problems (Fredericksen 1984), demonstrating practical intelligence (Sternberg 1984, 1985), and a range of divergent or "creative" production tasks, especially extended writing (Quellmalz 1985; Suhor 1985).

Deficiencies in the technology of objective measurement for higher-order skills are serious and long-standing. Steady, significant progress is being made, but there are as yet no general solutions. These skills may be especially difficult to address within a behaviorist framework because they are so much concerned with internal mental events. Examples include setting goals and subgoals, or monitoring comprehension.

Tendency toward Fragmentation

Reliance on objective tests may lead to a preoccupation with narrow, observable behaviors at the expense of any broader conception of the overall structure of the curriculum. This view of the curriculum is reflected in scope-and-sequence charts, where each measurable objective appears equally important, and central ideas and organizing principles are obscured. In a report by the National Coalition of Advocates for Students, *Barriers to Excellence* (NCAS 1985, 48-49), the CMLR system was cited to illustrate this problem. Under the CMLR program, reading for children in grades K-8 is reduced to a series of 273 separate "subskills," to be mastered and tested one at a time, in sequence. According to the NCAS report, reading instruction in some schools is so centered on the CMLR system that children have no opportunity to read actual books. "CMLR crowds out real reading" (NCAS 1985, 49). This fragmentation of the curriculum can exacerbate the neglect of higher-order skills. It is difficult to apply analysis, synthesis, or evaluation to a curriculum conceived as a mass of narrow, independent objectives.

Systems like CMLR that track each student's mastery of dozens or even hundreds of skills may become more attractive as use of computers for adaptive testing increases. Computers are preeminent bookkeepers, and existing psychometric models for tailored testing are perilously well suited to the testing of masses of tiny skills. If the technical development of such systems proceeds without sufficient attention to the limitations of a curriculum conceived in these terms, the computer's potential to improve learning is not likely to be realized. McBride (1985) predicts that computer-based adaptive testing will become much more prevalent in the near future.

Measurement-driven instructional programs, including computer-based testing programs, may cause poor and minority children to fall further behind the more advantaged in academic achievement. In large-city school systems serving a preponderance of at-risk students, such curricula may be implemented most rigidly. These are often highly bureaucratic school districts, which may find measurement-driven systems consonant with their concern for teacher accountability. Moreover, teachers in these less affluent systems are often less experienced than those in more attractive positions, reducing the probability that they will successfully adapt or supplement the curriculum to meet their students' needs. Finally, even if they possess the necessary skills to improve upon a test-driven curriculum, teachers in large-city districts may have limited access to supplementary curriculum materials.

Favoring of Instructional Activities Likely to Improve Test Performance

There has been a subtle shift, especially at the primary and upper elementary levels, toward instructional activities resembling objective test formats (Durkin 1978–79; Haertel and Calfee 1983). This shift reflects not only the importance of good student test performance, but also the effect of specifying intended learning outcomes in the language of measurable, behavioral objectives. Classroom discussion, simulations and small-group activities, and extended writing opportunities will do less to improve test scores than will worksheets requiring students to answer brief, isolated questions by filling in blanks or selecting among fixed choices. Of course, teachers use such activities not primarily to improve test scores, but to foster student learning. Nonetheless, their use of worksheets and practice tests is likely to increase if they accept objective tests as valid measures of most important learning outcomes. If teachers believe that the goal of schooling is to shape a certain behavioral repertoire, then worksheets and practice tests are the kinds of instructional activities that make sense.

Use of Classroom Time for Direct Instruction in Taking Tests

Students become proficient at what they practice. The surest way to improve test performance is to give students practice taking tests, and so high-stakes tests may lead to instruction on test taking itself. For example, coaching classes for the SAT are already part of many high school programs (Haertel 1986b). Perhaps more serious is the creation of remedial classes for high school students who fail minimum competency tests. Instruction in these classes sometimes consists of little more than worksheet exercises and practice tests resembling the MCTs required for graduation. This "spot remediation" serves only to get students past the hurdle of the test itself (Madaus 1988). Because low-income and minority students are at greater risk of failing MCTs, the distortion of curriculum and instruction toward narrowly targeted remediation following MCT failure is most likely to occur for these students.

Poor Prediction from School Success to Life Success

The foregoing influences of some testing programs on curriculum and instruction may culminate in a distortion of students' understandings of the goals of education, and of the future challenges they are preparing to meet. Objective tests offer poor models for the problems students are likely to confront after leaving school, and for the criteria of success in the world of work. Fredericksen (1984) has contrasted the well-structured problems on written examinations with single correct answers, unambiguous criteria for these answers, sufficient information provided or (presumably) known to the examinee, and well-defined solution procedures, with the ill-structured problems of the real world, where the rule is satisficing according to multiple, ambiguous criteria, and working from imperfect and incomplete information without the benefit of any procedures guaranteed to yield solutions. It is little wonder that school examinations so poorly predict life success (McClelland 1973). The academic skills measured by achievement tests are important, and the proper business of schooling is to teach and to test those skills, but students are not well served by the belief that test scores reflect their acquisition of the abilities required for success in life.

Centralization of Educational Decision Making

An externally mandated test confers a degree of power and influence on the agency responsible for its administration. This effect may be large or small—NAEP was originally designed to preclude state-level comparisons, in part to limit its influence and assuage fears that it would lead to a national curriculum. Measurement-driven instructional systems at the state level (for example, in California, Maryland, and Texas) are intended, among other purposes, to encourage greater conformity to state curriculum guidelines. This issue is ably discussed by Stern (1986) and by Madaus (1985, 1988). Curricular standardization in itself may not be undesirable, but it runs counter to strong national traditions of local control, and, as discussed above, the curricula defined by testing programs are likely to be seriously deficient.

External testing programs may influence local school practices in ways that go beyond influencing what is taught and how it is taught. Stern (1986, 338) suggests that principals might assign their best teachers to the grades or subjects tested, for example. Dropout prevention policies might be pursued less vigorously, and definitions of children as limited English proficient or learning disabled might be interpreted to exclude slower students from testing. Test preparation itself is likely to become part of the curriculum, both as part of regular classroom instruction and through special "coaching" classes. All of these possible influences represent compromises in which the amount, distribution, or quality of instruction is altered to improve test score averages.

Deprofessionalization of Teachers

Early in this century, when standardized achievement tests were coming into widespread use in the schools, they were viewed as tools of scientific educational management. Testing programs helped educational administrators to define themselves as specialized professionals. It is not surprising, perhaps, that practices which in the past enhanced the status of educational administrators should today be seen as detracting from the status of teachers. Most studies have found that teachers rely far more on their own judgment than on standardized tests for instructional decision making (Dorr-Bremme and Herman 1986; Kellaghan, Madaus, and Airasian 1982; Salmon-Cox 1982; Stetz and Beck 1981). When students are required to pass an externally mandated test before their educational attainments are recognized, it may be inferred that their teacher's judgment is not to be trusted. Numerous brief articles in *Phi Delta Kappan, Educational Leadership,* and similar journals attest to teachers' concern and resentment over tests that are used to reach automatic decisions about grade promotion, graduation, and entry into, and exit from, special instructional programs.

Discouraging Innovation

Once the curriculum has been reduced to a string of tiny hurdles, all equally important, it becomes difficult to experiment with alternative conceptions of content, organization, or instructional approach. Because each narrow objective is tested, it must be covered in sequence, often at a particular, appointed time. Thus, measurement-driven instruction legitimates a conception of the curriculum under which the only way to progress more rapidly is to run faster along the single track. Once such a system is in place, innovation is likely to be retarded.

Through their recognition of *instructional validity* as a desideratum of fair test use (Popham and Lindheim 1981), the courts may have lent further weight to this conservative force. Since *Debra P. v. Turlington,* many tests are validated against the content presently taught, at least as embodied in state curriculum guidelines (Rebell 1986). If tests so designed are used to track system performance, one can only expect that existing practices will be perpetuated.

Recommendations

Develop and Use Measures of Higher-Order Learning

Tests of critical thinking and problem solving divorced from academic content quickly degenerate into puzzles measuring only cleverness. These skills can only be measured in the context of particular content areas. There is an urgent need for better methods of testing such higher-order skills (Suhor 1985). Only the inclusion of such skills can justify testing programs intended to drive the curriculum. The required tests are likely to involve presentation of extended, complex stimuli rather than brief, separable questions, and to call for extended responses. Using computers, it may be possible to develop tests that require students to ask the right questions about a problem situation (for example, by using an information retrieval system), as well as finding the right answers. The goal should be to include some examination questions that more faithfully represent the requirements of ill-structured problems in out-of-school settings.

One important avenue to be explored is increased use of classroom performance testing (Stiggins and Bridgeford 1985; Stiggins, Conklin, and Bridgeford 1986). These are assessments involving the evaluation of products or performances produced by students according to specified directions and scored according to explicit criteria. Teachers already make extensive use of such assessments, but a need exists for higher levels of teacher skill in planning and using applied performance testing. There are some exciting examples of the potential of performance tests, even on a large scale, if resources are committed. One example is the alternative high school leaving examination in biology now in place in Israel, which involves actual laboratory work by each student and critical interpretation of experimental data not previously encountered (Tamir 1982, 1985). Some elements of the National Surveys conducted in Great Britain by the Assessment of Performance Unit (APU) also merit attention (Burstall 1986). One major area of application for performance testing is in the measurement of writing (Quellmalz 1985).

It was recommended in the previous section that a wider range of attainments in school be recognized. The development and use of different kinds of assessments, including ill-structured problems and performance assessments, can serve this goal. If schools can broaden the criteria of success, more students should be able to excel.

Evaluate Measurement-Driven Curricula with Respect to A Broad Range of Learning Outcomes

It has long been recognized (Cronbach 1963; Linn 1983) that for purposes of educational evaluation, there are benefits to a loose test/curriculum match. There may be important learning outcomes not covered in the prescribed curriculum, and these should be assessed whether they are taught or not. Even if, for example, teachers, schools, or districts espouse behaviorally oriented curricula, they should be held accountable for students' performance in solvng complex, ill-structured problems.

Seek Local Solutions to Educational Problems

The needs of individual students, classrooms, schools, and communities are unique. No single curriculum or instructional method can satisfy all of them. Individual teachers and administrators require latitude to fashion appropriate courses of action for their own particular circumstances. Any initiative to standardize the curriculum or impose particular assessment methods should be evaluated in the light of its probable effect on teacher professionalism and local autonomy, and should be sufficiently flexible to permit local adaptation and constructive innovation.

IV. TESTING AS AN INSTRUMENT OF PUBLIC ACCOUNTABILITY

Tests may influence policy by raising public interest or by bringing public pressure to bear on low-performing classrooms, schools, or districts. Reports in the news media of the relative standings of schools, districts, or states attract considerable attention, and those that do not fare well in these comparisons are likely to hear from their constituents. This public pressure may be employed deliberately, as with the School Performance Reports used in California to press school districts into conformity with state guidelines, or inadvertently, as when newspapers report annual achievement test rankings of public schools in the nation's great cities. The "crisis" precipitated by the SAT test score decline also reflected this mechanism of influence.

Issues

Testing as a Symbolic Response to Public Concerns about Education

Mandating a new test has become a popular legislative response to educational problems ranging from apparently illiterate high school graduates to apparently illiterate teachers. It costs little, gives the appearance of decisive action, and reduces a political problem to a technical one. Once a test is mandated, the details of its construction, validation, administration, and even interpretation are delegated to staff. In the case of minimum competency testing, the "solution" also shifts the responsibility for failure from the system to the student (Cohen and Haney 1980).

Testing as symbolic activity is not benign. It diverts attention from the root causes of low student achievement, and encourages the simplistic idea that if policymakers just insist upon results, then teachers and administrators can somehow manage to provide them. This idea is consistent with the "factory" model of education implicit in measurement-driven approaches to school system accountability. The risks of this approach include negative impacts on curriculum and on teacher morale, diversion of instructional time and resources from teaching to irrelevant testing, and stigmatizing schools or districts serving lower-achieving students.

Proliferation of Tests and Testing Programs

It is useful to consider testing in relation to Downs's (1972) policy cycle of "alarmed discovery," "crisis activity," "disillusionment with results," and "return to neglect." Successive waves of concern over different educational issues may spawn one testing program after another, and when the issues once more fade, these testing programs may be left behind. When attention was focused on the problem of high school graduates weak in basic skills, for example, it may have seemed inevitable to prescribe MCTs as part of the solution. Following "return to neglect," however, these tests are left in place to divert resources, including student time, from more beneficial pursuits.

Recommendations

Beware of Tests as Apparent Solutions to Educational Problems

Carefully designed testing programs may be useful in analyzing and responding to educational problems, but only as adjuncts to actual remedies. Testing alone cannot substitute for better prepared teachers, improved instructional materials, or better allocation and use of resources.

If a new testing program is started and scores are publicized, no one should be surprised to see annual score improvements for several years, but it must not be assumed that such improvements automatically signal the amelioration of whatever problems prompted the testing requirement in the first place. It may be possible for teachers and students to turn out higher test scores on demand, but in the process some other good is probably being sacrificed. Madaus (1988) observes that policymakers have a vested interest in the testing programs they create, and may have little incentive to question seriously the meanings of the test scores, or the possible negative consequences of testing programs. It is essential, therefore, that educational leaders and thoughtful citizens monitor this use of tests, and call attention to the need for authentic responses to educational concerns.

V. TESTING TO MONITOR PERFORMANCE AND INFORM POLICY

Informed deliberation about educational policy requires data, and the information available is far from adequate. Smith (1984, 3) wrote that "the present state of educational indicators is a shambles." Questions about funding levels, the needs of specific groups, curriculum revisions, or students' preparation for the world of work all depend on accurate, comprehensive achievement data. The best available data for the nation as a whole come from the National

Assessment of Educational Progress (NAEP), and even these data have serious weaknesses (Messick, Beaton, and Lord 1983; Smith 1984; Stedman and Smith 1983; Selden 1986). Needed improvements in NAEP include stronger measures of higher-order skills, a sampling design permitting comparisons at least at the state level, and the coordinated collection of student background and school process measures linked to achievement scores (Alexander and James 1987). For all its limitations, NAEP is superior for many purposes to any available alternatives. Testing programs within districts and states are for the most part noncomparable, and are even more limited than NAEP in the range of learning outcomes they sample.

Issues

Achievement Tests in an Educational Indicator System

When NAEP was first conceived over twenty years ago, it was expected to provide a source of accurate, comprehensive, and consistent information on student achievement, to improve educational decision making and policy formation. The limited impact of NAEP over the past two decades shows clearly that a model of improving policy by simply providing information is naive. Findings from NAEP have been occasionally seized upon, sometimes reported accurately and other times distorted (Forbes 1985), when they happened to support particular policies and positions. For the most part, however, NAEP has generated little interest. (Attention to NAEP findings has increased in recent years, in part due to vigorous dissemination of information by the present NAEP contractor.)

The usefulness of NAEP or other achievement data would be substantially enhanced if they were placed in the context of information about other policy-relevant variables. Information about patterns and levels of achievement would be far more useful to policymakers if it were tied to information about variables over which they had some direct control. Ideally, achievement data would be reported as part of an integrated system of educational indicators, in which inputs were tied to outcomes, and standards were available to judge the adequacy of indicator levels and to monitor improvement (Smith 1984).

Proper Use of Test Results in Educational Policy Debates

Stedman and Smith (1983) indicate forcefully that the misuse of test data in policy debates is *not* a problem to be solved by better psychometrics alone. In their analysis of four recent national reform reports, they found careless handling of data, selective reporting, and inconsistencies between policy conclusions and the background papers on which they were ostensibly based. Forbes (1985) likewise documents the failure of government officials and the public to properly read data on levels of students' basic skills. As one striking example, advocates of "Back to Basics" capitalized upon the SAT test score decline to support their position at a time when NAEP data indicated that basic skills were probably improving even as the more complex skills measured by the SAT declined.

Responsible Interpretation of Group Differences

Although gaps between the achievement levels of Anglo whites and of most minority groups have narrowed over the years, significant disparities remain. An issue arises when these disparities are reported and interpreted. The existence of stable group differences must not be used to justify differential performance expectations across groups; the existence of a technology to measure and predict group differences neither explains nor excuses them. Any interpretative system that involves differentiated performance expectations according to student background characteristics, even something as simple as the pervasive "large city" norms available for most standardized achievement batteries, has the potential to legitimate existing differences and thereby weaken efforts to eliminate them.

This risk is illustrated in one of the score reports available from the publisher of a widely used achievement test battery, discussed by Haertel (1985). This score report presents comparisons of observed school means to predictions based on indices of teacher-reported or student-reported parent educational level. The intent of the report is to provide a fairer basis for comparing schools to one another, especially in school districts serving diverse communities. Schools enrolling a greater proportion of low-income and minority students are likely to be those in which parent educational levels are lower, in which case they will be held to lower standards than are schools serving traditionally higher-achieving populations. It may be all too easy to conclude that if children in these respective schools are performing at the different levels predicted, then the school district has no responsibility to try to eliminate remaining achievement disparities.

Responsible Reporting of Group Differences

There is a second, related concern in reporting achievement patterns across groups. Simple tabulations according to levels of one variable at a time may exaggerate the magnitude of group differences, and may suggest incorrect and simplistic explanations. The black-white achievement gap is greater for the nation as a whole, for example, than within any one of the four major geographic regions, because blacks are represented disproportionately in the region showing the lowest overall achievement both for blacks and for whites. Thus, a one-way tabulation of achievement by race for the nation as a whole is more invidious than a two-way tabulation of achievement by both race and geographic region. Further controls for household income, parent educational level, and so forth, reduce apparent disparities by race still further. Where such additional variables are available, it appears irresponsible to report results in such a way that the possible contributions of these additional variables to racial and ethnic group disparities are not made apparent. If one-way tabulations were desired, these could be standardized, in effect producing, for example, racial or ethnic comparisons for hypothetical populations equated on parent education, income, and so forth. There are, of course, good reasons to report raw one-way tabulations as well, but this can be done in such a way that improper causal attributions are discouraged.

Note that demographic patterns should be reported responsibly, not avoided. Stedman and Smith (1983, 88) rightly criticize the report *A Nation at Risk* for presenting the functional illiteracy rate of seventeen-year-olds from the 1974 and 1975 NAEP assessments without acknowledging that "it [was] clear from almost every recent report that the problem of illiteracy for young adults is very heavily concentrated in the poor and minority (particularly male) population."

Recommendations

Encourage Development of an Integrated Indicator System for Education

There is a pressing need for better information on the achievement of students in the nation as a whole, in different geographic regions, and among specific subgroups. NAEP can inform such questions as the relation between higher-order and lower-order literacy skills, the achievement test score decline of the 1970s, and trends in the achievement gaps among racial and ethnic groups at different age levels. That these data have been underused does not detract from their importance. The collection of nationally comparable achievement data and their use in policy study and policy formulation requires serious attention.

Encourage Development of a Comprehensive System for Monitoring Student Achievement

At its best, a standardized achievement testing program could embody a far richer conception of curriculum and of education than is found in almost any of the tests now in use. The New York Regents examinations (Ambach 1984), AP tests, and the International Baccalaureate (Peterson 1972) suggest models for a comprehensive assessment system that might offer a common, psycho-metrically grounded vocabulary for discussing cognitive learning outcomes, permitting more focused comparisons across districts, states, or other school systems, more rational consideration of the tradeoffs inherent in policy decisions, and more responsible specification of educational standards.

VI. SUMMARY

In this chapter, four ways of using externally mandated tests in educational policy have been described. High test scores or score averages may be rewarded directly; tests may be used to encourage conformity to a particular curriculum; test outcomes can influence public opinion; and they can inform educational decision making. None of these uses of tests as policy tools is improper or detrimental in itself, but each carries certain risks. Responsible test use requires thoughtful attention to the likely consequences of testing for the entire educational system.

In considering different uses of externally mandated tests, several themes recur. First, most externally mandated achievement tests could address a broader range of learning outcomes. These tests are unlikely ever to assess all intended outcomes of schooling, but movement in that direction would be an improvement. Use of different assessment formats should be encouraged, including exercises that allow for more extended consideration of complex problems, that require students to produce a response rather than to select one, and that have more than one correct answer.

Second, in addition to improving the tests, the uses of tests can be improved. The power of test scores to summarize and simplify makes them invaluable for analysis and discussion of the educational system, but can also encourage an uncritical reliance on test scores alone as sufficient indicators of schooling outcomes for students, schools, states, or the nation. Test scores should be reported and used in the context of additional information. At a minimum, there must be adequate attention to those learning outcomes that resist simple quantification. When students, schools, districts, or larger units are compared, sufficient attention must be given to background and demographic variables that help to explain achievement disparities. At the same time, demographics must never be used to excuse disparities in schooling outcomes.

Finally, the media, policymakers, and the public should greet reports and interpretations of test scores with healthy skepticism. Achievement tests can answer some important questions with unrivaled precision, but they cannot answer other questions at all. In considering any report of testing outcomes, it would be well to ask what the reported results really signify, whether reported differences among units or over time are large enough to matter, what plausible explanations might be advanced for the findings reported, and what other schooling outcomes are left unaddressed. Raising these four questions could go far toward improving the use and interpretation of tests for educational policy.

REFERENCES

Alexander, L., and H. T. James. 1987. *The nation's report card: Improving the assessment of student achievement.* Washington, DC: Office of Educational Research and Improvement, United States Department of Education.

Ambach, G. M. 1984. State and local action for education in New York. *Phi Delta Kappan* 66:202–4.

American Educational Research Association, American Psychological Association, and National Council on Measurement in Education. 1985. *Standards for educational and psychological testing.* Washington, DC: American Psychological Association. (Known as APA *Standards.*)

Anderson, L. W., and R. B. Burns. 1987. Values, evidence, and mastery learning. *Rev. Ed. Res.* 57:215–23.

Arlin, M. 1984. Time, equality, and mastery learning. *Rev. Ed. Res.* 54:65–86.

Bloom, B. S. 1976. *Human characteristics and school learning.* New York: McGraw-Hill.

Bloom, B. S., M. D. Engelhart, E. J. Furst, W. H. Hill, and D. R. Krathwohl. 1956. *Taxonomy of educational objectives. Handbook I: Cognitive domain.* New York: McGraw-Hill.

Burstall, C. 1986. Innovative forms of assessment: A United Kingdom perspective. *Ed. Meas.: Issues and Practice* 5 (1): 17–22.

Cohen, D., and W. Haney. 1980. Minimums, competency testing, and social policy. In *Minimum Competency Testing,* ed. R. Jaeger and C. K. Tittle. Berkeley, CA: McCutchan.

Cole, N. S. 1973. Bias in selection. *J. Ed. Meas.* 10:237–55.

———. 1981. Bias in testing. *Am. Psychol.* 36:1067–77.

Connell, W. F. 1950. *The educational thought and influence of Matthew Arnold.* London: Routledge and Kegan Paul.

Cronbach, L. J. 1963. Course improvement through evaluation. *Teachers Col. Rec.* 64:672–83.

Cuban, L. 1984. School reform by remote control: SB 813 in California. *Phi Delta Kappan* 66:213–15.

Dorr-Bremme, D. W., and J. L. Herman. 1986. *Assessing student achievement: A profile of classroom practices* (CSE Monograph Series in Evaluation, 11). Los Angeles: Center for the Study of Evaluation, University of California.

Downs, A. 1972. Up and down with ecology: The issue attention cycle. *Public Interest* 29:39–50.

Durkin, D. 1978–79. What classroom observations reveal about reading comprehension instruction. *Reading Res. Quar.* 14:481–533.

Fine, M. 1986. Why urban adolescents drop into and out of public high school. *Teachers Col. Rec.* 87:393–409.

Forbes, R. H. 1985. Academic achievement of historically lower-achieving students during the seventies. *Phi Delta Kappan* 66:542–44.

Fredericksen, N. 1984. The real test bias. *Am. Psychol.* 39:193–202.

Gallup, A. M. 1985. The 17th annual Gallup poll of the public's attitudes toward the public schools. *Phi Delta Kappan* 67:35–47.

———. 1986. The 18th annual Gallup poll of the public's attitudes toward the public schools. *Phi Delta Kappan* 68:43–59.

Gallup, A. M., and D. L. Clark. 1987. The 19th annual Gallup poll of the public's attitudes toward the public schools. *Phi Delta Kappan* 69:17–30.

Glass, G. V. 1978a. Matthew Arnold and minimum competence. *Ed. Forum* 42:139–44.

———. 1978b. Minimal competence and incompetence in Florida. *Phi Delta Kappan* 59:602–5.

Guskey, T. R. 1985. *Implementing mastery learning.* Belmont, CA: Wadsworth.

Guskey, T. R. 1987. Rethinking mastery learning reconsidered. *Rev. Ed. Res.* 57:225–29.

Haertel, E. H. 1985. Review of *Metropolitan Achievement Tests, 5th Edition* (1978). In *The Ninth Mental Measurements Yearbook* 1:963–65, ed. J. V. Mitchell. Lincoln, NE: Buros Institute of Mental Measurements, University of Nebraska–Lincoln.

———. 1986a. Choosing and using classroom tests: Teachers' perspectives on assessment. Paper presented at the meeting of the American Educational Research Association, San Francisco.

———. 1986b. Measuring school performance to improve school practice. *Ed. and Urban Soc.* 18:312–25.

———. 1986c. The valid use of student performance measures for teacher evaluation. *Ed. Eval. and Policy Anal.* 8:45–60.

Haertel, E. H., and R. C. Calfee. 1983. School achievement: Thinking about what to test. *J. Ed. Meas.* 20:119–32.

Haertel, E. H., S. Ferrara, M. Korpi, and B. Prescott. 1984. Testing in secondary schools: Student perspectives. Paper presented at the meeting of the American Educational Research Association, New Orleans.

Hamilton, S. F. 1986. Raising standards and reducing dropout rates. *Teachers Col. Rec.* 87:410–29.

Kellaghan, T., G. F. Madaus, and P. W. Airasian. 1982. *The effects of standardized testing.* Boston: Kluwer-Nijhoff.

Linn, R. L. 1973. Fair test use in selection. *Rev. Ed. Res.* 43:139–61.

———. 1983. Testing and instruction: Links and distinctions. *J. Ed. Meas.* 20:179–89.

———. 1984. Selection bias: Multiple meanings. *J. Ed. Meas.* 21:33–47.

Linn, R. L., G. F. Madaus, and J. J. Pedulla. 1982. Minimum competency testing: Cautions on the state of the art. *Am. J. Ed.* 91:1–35.

McBride, J. R. 1985. Computerized adaptive testing. *Ed. Lead.* 43:25–28.

McClelland, D. C. 1973. Testing for competence rather than "intelligence." *Am. Psychol.* 28:1–14.

Madaus, G. F. 1985. Test scores as administrative mechanisms in educational policy. *Phi Delta Kappan* 66:611–17.

———. 1988. The influence of testing on the curriculum. *Yearbook of the National Society for the Study of Education: Critical Issues in Curriculum* 87 (1): 83-121.

Mager, R. 1962. *Preparing instructional objectives.* Belmont, CA: Fearon.

Messick, S. A., A. Beaton, and F. M. Lord. 1983. *National Assessment of Educational Progress reconsidered: A new design for a new era.* Princeton, NJ: Educational Testing Service.

National Coalition of Advocates for Students. 1985. *Barriers to excellence: Our children at risk.* Boston, MA: Author.

Natriello, G., A. M. Pallas, and E. L. McDill. 1986. Taking stock: Renewing our research agenda on the causes and consequences of dropping out. *Teachers Col. Rec.* 87:430–40.

Ogura, Y. 1987. Examination hell: Japanese education's most serious problem. *Col. Bd. Rev.* 144:8–11, 26–30.

Peterson, A. D. C. 1972. *The international baccalaureate.* London: George G. Harrap.

Popham, W. J. 1981. The case for minimum competency testing. *Phi Delta Kappan* 63:89–91.

Popham, W. J., K. L. Cruse, S. C. Rankin, P. D. Sandifer, and P. L. Williams. 1985. Measurement-driven instruction: It's on the road. *Phi Delta Kappan* 66:628–34.

Popham, W. J., and E. Lindheim. 1981. Implications of a landmark ruling on Florida's minimum competency test. *Phi Delta Kappan* 63:18–20.

Quellmalz, E. S. 1985. Needed: Better methods for testing higher-order thinking skills. *Ed. Lead.* 43:29–35.

Rebell, M. A. 1986. Disparate impact of teacher competency testing on minorities: Don't blame the test-takers—or the tests. *Yale Law and Policy Rev.* 4:375–403.

Rogosa, D. R. 1985. Understanding correlates of change by modeling individual differences in growth. *Psychometrika* 50:203–28.

Salmon-Cox, L. 1982. *Technical report: Social functions of testing, school building studies.* Pittsburgh, PA: Learning Research and Development Center, University of Pittsburgh.

Selden, R. 1986. *White paper: Strategies and issues in the development of comparable indicators for measuring student achievement.* Denver, CO: State Educational Assessment Center, Council of Chief State School Officers.

Shepard, L., G. Camilli, and M. Averill. 1981. Comparison of procedures for detecting test-item bias with both internal and external ability criteria. *J. Ed. Stat.* 6:317–75.

Shepard, L., G. Camilli, and D. M. Williams. 1985. Validity of approximation techniques for detecting item bias. *J. Ed. Meas.* 22:77–105.

Shimahara, N. K. 1978. Socialisation for college entrance examinations in Japan. *Comparative Ed.* 14:253–66.

———. 1985. Japanese education and its implications for U.S. education. *Phi Delta Kappan* 66:418–21.

Shoemaker, D. M. 1975. Toward a framework for achievement testing. *Rev. Ed. Res.* 45:127–47.

Slavin, R. E. 1987a. Mastery learning reconsidered. *Rev. Ed. Res.* 57:175–213.

———. 1987b. Taking the mystery out of mastery: A response to Guskey, Anderson, and Burns. *Rev. Ed. Res.* 57:231–35.

Smith, M. S. 1984. A framework for the development of national educational indicators. In *Education evaluation and assessment in the United States.* Position paper and recommendations for action by the Council of Chief State School Officers. Washington, DC: Author.

Stedman, L. C., and M. S. Smith. 1983. Recent reform proposals for American education. *Contemp. Ed. Rev.* 2:85–104.

Stern, D. 1986. Toward a statewide system for public school accountability: A report from California. *Ed. and Urban Soc.* 18:326–46.

Sternberg, R. 1984. What should intelligence tests test? Implications of a triarchic theory of intelligence for intelligence testing. *Ed. Researcher* 13 (1): 5–15.

———. 1985. Teaching critical thinking, Part 2: Possible solutions. *Phi Delta Kappan* 67:277–80.

Stetz, F. P., and M. D. Beck. 1981. Attitudes toward standardized tests: Students, teachers, and measurement specialists. *Meas. in Ed.* 12:1–11.

Stiggins, R. J., and N. J. Bridgeford. 1985. The ecology of classroom assessment. *J. Ed. Meas.* 22:271–86.

Stiggins, R. J., N. F. Conklin, and N. J. Bridgeford. 1986. Classroom assessment: A key to effective education. *Ed. Meas: Issues and Practice* 5 (2): 5–17.

Strike, K. A. 1982. *Educational policy and the just society.* Urbana, IL: University of Illinois Press.

Suhor, C. 1985. Objective tests and writing samples: How do they affect instruction in composition? *Phi Delta Kappan* 66:635–39.

Sutherland, G. 1973. *Policy-making in elementary education, 1870–1895.* London: Oxford University Press.

Tamir, P. 1982. The design and use of a practical tests assessment inventory. *J. Bio. Ed.* 16:42–50.

———. 1985. The Israeli "Bagrut" examination in biology revisited. *J. Res. in Sci. Teaching* 22:31–40.

Wehlage, G. G., and R. A. Rutter. 1986. Dropping out: How much do schools contribute to the problem? *Teachers Col. Rec.* 87:374–92.

Weinstock, R. 1984. A Title I tale: High reading/math gains at low cost in Kansas City, Kansas. *Phi Delta Kappan* 65:632–34.

Making Sense of School Testing

Walter M. Haney

I. INTRODUCTION

Making sense of school testing programs nowadays is difficult for a variety of reasons. One aspect of testing in the nation's schools nevertheless seems clear—the sheer volume of standardized testing is increasing. As Chris Pipho wrote in 1985:

> Testing is on the increase! Business for commercial test publishers is up and new companies are eyeing the market, ready to jump into a business that looks like it is firmly standing on the up escalator. Nearly every large education reform effort of the past few years has either mandated a new form of testing or expanded uses of existing testing. (Pipho 1985, 19)

But it is perplexing *why* there is such emphasis on testing in education in recent years. Let me cite two kinds of examples from comments previously made at this conference and from recent literature on testing.

If you were sitting in the audience at this conference and paid attention to what has been going on in the field of standardized testing recently, you may well wonder what is happening. We heard from Eva Baker that there is a lot of meaningless testing going on. Testing is not doing what people think it is doing. Ed Haertel's analysis indicates that most testing programs are pretty grim. They are not working as they are supposed to work. We find, according to Jim Crouse, that the claims of one of the most prestigious educational testing organizations, the Educational Testing Service (ETS), regarding the validity of its tests and the analyses of its technically sophisticated experts do not always hold up under scrutiny.

How do we make sense out of all this? If testing programs are working out as poorly as Baker, Haertel, and Crouse seem to think, why all the increase in testing?

Recent Literature

Before attempting to help sort out answers to these questions, let me refer briefly to recent literature on how school testing programs are working out in practice. Since mid-century several major studies have sought to determine how tests and their results are actually used in schools (Hastings et al. 1960; Hastings, Runkel, and Damrin 1961; Goslin, Epstein, and Hallock 1965; Goslin 1967; Radwin 1981; Resnick, D. 1981; Resnick, L. 1981; Salmon-Cox 1981; Sproull and Zubrow 1981; Kellaghan, Madaus, and Airasian 1982; Glass and Ellwein

1986; and Dorr-Bremme and Herman 1987. See also Rudman et al. 1980, for a review of older literature.)

For the moment, I refer only to one of the more recent contributions to this genre of research, namely the study of recent efforts at educational reform "by raising test standards" conducted by the federally funded Center for Research on Evaluation, Standards and Student Testing (CRESST). After studying six of these large-scale efforts to raise test-score standards for elementary and secondary school students, CRESST researchers concluded that the standards-raising movement "emanates not so much from a desire to improve learning and instruction as from a desire to gain political control of education" (Glass and Ellwein 1986, 5). They suggested that the purposes and political interests served by raised standards "have little to do with the accomplishments and chances for 'life success' of the pupils in whose name the reforms are undertaken" (5–6). Regarding the effects of the reform-by-raising-test-standards movement, they observed, "Teachers are bearing the brunt of both the blame for the crisis that brought about the reforms and the busy work that the reforms have engendered. Pupils take what is dished out and move on" (Glass and Ellwein 1986, 6).

Glass and Ellwein conclude that recent test-based reforms are of more symbolic than instrumental consequence. They also observe that how one views the symbolic value of the test-based reforms depends on how close one is to the day-to-day stuff of teaching and learning:

> The nearer the individual is to the classroom, the less sympathetic he or she is with the symbolic activities of the schools. Persons so situated regard the instrumental goals and acts of the schools as paramount and the symbolic acts as wasteful, unnecessary, hypocritical or self-serving. Those individuals situated in the district central office see things differently. They point out to us that for them the symbolic is instrumental. To neutralize conflict, to shield the system from outside political pressures, to provide for continuity in leadership—these things maintain the environment in which the instrumental goals of education can be pursued. (Glass and Ellwein 1986, 5)

Again, we must ask what in the world is happening? Are all of the effort and money devoted to developing new testing programs as part of educational reform efforts over the last few years largely symbolic charades, having little to do with life behind the classroom door? What happens in the classroom when individual teachers try to teach individual students?

To help understand some of these issues, a historical perspective is useful to indicate both how we have come to be where we are and some of the possibilities and limits on testing in the schools in the future.

II. HISTORICAL PERSPECTIVE

It is very hard to track what has happened in testing in the schools, so I have adopted the strategy of looking at interest in testing somewhat indirectly by examining coverage of testing in the published literature. Figure 1 shows the average number of annual entries in the *Reader's Guide to Periodical Literature* under three different rubrics: Educational Tests, Intelligence Testing, and Intelligence Quotient from 1912 to the early 1980s. The figure shows something of the ebb and flow of interest in testing in the general periodical literature. What figure 1 indicates clearly is that popular attention to testing goes back a long time. Moreover, by the crude measure of average annual number of entries in the *Reader's Guide,* the amount of attention testing received in the popular literature was *higher* in the second decade of this century than it has been since then. Without going into the details of events associated with some of the peaks and valleys in this chart (for more detail on how this figure was constructed and the historical events reflected in it, see Haney 1984), I note that there was a lot of testing a long time ago. The Stanford Achievement Test was selling over a million and a half booklets annually in the 1930s, so large-scale standardized testing in the schools has a long history. Understanding the historical trends associated with the upsurge of testing in the schools will help to explain some of the seeming anomalies of current testing.

FIGURE 1

Average Annual Number of Entries in
Readers' Guide to Periodical Literature
Under Educational Tests,
Intelligence Testing, and Intelligence Quotient

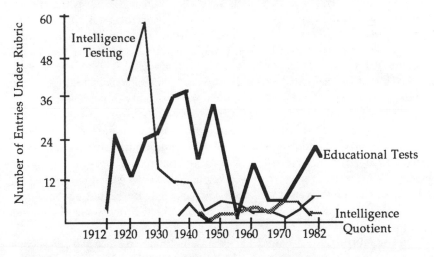

Three general trends have clearly influenced the growth of testing. First, testing became widely used in the schools starting in the second decade of this century, 1915 to 1920. Use of standardized tests in the schools expanded dramatically in the 1920s and 1930s. This was a period of immense growth in the schools and also in the bureaucratization of education, both of which contributed to the growth of testing.

The second trend worth noting is the commercialization of testing. Standardized tests had been around even before the turn of the century, but their use became widespread in the schools in the 1920s only after the *World Book Company* and several others began to sell tests.

Third, standardized testing gained widespread popularity in the schools only with the help of academics and would-be scientists, who, starting even before 1900, had promoted testing. Their efforts were greatly aided by the prominence publicly given to testing by the apparent success of "scientific" instruments of human selection during World War I.

This early history helps us to make some sense of what is happening today. Even though I am enamored of the history of testing, I will not elaborate here on the more recent history of educational testing, except to point out several major new influences since mid-century. First, testing has become much more a national enterprise—not just a federal enterprise, but also a national enterprise. Thus, even when the federal government is not directly involved, we see coalitions of governors and other state-level officials, for example, Lamar Alexander's committee, promoting coordinated uses of tests. So even if it is not federal, the recent growth in testing in the schools is still a national phenomenon.

Second, since the 1950s, there have been repeated controversies concerning the educational and social role of testing. Controversies have erupted publicly, for instance, about the fairness of testing in general, biases in testing regarding sex, ethnicity, and social class, and the effects of test results on teachers' judgments (see Haney 1984, 1981, for more detail).

Third, there has clearly been an effort to "professionalize" testing. In this volume, for instance, Ed Haertel mentions the possibility of developing better standards regarding testing. Though Haertel is likely aware of this, I would simply point out that efforts to develop "professional" standards for testing (intended to prevent abuses) go back well before mid-century. In my view, such professional standards have had very little impact on preventing abuse. Indeed, if you look at the ways in which some people have tried to use the test standards in defending what I take to be egregious abuses of testing, you have to conclude that such "professional standards" hold little potential for preventing significant abuse.

The fourth factor I would like to note is litigation since the 1950s concerning testing. Litigation on employment testing has a long history, but only in the 1960s do we begin to see significant amounts of litigation concerning educational testing. And if you look at influences on school testing practices and the elimination of certain uses of tests (only some of which I think were harmful), what has prevented these uses has not been professional associations' enforcement or vigorous application of test standards. Rather, it has been the use of test standards and innovative use of legal precedent in litigation by advocacy groups supported by selected members of this testing profession. Among the examples worth mentioning are the *Hobson v. Hanson*, the *Larry P.*, and the *Debra P.* cases. Not the test companies, not the professional associations, per se, but selected experts on testing are the ones who make use of test standards to help prevent abuse—or at least what they perceive as abuse—of tests.

III. THE CURRENT SITUATION

So, there is currently a whole lot of testing in the schools. Nobody knows exactly how much because there are so many different tests given by different sponsoring agencies—the schools themselves, the federal government (for example, through mandates issued originally through Title I, now Chapter I), and the states. Especially since 1970, there has been a great increase in state-sponsored tests, originally called minimum competency tests and now increasingly called basic skills or scholastic skills tests. Moreover, not only has there been an increase in state-mandated uses of tests, there have been specifically legislated or mandated policy uses of the tests—for example, in New Jersey, to identify low performing schools, and in California, the "Cash for CAPs" program. Some wonderful anecdotes have been passed along to me about the way in which the "Cash for CAPs" program has been working out in practice, but I will not take the time to mention them here.

Research going back to 1960 on how tests are used or not used in schools has yielded some general findings worth mentioning. Here I refer to works such as those done by Hastings et al. (1960, 1961), Goslin (1967), Goslin et al. (1965), the University of California at Los Angeles Center for the Study of Evaluation (1987), and George Madaus (see Madaus, this volume).

First of all, since the 1960s, school people consistently seem quite uninformed about some of the basics of the technology of testing, for example, percentiles and grade equivalent scores. Some have suggested we ought to teach school people more about the technology of testing. I am not sure that is the solution, but studies do show that many teachers, administrators, and others who are expected to use the test results do not know much about the technology of testing.

Second, run-of-the-mill testing programs, traditional standardized achievement testing programs, do not seem to be much used by administrators or teachers. Probably the clearest exception to this general trend in research findings is the study that received a lot of publicity in the late 1960s and early 1970s, the Rosenthal and Jacobsen study *Pygmalion in the Classroom* (1968). In this study, researchers gave false IQ test results to teachers and found that as a result the teachers' behavior changed and actually affected how kids did on subsequent tests.

Controversy surrounded the Rosenthal and Jacobsen study and a lot of people tried to replicate it; the results were mixed. Some people thought the original study was severely flawed and many researchers failed to confirm its findings, which raised many interesting methodological issues. One particularly interesting reanalysis of the Rosenthal and Jacobsen study was by Raudenbush (1984), in which he performed a meta-analysis looking at what factors seemed to explain whether or not people found effects from efforts to replicate the Rosenthal and Jacobsen study. Raudenbush found that when he put dummy variables into his meta-analysis to control for various aspects of study design, one variable seemed to account for whether or not effects showed up. The variable was how much contact teachers had had with individual students *prior* to getting the false test information. Specifically, he found that when there was less than two weeks of prior contact between the teacher and the students, the effects seemed to be greater. Effects also seemed to be greater at grade one and grade seven—transition points in the bureaucratic structure of our schools. At least to my mind, Raudenbush's reanalysis seems indirectly to reinforce the historical fact that testing has largely served as an aid to the bureaucratic structure of education in this country. Test results have very little influence on the day-to-day activities of most teachers. Where they do have an impact is at the bureaucratic interstices of schooling.

I would like to reiterate a point that Eva Baker made previously (see Baker, this volume)—much of what goes on in the name of testing has to do with the symbolic values associated with testing, values associated with objectivity, science, standards, and so forth. Moreover, many of our assumptions—and I include myself—regarding the instrumental value of testing probably do not have a great deal of substance behind them.

In this regard I cite three examples. First, a lot of people suggest that tests in the schools are useful in providing diagnostic information so that teachers can "remediate" students. Research on how tests are used in schools indicates that this does not happen very often. Moreover, how much time do teachers have to perform the kind of analyses that often are suggested to be associated with diagnostic use of test results? Indeed, whenever I hear people talk about the diagnostic value of test information, I always think of the anecdote that Sheldon White told when he was head of a previous national commission on testing:

> Whenever anybody tells me I need more information to make better decisions, I look at my desk. It's piled with information. I can't find specific information when I need it, because I've got so

much paper. The solution to my problem in making better decisions, is not more information, it's less information.

I think most teachers are in exactly the same position. They do not need
more test information to make decisions, they need less information, or maybe
more time.

A second example concerns what is loosely said to be evidence about
the validity of tests. I would point out that many testing programs have far less
reasonable or even plausible evidence concerning their validity than the kind
of evidence Jim Crouse (1985) critiques regarding the SAT. The kind of "content
validity" studies that have been conducted to bolster the use of certain tests,
for example, teacher compeency tests, have very little to do with validity as it is
described by some of the best researchers on test validity, and is set out again,
to my mind, in the standards on tests. But people still claim that these tests
have validity even though they have scarcely even considered the kinds of
inferences that are made on the basis of test results. As the test standards
clearly point out, validity has to do not with tests themselves, but with the inferences that are made on the basis of test results. But if you push very hard with
regard to the inferences made on the basis of most commonly used tests, you
find very little evidence.

A related issue that I think has been a source of great confusion over the
past twenty years is test bias. A lot of test specialists claim that there is little
evidence that tests are biased according to commonly accepted psychometric
definitions of bias. Well, if you accept the definitions, the *psychometric* definitions of bias, I think they are probably correct. But if you look up the word bias
in the dictionary, or if you talk to nonspecialists about what it means to say that
a test is biased, the notion of bias has very little to do with the psychometric
definitions. What "bias" means in the common lexicon is that if something is
biased, it is unfair. In this sense I think that most public concern about test bias
has a lot more to do with what the testing literature calls group parity models of
fair selection than it does with the psychometric definitions of bias. And I think
that if you try to ferret out the symbolic value, what is really behind people's
concern about bias, it is more similar to this issue of group parity than to bias as
psychometrically defined. Yet testing experts have retreated from considerations of group parity because they say those group parity models deal with
issues of social and political values. Since we are technical experts, they say, we
have no special insight into which models of group parity are most appropriate.
Incredibly enough, however, people who advance such arguments pretend that
the psychometric models for analyzing bias are somehow technically above the
fray and do not involve implicit assumptions about social and political values.

IV. THE FUTURE

Each of these points may be worth elaborating, but I will not attempt such elaboration here. Instead, in closing, I would like to point out things that I see that may or may not happen on a couple of fronts. Before doing that, let me show one more figure which will help to demonstrate that standardized testing is not simply distorting curriculum concerns. Rather it seems clear that testing is becoming more and more the coin of the educational realm and is coming to define the goals of schooling. Again, it is hard to get evidence on this, but one thing that I did, just to try to get a sense for how educators have paid attention to curriculum concerns versus testing, was to do another analysis of the coverage of these subjects in published literature. Here I used the *Education Index*, which is useful because it goes back more than fifty years and over that time has employed fairly consistent indexing rubrics. What I did was to simply measure the annual number of column inches of references in the *Education Index* from 1930 to 1985 under two general rubrics: Curriculum, and Tests and Scales. I will not go into the details of how I did this, but the results, shown in figure 2, are striking. Note that from the 1930s until the middle 1960s, the material on curriculum seems to be as voluminous as the information on testing. After the mid-1960s, however, notice what has happened. Why is it that since the 1960s more has been published on testing than on curriculum?

FIGURE 2

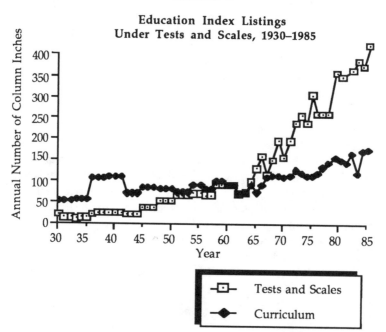

Beginning in the mid-1960s, among the many factors that contributed to the increased prominence of testing were the National Defense Education Act (NDEA), which provided federal funds for training in educational testing; the civil-rights movement, which sought to use testing to help ensure equal educational opportunities for minorities; and the Elementary and Secondary Education Act (ESEA) of 1965, which clearly contributed to growth in school testing via federal mandates for program evaluation. But whatever the historical causes, it is clear that testing now receives much more attention in the educational literature (the *Education Index* is based exclusively on education literature) than curriculum. At least in theory, according to what educators say, we ought to start with curriculum and then decide later what to test on the basis of curricular concerns.

What this pattern suggests to me is that testing is increasing not just as a measurement technique, but also as a signaling device to communicate what is valued in our schools. In this regard, I do not view the symbolic value of testing as being totally negative. I think that if we are really concerned about making tests more useful to educators in the schools, we have to take the notion seriously that tests communicate what is valued. This perspective suggests to me that we ought not to worry so much about the strictly technical issues, but instead must concern ourselves more with tests not only as measurement devices, but as means of communicating what we want our schools to be doing.

With regard to tests as signaling devices, there is not a lot of evidence, but I know of several items that shed light on this perspective. One interesting study was done by Charles Suhor (1985), who was affiliated with the National Council of Teachers of English and interested in the effects of objective tests versus essay exams on the teaching of writing. First, he informally surveyed about three hundred people involved in the teaching of English around the country, and then he tried to find what he could in the published literature. He concluded that there seemed to be unanimity of opinion that the essay testing of writing has a beneficial impact on the teaching of writing, whereas multiple-choice items have a negative impact on the teaching of writing. The apparent reason was that essay testing helped to focus attention on actual writing whereas multiple-choice testing did not.

Another example of viewing tests as signaling devices comes from the College Board and the Educational Testing Service when they reintroduced the essay portion of the English Composition Test. The essay test was reintroduced in 1977 not because there was any new evidence concerning the validity of the essay test but because there was so much demand from high school English teachers for the reintroduction of the essay form of the exam: "As the writing crisis became a major concern in American education, the College Board responded by introducing the 20-minute essay once again in December 1977,

in order *to signal the importance of writing in the secondary curriculum"*(Donlon 1984, 90, italics added).

V. CONCLUSION

Some technical developments on the horizon offer the potential for making
testing more useful educationally. I think some of the new scaling technologies
that will allow more useful equating of test results with instructional materials
show promise. I am intrigued with what people are doing with computerized
testing, though I am highly skeptical of some of the tentative claims made
about the functional equivalence of computerized tests and paper-and-pencil
tests. Everything we know about method variance from a long history of research in testing suggests they are not likely to be functionally equivalent. And
I think that some of the test development methods that will allow more
openness in both the content and form of testing hold considerable potential
for improving things marginally.

Some of the broader social controversies about testing and some of what
I perceive in previous prescriptions about misuses of tests, technical developments, and standards regarding test use seem to have only a small potential
for affecting practice. If we look at the political history of testing, we have to
conclude that the worst abuses of testing have not been curtailed by any kind
of technical analysis, any kind of professional unanimity, but rather by political
organization, political protests, and litigation. So I believe that these technical
developments and elaboration of standards may improve things only at the
margins. But if we look at the history of testing, and at past social controversies
and litigation concerning testing, we are led to conclude that to curb the worst
abuses, we cannot rely on professional organizations or technicians. History
tells us quite clearly that political action, litigation, and legislation are more
effective means of affecting educational and other social applications of
testing.

REFERENCES

Crouse, J., 1985. Does the SAT help colleges make better selection decisions? *Harvard Educational Review* 55 (2): 195–219.

Dorr-Bremme, D. W., and J. L. Herman. 1987. *Assessing student achievement: A profile of classroom practices.* Los Angeles, CA: Center for the Study of Evaluation, University of California.

Donlon, T. F., ed. 1984. *The College Board technical handbook for the Scholastic Aptitude Test and Achievement Tests.* New York: College Entrance Examination Board.

Glass, G. V., and M. C. Ellwein. 1986. Reform by raising test standards. *CRESST Evaluation Comment* (December): 1–6.

Goslin, D. 1967. *Teachers and testing.* New York: Russell Sage Foundation.

Goslin, D., R. R. Epstein, and B. A. Hallock. 1965. *The use of standardized tests in elementary schools.* New York: Russell Sage Foundation.

Haney, W. 1984. Testing reasoning and reasoning about testing. *Review of Educational Research* 54 (4): 597–654.

Haney, W. 1981. Validity, vaudeville, and values: A short history of social concerns over standardized testing. *American Psychologist* 36 (10): 1021–34.

Hastings, J., P. Runkel, and D. Damrin. 1961. *Effects of use of tests by teachers trained in a summer institute.* Urbana: Bureau of Educational Research, University of Illinois. (ERIC Document Reproduction Service No. 002925).

Hastings, J., P. Runkel, D. Damrin, R. Kane, and G. Larson. 1960. *The use of test results.* Urbana: Bureau of Educational Research, University of Illinois.

Kellaghan, T., G. F. Madaus, and P. W. Airasian. 1982. *The effects of standardized testing.* Boston: Kluwer-Nijhoff.

Pipho, C. 1985. Tracking the reforms. Part 5: Testing—Can it measure the success of the reform movement? *Education Week* (May 22): 19.

Radwin, E. 1981. *A case study of New York City: Citywide reading testing program.* Cambridge, MA: The Huron Institute.

Raudenbush, S. 1984. Magnitude of teacher expectancy effects on pupil IQ as a function of the credibility of expectancy induction. *Journal of Educational Psychology* 76 (1): 85–97.

Resnick, D. 1981. Testing in America: A supportive environment. *Phi Delta Kappan* 62:625–28.

Resnick, L. 1981. Introduction: Research to inform a debate. *Phi Delta Kappan* 62:623–24.

Rosenthal, R., and L. Jacobsen. 1968. *Pygmalion in the classroom.* New York: Holt, Rinehart and Winston.

Rudman, H., J. Kelly, D. Wanous, W. Mehrens, C. Clark, and A. Porter. 1980. *Integrating assessment with instruction. A review (1922–1980).* East Lansing: Institute for Research on Teaching, Michigan State University.

Salmon-Cox, L. 1981. Teachers and standardized tests: What's really happening? *Phi Delta Kappan* 62:631–34.

Suhor, C. 1985. Objective tests and writing samples: How do they affect instruction in composition? *Phi Delta Kappan* 66:635–39.

Sproull, L., and D. Zubrow. 1981. Standardized testing from the administrative perspective. *Phi Delta Kappan* 62:628–31.

The Irish Study Revisited

George F. Madaus

When Bernard Gifford asked if I would write about the results of the "Irish study," a large-scale experimental study of the effects of standardized testing, I quickly agreed. It was an offer I could not refuse. After all, the Irish study had consumed better than ten years of my professional life, and here was an eleventh-hour opportunity to publicize the findings which, unfortunately, are not widely known outside some testing circles. I was, however, in a curious position; the book detailing our findings is readily available (Kellaghan, Madaus, and Airasian 1982), so perhaps all that was needed was to call attention to the book. Further, my recent work has led me to realize that the Irish results do not speak directly to many of the current policy uses of tests in the schools. This is not because the results are contextually bound to Ireland—quite the contrary. I believe that the Irish results still speak powerfully to the use of tests in our traditional school-district testing programs, which I will describe in more detail presently. What has changed since the days of the Irish study is the way standardized test results are being used.

The Irish experiment can be characterized as a low-stakes testing program (Madaus 1988). A low-stakes testing program, in contrast to a high-stakes program, is one where people do not perceive that important rewards or sanctions are tied directly to test performance. In such programs, results are reported to teachers but there is no immediate, automatic decision linked to performance. Further, the teachers do not perceive that the results are used to evaluate their teaching. This does not mean that results from such programs do not affect teachers' perception of students, nor that student-placement decisions are not sometimes related to test performance. The important distinction is that teachers, students, and parents do not perceive test performance as a *direct* or *automatic* vehicle of reward or sanction. This is the type of program we simulated in the Irish study. While the Irish study was unfolding, however, test information started to be used in the United States in dramatically new and powerful ways. In the mid-seventies test results began to be used seriously for policy purposes, first at the state level but eventually at the school-district level as well.

Therefore, given this switch in testing emphasis, I decided to present the background of the Irish study—what we did, and the highlights of what we found—and then discuss the findings in light of changes in test use since the study was completed. My hope is that by doing this I can put in proper perspective the impact of both the older, traditional uses of standardized tests, and their contemporary uses.

First, I shall describe the background of the Irish study. Second, I will briefly outline the design of the study and what we did. Third, I will discuss how providing teachers with information about student performance on standardized tests affected the schools, teachers, parents, and, of course, students. I shall also describe what to me was the most interesting aspect of our study: our investigation of testing and the expectancy process (at the time popularly referred to as the Pygmalion effect). Fourth, I will discuss the limitations of the results in terms of more recent uses of standardized test information in the policy sphere. Finally, I shall describe a set of seven general principles that describe the consequences of using standardized tests in the schools.

I. THE BACKGROUND OF THE IRISH STUDY

During the late sixties and continuing into the seventies there was considerable controversy over the widespread use in American schools of commercially available norm-referenced standardized tests of achievement and ability. While such tests had been a common feature of annual school-district testing programs since the 1920s, and while they had been criticized by some academicians since their inception after World War I, they were, until the late sixties, regarded by most educators as simply a normal, largely nonthreatening, annual aspect of school life.[1] Travers captures best the general acceptance by educators of the enormous growth of the achievement testing movement between the two wars:

> Many principals must have felt that, by participating in the new achievement testing enterprise, they placed themselves on the frontier of progress. Also, teachers and children did not seem to be bothered by the taking of standardized tests. They knew virtually nothing was ever done with the results. When the teacher spent the morning giving a test, it was an easy morning for him or her, and a not unpleasant one for most of the pupils. Such tests were much less threatening to the children than a test prepared by the teacher on which a grade might depend (1983, 145).

Starting in the sixties, however, a formidable array of criticism directed at the use of these tests emerged, perhaps epitomized by the National Education Association's call in 1971 for a moratorium on such testing.[2] The criticism ranged from charges of bias in test content (Clark 1963) to criticisms of the functions for which tests were used, in particular, the selection and

---

[1] There were notable exceptions to this description, of course, but in general I feel it is an accurate characterization of school testing programs.

[2] Calls for moratoriums are not new. In the mid-to-late-1920s there was a movement to declare a moratorium on research, or declare a science holiday (Carroll 1986).

labeling of students (Pidgeon 1970; Rosenthal and Jacobsen 1968). The effects of tests on the general educational environment were also criticized; for example, tests were accused of "arousing fear" and "satisfying greed" in students (Holt 1968); one commentator went so far as to describe some tests as "pretty strong poison" (Houts 1975).[3]

During this period, testing also had its defenders. Those who saw standardized tests of achievement and ability as beneficial argued that, when used properly, they are more "objective" and reliable than other, more impressionistic measures of student attainment. Thus, it was argued, tests provided information about students, individually and in groups, that was helpful in teaching and guidance. Proponents also claimed that school testing programs assisted administrators as well as teachers in monitoring the educational programs of schools and in evaluating new curricula, instructional materials, and teaching methods. Finally, when test information is given to students and parents, it acts as a source of motivation and contributes to the improvement of students' learning and the enhancement of their self-concepts (see Adams 1964; Bloom 1969; Ebel 1966; Findley 1963; Tyler 1968, 1969).

This small sample of the supposed advantages and disadvantages of tests, taken from the literature of that period, indicates that the questions surrounding their use were many and complex. Several difficulties, all interrelated, became apparent when one tried to discuss and evaluate the arguments on both sides of the issue. First, many of the arguments were diffuse. For example, critics frequently failed to distinguish between types or uses of tests. Second, empirical evidence to support statements on either side was rarely cited. The criticisms in particular seemed to be based on critics' political and ideological positions on the educational system in general; testing became the subject of criticism insofar as it was seen to support and reinforce

---

[3]Controversy over testing was not a new phenomenon. For example, in a historical survey of examinations from ancient times through the mid-1940s, O'Meara compiled a comprehensive and rather amusing list of ills associated with testing:

> carelessness, hatred, favoritism, labor unrest, unprogressiveness, defective art, dishonesty, discontent, poverty, fraudulency, laziness, a generator of mental defectiveness and physical degeneration, serfdom, radicalism, suffering, death, strikes, and war (O'Meara 1944).

that system.[4] The arguments in support of testing were also rooted in a particular world view that colored perceptions of education and testing.[5] Finally, much of the criticism came from people outside the testing profession and was made in the public arena rather than within the confines of scholarly publications (Cronbach 1975; Jensen 1980), which meant that the debate did not abide by the canons that normally apply in scholarly publications. It also meant that a wide range of publics considered the issues important.

Thus, while many effects had been attributed to testing during this controversy, surprisingly little empirical evidence about the effects of testing was available. Because the use of standardized tests had grown so widely in the United States over the previous fifty years, it was extremely difficult to identify school systems, teachers, or students who had not experienced standardized testing, and who thus could be used as a reference group with which systems, teachers, and students who had experienced such testing programs might be compared.

While the controversy raged over testing in this country and in Great Britain as well, I had been working in Ireland on an evaluation of its Leaving Certification Examinations (Madaus and Macnamara 1970). In discussing the debate over testing in America and the British Isles with Tom Kellaghan, the director of the Educational Research Centre, St. Patrick's Training College in Dublin, it occurred to us that Ireland offered a unique opportunity to empirically examine the arguments about the effects of standardized testing. Even though Ireland had a well-developed educational system, very little use was made of standardized testing. Thus, the conditions existed in which an experimental design could be implemented, with some schools testing and receiving test information, while others would not. Differences between schools

---

[4]Ideological positions that opposed testing were strongly represented—but by no means limited to—people who held egalitarian or Marxist views, particularly in Europe. For example, Neander from West Germany, summarized the Marxist position this way:

> The system of objectivized measurement of success is not only a means of guaranteeing the enforcement of subject matter class . . . in the hands of the representatives of capital interests. . . . The system reveals its bourgeois class attributes in particular by the fact that, even under the pretense of aiming at reform, it acts contrary to the interests of the wage earners, in this instance especially the workers, and consequently in the interests of capital (quoted in Ingenkamp 1977, 15–16).

The egalitarian view can be best seen in the writing of Ivan Illich and Paulo Freire.

[5]Many defenders—but like the critics, by no means all of them—held a logical positivistic, utilitarian view of the world, a view that saw education in terms of an input-output factory or engineering model.

following these two conditions should be attributable to the testing program. Joined by Peter Airasian, we developed a proposal to implement such a study in Ireland. Eventually the study was funded by the Russell Sage Foundation, the Carnegie Corporation, the National Institute for Education, and the Spencer Foundation. The Department of Education of the Irish government supported the development of tests and the administration of the testing program.

Our objective was to assess the impact of standardized testing and test information over a wide range of variables. We sought to monitor possible effects on pupils' attitudes, perceptions, and scholastic performance. We asked such questions as:

- Does the availability of standardized test information affect teachers' perceptions of pupils?
- Does it affect students' level of achievement?
- How much weight do teachers give to standardized tests relative to other types of evidence in making decisions about pupils?
- Do teachers perceive standardized tests as biased against certain groups of pupils?
  Does the availability of test information affect teachers' grouping practices?
- Does the content of standardized tests affect the nature and emphasis of classroom instruction?
- Do standardized test results influence a student's self-perception?
- Is testing perceived by teachers as fostering fear and competitiveness?
- Does a testing program in schools have any impact on parents' perceptions of their children?

The answers to these and other related questions had relevance primarily for the initiation, continuation, or elimination of school testing programs that focused primarily on providing *the classroom teacher* with ability and achievement information about individual pupils.

Thus, the model we were testing was that of the traditional, annual, school-district testing program initiated and controlled by the school district, where students are tested and, some weeks later, teachers are given information about the performance of each student. Such testing programs did not involve high stakes such as graduation or promotion decisions, teacher evaluations, merit pay allocations, the awarding of compensatory funds, automatic placement of students in remedial programs, or school or district certification, which are characteristic of many such programs today. Ours reflected the gentler use of test information described in the Travers quote above. It is important to keep this perspective in mind.

II. THE DESIGN OF THE IRISH STUDY

In an attempt to obtain empirical evidence that would speak to these and other issues relating to standardized testing, a classroom-based standardized testing program was introduced experimentally to a stratified random sample of Irish schools in 1973, and continued for a period of four years.

Basically we simulated the mechanics of a traditional school-based testing program in the United States. An external agency (the Educational Research Centre, St. Patrick's College) provided schools with standardized norm-referenced tests of ability and achievement. Classroom teachers administered the tests to the students and returned completed answer sheets to the research organization for scoring and processing. Test results were then returned by mail to teachers.

The test battery for the program was made up of a test of general ability or intelligence (an Irish adaptation of the Otis Lennon, Form J at grades two, three, and four, and the Drumcondra Verbal Reasoning Test at grades five and six), attainment tests in English and Mathematics in grades two through six (Drumcondra Attainment Tests, Level I in grade two, Level II in grades three and four, and Level III in grades five and six), and an attainment test in Irish in grades three and four, and Level III in grades five and six. All tests were developed and normed for Irish pupils.

In most respects the attainment tests were very similar to American ones. Each test was made up of several sections. For example, the mathematics tests have separate sections for computation, concepts, and problem solving, and the language tests have separate sections measuring vocabulary, spelling, language usage, and reading comprehension. Most items on the tests used a selection-type format (that is, multiple-choice). However, for some items on the verbal reasoning test and some on the lower level attainment tests, the pupil was required to supply his or her answer. For all tests except attainment tests taken in grades five and six (Level III), pupils made their answers in the test booklets; at grades five and six, separate machine-scorable answer sheets were used.

In this investigation, we were primarily interested in the use of standardized norm-referenced tests of ability and achievement and the information derived from such tests. However, some provision was also made for examining the effects of variation in the type of information supplied (normative information and diagnostic information based on item data). It should be noted that some of the emerging testing approaches that endeavored to wed instruction and evaluation (for example, mastery learning and continuous achievement monitoring) were not examined.

The sample of schools for the investigation was drawn from the population of elementary schools in the Republic of Ireland. Altogether 170 schools began the study, and these were divided into a number of treatment groups. The treatment groups were actually more complex than we shall outline here; a full description is provided in Kellaghan, Madaus, and Airasian (1980). The present outline should suffice for the purpose of this discussion.

In the main treatment group, standardized testing of ability and achievement was carried out in grades two through six at the beginning of the school year, and norm-referenced information in the form of standard scores and percentile ranks on the performance of students was returned to all teachers.

In the second treatment group, limited to grades five and six, the standardized testing program was similar to that in the preceding treatment. In addition, teachers received a more detailed breakdown of students' performance on tests in terms of the skills and contents assessed by the tests. For example, in mathematics, details were provided on the performance of students on groups of items designed to measure a student's ability to multiply and divide fractions, while in reading comprehension, information was provided on items that involved the drawing of inferences from passages. Thus, an attempt was made to provide diagnostic information on students' performance.[6]

Two other groups acted as controls for the experiment. In the first of these, no testing was carried out until the end of the study. In the second control group, standardized tests of ability and achievement were administered, as in the main treatment group, at the beginning of each year in grades two through six. However, no feedback on students' performance was provided to teachers.

Throughout the study, information was collected in questionnaires on schools, teachers, and students. Principals supplied information on school practices and organization as well as on the use of test results. Teachers supplied information on their perceptions of and use of evaluation procedures in general and their perceptions of standardized tests in particular. They also provided information on their use of the test results provided to them during the course of the study. Data on students were also obtained from teachers. Teachers were asked to rate each student in their class on a variety of cognitive and noncognitive characteristics. This information was collected at the beginning of the school year before teachers had received test results and again at the end of the school year. Students themselves also completed questionnaires to ascertain their general attitudes about school work, their concepts of themselves as learners, and their educational expectations. These questionnaires were limited to sixth grade. A final source of evidence on

---

[6]We are using the term diagnostic in the limited sense of giving to teachers information that identified students who were weak or deficient in the particular areas reported on; not in the medical sense of giving the teacher reasons why the student was weak in the content area or skill.

students was their performance on standardized tests administered in all treatment and control groups at the end of the investigation.

Overall, then, the main treatment variables concern information from test results (as against no information), type of information (simple norm-referenced information or norm-referenced with more detailed diagnostic information), and type of test (ability, norm-referenced achievement, and criterion-referenced achievement).

III. THE MAIN FINDINGS

Before considering the main findings of our experiment, the reader should know that a survey of school practices at its beginning confirmed our belief that the use of standardized tests of ability and achievement were rare indeed in Irish schools. What did we find when we introduced standardized test information into this kind of environment? Two sets of findings are of particular interest. The first relates to the general reactions of teachers and students to tests and the testing program; the second, to the congruence between the test results and teachers' already formed judgments of pupils.

Reactions of both teachers and pupils to the testing program were very positive. Teachers perceived standardized ability and achievement tests as accurate measures of pupils' scholastic ability—more accurate in fact than the public examinations, though somewhat less accurate than their own classroom tests. The reports of pupils as well as of teachers indicated that the pupils approached the tests seriously; a large majority enjoyed sitting for the tests (80%), and did not feel afraid (85%), nervous (70%), or bored (83%).

The testing was carried out in a basically hospitable, nonthreatening environment. Further, the test scores supplied to teachers were not expected to have a large impact. That is, when teachers' ratings of pupils' ability and achievement, and pupils' test scores for the same variables are compared, we find considerable agreement. No matter how we analyzed the data, test scores on the whole served to confirm teacher ratings.

Thus, we found that the potential for testing and test information of the type described above to upset the existing evaluative ecology of the classroom was quite limited. After all, teachers were operating on the basis of well-established evaluative systems and the provision of standardized test information largely confirmed the judgments they had already formed about pupils. Given this fact, some of our findings on the effects of testing on teachers and pupils indicates that test information did indeed have a surprisingly strong impact.

School-Level Effects

Our findings on the effects on schools of a four-year program of standardized testing were surprising in at least two respects. The first surprise related to the almost total lack of effects on school practices and organization as reported by school principals. When we compared the responses of principals in the experimental and control groups relating to various aspects of school organization and practice, we were forced to conclude that the overall impact of the testing program was slight.

The second major surprise in our findings relating to the effects at the school level concerns the test performance of pupils at the end of the study. If testing and giving information about performance to teachers have a beneficial effect on the scholastic achievement of pupils, then we expected that effect to be reflected in the improved test performance over time of the group which had received test information. While our findings about pupil test performance are complex, they certainly cannot be interpreted to support the view that the provision of test information to teachers invariably leads to increases in *school mean performance* of pupils on standardized tests. In fact, while on the ability test the group that received information showed the best performance, on the achievement tests it was the group with no prior test experience that performed best. Secondly, the two tested groups (one with information, one without) never differed significantly from each other in their performance. When we looked at variations in the type of information provided (norm-referenced, diagnostic), we had to conclude that the type of information the teachers received was not a significant factor in determining school-level achievements.

In a final set of school-level analyses, we examined the distribution of ability, achievement, and socioeconomic background of students within and between classes in schools that had more than one class at a grade level. If test results are used to stratify pupils, then we would expect that classes in schools that had information would become, relative to classes in schools without such information, internally more homogeneous in terms of ability/achievement. Further, class means at a grade level should become more widely dispersed. These hypotheses were not substantiated. Classes in schools with test information did not exhibit greater homogeneity in ability, achievement, or socioeconomic background than classes in schools without such information.

Teacher-Level Effects

At the end of the study, data were collected from teachers relating to their activities, beliefs, and opinions about standardized tests and test results. Teachers were also asked about their use of tests in making decisions about pupils. On most topics, information was obtained at two points in time and thus it was possible to examine changes over time in teachers' perceptions of standardized testing.

In general, teachers in all treatment groups expressed positive attitudes toward the standardized tests used in the study. They liked the tests and perceived that their pupils liked them. Thus, while there were changes in teachers' perceptions, beliefs, and reported practices associated with the availability of standardized test results, and these were in the predictable direction, they were not extensive or radical. This conclusion is compatible with the finding discussed above that teachers, at the beginning of the study and at its end, in all treatment groups, perceived themselves as being the most accurate judges of a pupil's intelligence and achievement. It is unlikely that providing teachers with one further piece of information would seriously disrupt this view, even if the information differed radically from already formed judgments. When you consider that teachers had rated the accuracy of standardized tests very highly, and that the results from such tests basically confirmed their judgments about and perceptions of pupils, based on a multiplicity of cues and a variety of information sources, then it is clear that major changes in the perceptions and behavior of teachers would be very improbable indeed.

The results were clear. The availability of standardized test information did not substantially alter the evaluative criteria on which teachers report they would most rely in making a variety of decisions about their pupils. Rather than replacing teacher judgments and observation, classroom tests, and recommendations from other teachers, standardized test results were integrated into existing information about pupils and probably were seen as basically confirming, rather than replacing, other sources of information. Thus, their impact did not become very apparent in terms of reported practice.

In terms of the impact of the kind of information received, we found that teachers who received diagnostic information were more likely than teachers in other treatment groups to report using the test results. They were also more likely to have seen pupil results from previous years, and more likely to communicate results to more pupils and parents. However, as we saw above, this did not result in higher school mean achievement scores for the diagnostic information treatment group.

Parent-Level Effects

Our survey of parents revealed that the standardized testing program had little effect on parents. Perhaps the only finding of any note was a negative one—that parents, on the whole, reported they were unaware of any such program. This is surprising because a large percentage of sixth-grade pupils (about 80%) said they told their parents they had sat for standardized tests. Perhaps the communication was not effective and either parents or children misunderstood what was involved in the testing program, or in the interviews parents had forgotten about the information, probably because they did not perceive it as relating to anything very important in their children's education. It would be hard to imagine a finding like this in relation to present-day testing programs in the United States. This finding indicates how traditional school-based standardized testing programs have changed since the situation

Travers described prevailed, and even since the days in which the Irish study was planned. We will return to this point presently.

Despite lack of specific information about our standardized testing program, Irish parents' attitudes toward such testing was positive. For example, about half the parents interviewed thought the provision of norm-referenced intelligence and achievement tests would be a change for the better in Irish education, and a large majority said they would be interested in receiving information on the performance of their children on such tests, if such information was available. However, a question must be raised about their understanding of what such tests precisely involve. Even if they had some idea of the nature of standardized tests, we can be fairly certain that few of them had any idea of controversies surrounding the use of standardized tests in the United States.

Pupil-Level Effects

When we began the Irish study, the effects of standardized testing were most widely debated in terms of its impact on pupils. We sought evidence relating to such effects in a number of areas. The findings are extensive and complex, so I will highlight only some of them.

In the case of achievement-test performance, there seems to be a unique effect associated with the provision of diagnostic information. Pupils for whom both diagnostic and norm-referenced information was available out-performed pupils in all other groups. On the intelligence test, the performance of pupils in this group was similar to that of other tested groups. Thus the effect was specific to the tests for which the diagnostic information had been provided, that is, the achievement tests.

These findings are not unreasonable. The aim of providing diagnostic information is to make available to teachers sufficiently detailed information to help them in the identification of individual students' learning difficulties. We saw above that teachers make more use of such information than they do of simple norm-referenced information. Our findings seem to indicate that this use paid off in terms of improved test performance.

However, these findings must be tempered by our failure to find any specific effect associated with the provision of diagnostic information in our school-level analysis. There are a number of possible explanations for this discrepancy. First, the larger number of degrees of freedom available for the pupil-level analyses meant that smaller differences between treatment groups would exhibit significance. Second, in our pupil-level analyses we departed from our experimental unit, which was the school. Third, it may be that aggregating scores to the level of the school masked within-school differences, differences which may have existed either between teachers or between pupils. Indeed, it might be argued that the teacher or pupil is a more appropriate unit of analysis than the school to test the effects of the provision of test information. If one accepts this argument, then the pupil-level results may be seen as of greater import than the school-level ones. In order to obtain significant results, however, we had to depart from analyses based on our experimental unit, the school.

Analyses of differences between treatment groups relating to pupils' perceptions of scholastic work and of related behaviors revealed that students in the group in which teachers had received norm-referenced test information tended to rate themselves lower in a number of areas (spoken Irish, English composition, interest in school, keenness to do well in school, and originality) than students in groups which had not received test information. We also found that students in general tended to rate themselves highly by comparison with other criteria (test scores and teacher ratings). Perhaps the availability of test information had the effect of moving pupils' ratings somewhat toward those other criteria. There are, however, a number of factors which caused us to hesitate before accepting this conclusion. First, the finding applied only in some of the areas that were directly tested, while it also applied in areas not closely related to tested areas at all (for example, originality). Thus, the effect seems too diffuse and haphazard to be attributed to the test information supplied to teachers. Second, if the test information affected students' self-ratings of their scholastic performance, we would have expected the effect also to have manifested itself in a closer congruence for the information group between pupils' own ratings and teacher ratings of their scholastic achievement, and even more so, between the pupils' ratings and their test scores. However, we did not find this to be true. Finally, when we examined students' self-concepts, a measure of which was composed of students' views of themselves as students and of their perceptions of their performance levels in various scholastic areas, we found no statistically significant differences that could be associated with testing or the availability of test information to the students' teachers.

IV. TESTING AND THE EXPECTANCY PROCESS

The Irish study afforded a unique opportunity to examine the expectancy or "Pygmalion" effect popularized by Rosenthal and Jacobsen (1968) in their famous study. Rosenthal and Jacobsen concluded that providing teachers with falsely inflated test information about pupils' ability altered teachers' expectations for these pupils, which in turn led to an improvement in the pupils' measured scholastic ability.

Four basic steps had been postulated in the expectancy process, and these steps take place whether or not test information is available to teachers. First, teachers form differential expectations for pupils. Second, teachers treat pupils in line with these expectations. Third, pupils react in accordance with the expectations. And finally, teacher expectations come to be reflected in the pupils' measured ability and achievement.

Unlike Rosenthal and Jacobsen, we did not attempt to mislead teachers about their pupils' ability or achievement. The information we supplied was, as it is in the normal school setting, the pupils' *actual* test performance. Our design also allowed for a control group (Treatment 2) in which teachers did not have access to test information. Because the test results Rosenthal and Jacobsen provided were inflated, they were, for ethical reasons, only able to examine the expectancy "advantage" situation: that is where the test information was more favorable than the teacher's perceptions of a pupil. Since in a normal testing program one would also expect instances in which the test information would be less favorable than the teacher's perception, we were also able to examine the situation in which an expectancy "disadvantage" could occur.

We were interested in a series of questions related to the expectancy process, both when test information is given and when it is withheld.

- How close are teachers' estimates of pupils' ability and achievement to the estimates obtained from tests?
- When test information did not agree with teachers' perceptions, did this lead to a change in their perceptions?
- After a period of time in which teachers' perceptions and test informa–tion had had an opportunity to affect pupils, was there evidence that the pupils' test performance was influenced by the teachers' initial percep–tions and/or by the test information?

We examined our data in several ways in search of an expectancy effect—across grades (two, four, and six), over five different constructs (general ability, mathematics, English reading, Irish reading, and pupil self-concept), and by various pupil characteristics (gender, socioeconomic status, and location of school). With the exception of pupil self-concept, our analyses clearly show that for the total sample we examined, expectancy processes were at work, *both* when teachers had test information and when they did not. Predictions based on our original model relating to an expectancy effect on teachers' subsequent perceptions of pupils, and on pupils' subsequent test performance, were confirmed more often than not. While our results were not uniform across all grades or constructs, the clear trend of our data indicated that when teachers were given test information, their ratings of pupils tended to move in line with that information. On the other hand, when test information was not available, pupils' end-of-year test performances tended to align with teachers' initial perceptions of the pupils' achievement and ability.

When we looked at our data by gender, we were forced to call into question the four-step expectancy model postulated above. While our results relating to gender were equally consistent, they raised some difficulties for the model in that the effects of test information or lack of test information on the expectancy process differed for boys and girls. While again there were inconsistencies across grade and construct, the general pattern that emerged indicated test information and teacher perceptions did not interact in the same way for boys and for girls. Generally, teachers' perceptions of boys aligned with the test information or with the altered teacher perception. On the other hand, while test information was not usually related to changes in teachers' perceptions of girls, it was related to shifts in the girls' test performance. In other words, within the group that received test information, the effect of such information on *subsequent teacher perceptions was strongest for boys*, while within the group that did not have such information, the impact of the teacher's original perception on *subsequent pupil test performance was strongest for girls*. While our model had led us to expect the boys' subsequent test performance to align with the altered teacher perceptions, we found that they did not. At the same time, while girls' subsequent test performance tended to align with the original teacher perceptions as predicted, the teachers' subsequent perceptions of girls were not found to align with the test information as predicted.

The reasons that predictions based on the model were not borne out when the data were analyzed by gender are not at all clear. It may be that the model has to be modified if it is to encompass boys and girls. It would appear that boys do not react as strongly to teacher perceptions as do girls. Perhaps teachers do not communicate expectations as clearly to boys as they do to girls. Or it may be that our measures of perceptions were not sensitive enough.

When we examined the expectancy process in different school locations, we found some evidence that test information had a stronger impact on the expectancy process in urban than in town or rural schools. At grade six, test information influenced the perceptions of city teachers more than it did those of town and rural teachers. At grade four, test information had a more pervasive effect on the subsequent test performance of pupils in city schools. Results of analyses in which pupils were stratified by socioeconomic status provided little support for the claim that test information is likely to be most effective (and the literature would argue most detrimental) in the case of children from low socioeconomic backgrounds.

While the provision of test information tended to benefit pupils whose test scores were higher than their teachers' assessments of their ability or achievement, it tended to work to the detriment of pupils for whom the teacher's original assessment was more favorable than the test results. But further, our results also clearly showed that when test information is *not* available, an analogous process operates. If a teacher had a low opinion of a pupil and did not have access to test information that would have shown the pupil in a better light, this situation tended to work to the pupil's "disadvantage." Conversely, if a teacher had a favorable initial opinion of a pupil but was unaware of the pupil's relatively poorer test performance, the uncorrected teacher expectations tended to "benefit" the pupil.

What can we say about the net effect on pupils of the provision of test information? The literature often emphasizes the negative outcome—the expectancy disadvantage. For some indication of the extent of advantage and disadvantage, we looked at the discrepancy data using collapsed test scores (a five-point scale to correspond to the rating forms used), and found that the presence of test information, on balance, worked to pupils' advantage. When we examined shifts in teacher ratings that became more favorable over the course of the year, we found that the provision of test information led to a significantly higher proportion of such shifts for perceptions of mathematical achievement at all grades. The provision of test information also resulted in larger proportions of pupils at grades two and six for whom teachers' ratings of English reading went up. On the other hand, when we looked at teachers' ratings that became less favorable over time, we found that such shifts were not attributable to the receipt of test information. We estimated the "net advantage" associated with the receipt of test information to be between 4% and 11%. More favorable shifts occurred among teachers who received information than among those who did not.

When we looked at the impact of the provision of diagnostic information on the expectancy process, we found that it had no unique impact on subsequent test performance beyond that of norm-referenced information on ability and achievement. Additional analyses by gender, location, and socioeconomic status did not alter this conclusion. Similarly, we did not find any evidence of a unique expectancy effect associated with the limitation of the kind of test information supplied to either norm-referenced achievement test information or norm-referenced ability test information.

We feel that our expectancy results are striking in light of the numerous factors at work to limit a demonstration of the effects of test information. First, there was strong agreement between initial teacher perceptions and initial test scores. After correcting for unreliability in our estimates, the amount of unexplained variance between the two initial assessments of the pupils' scholastic standing was only between 16% to 19%. Thus, while there was some room for test information to influence teacher perceptions, there was not a great amount. The relationship between ratings and test scores collapsed to a five-point scale can also be represented by the discrepancies between them. Over grade level and treatment, the two assessments were in perfect agreement for 46% to 60% of all pupils. Nearly 40% of the ratings diverged from the collapsed test score by only a single unit, while larger discrepancies occurred for only 4% to 11% of pupils. These two ways of looking at the data show that while knowledge of test results can provide teachers with information about some pupils that is discrepant from their assessment of the pupils' ability or achievement, the potential impact of test information is severely limited by the relatively close agreement between the two assessments.

A second factor may have limited our capability to demonstrate an expectancy effect: within the groups that were provided with test information, not all teachers attended to that information. Our best estimate was that only about half the teachers could be classified as "test users." Thus the provision of test information to teachers, even when that information was discrepant from teachers' own estimates of pupils, cannot be regarded as ensuring that they will attend to it—a necessary first step if the information is to have any effect on teacher perceptions.

Third, the test information we provided was not generally communicated directly to parents, pupils, or other teachers. Thus, while test information was communicated, it was not made available to a majority of parents or pupils. It would appear that in this situation, the potential impact of test information on pupil behavior and subsequent test performance was diminished.

Finally, the four-step expectancy model obviously oversimplifies the process. The provision of test information does not necessarily trigger the predicted chain of events. Some teachers may not perceive the information as discrepant; others, while perceiving the discrepancy, may ignore it. Even when test information is perceived as discrepant, teachers can handle the discrepancies in ways that can weaken or strengthen the impact of the information. And, of course, some teachers may change their estimates of pupils on the basis of information quite unrelated to test scores, and this may happen in the period between the testing and the receipt of test results.

Even when teachers change their perceptions of pupils on the basis of test information and alter accordingly their treatment of pupils, the behavior of some pupils may remain unaffected. Pupils may not perceive the altered teacher behavior or, if they do, they may not react to it in the way suggested by the model. This would appear to be what happened for the boys in our sample. The extent to which pupils react to teachers' expectations and behavior is probably a function of some aspects of the relationship already established between the two. For example, the degree of a pupil's dependency on a teacher, or the extent to which a pupil identifies with a teacher, may be relevant. The impact of a teacher's behavior could also be offset by parental or peer group influences.

In view of these mitigating factors, we feel that our results provided strong evidence that expectancy processes were operating in our classrooms. And this was true whether or not test information was available; the expectancy process worked to the "advantage" of some pupils and to the "disadvantage" of others. However, on net, more pupils seemed to be at an expectancy "advantage" than "disadvantage" when their teachers had test information than when they did not. Finally, our results, while clear and consistent, also demonstrated that the expectancy process works in a relatively small proportion of cases. In most instances, teacher perceptions and test performance agreed rather closely, thereby greatly reducing the number of pupils for whom test information could trigger the expectancy process.

V. LIMITATIONS OF THE IRISH STUDY RESULTS IN LIGHT OF CURRENT PRACTICES

The Irish study was designed to test the effects of providing classroom teachers with traditional forms of standardized test information. Test results were returned to teachers, and they could use, or not use, the results as they saw fit. This was the type of testing program we simulated in the Irish study, and our results must be understood within the context of the teacher as the principal user of test information.

In the United States, from the 1920s through the 1960s, with some notable exceptions, this was also the general practice in most school-district testing programs; teachers received the annual standardized test results for their classes, but were seldom under any pressure to use them in specific ways.[7] For example, a national survey of teachers conducted in the mid-sixties found that most reported that they did not use standardized test results in grouping, planning instruction, and similar activities (Goslin 1967). Thus, as noted at the outset, the Irish experiment can only be characterized as a low-stakes testing program. Further, as noted in the introduction, around the mid-seventies test results began to be used seriously for policy purposes, first at the state level, but eventually at the school-district level as well.

Two principal uses of test results in the policy sphere emerged. The first was the use of test information to *inform* policymakers about the current state of education. The second was the use of tests as *administrative devices* in the implementation of policy. In the former case, test results are used exclusively to describe the present state of education or some aspect of it, or to support lobbying efforts for new programs or for reform proposals. The effects of this informational, descriptive use of test results on the educational process are indirect. This is in sharp contrast to the administrative use of test results, whereby results automatically trigger a direct reward or sanction being applied to an individual or institution. While this latter use of test results began at the state level with the minimum competency testing movement, policymakers at the local level were quick to jump on the fast-moving accountability bandwagon. They realized the accountability potential of their own school-district testing programs. They saw that they could influence teacher and

---

[7] An exception was the use of "intelligence" tests to place children in classes for the educationally mentally retarded (EMR). Even this exception, however, could be considered outside the normal course of school-district testing programs since it generally involved the use of individually administered "intelligence" tests.

student behavior by the elegantly simple stratagem of attaching rewards and sanctions to their standardized, multiple-choice test results.

Thus today many school-district testing programs can be characterized as high-stakes testing programs: that is, programs where the results are seen—rightly or wrongly—by students, teachers, administrators, parents, or the general public, as being used to make important decisions that immediately and directly affect them. Examples of high stakes include linking standardized test scores to such important decisions as (1) graduation from high school, promotion from grade to grade (sometimes called "gates" tests), or automatic placement in a remedial program; (2) the evaluation of teachers or administrators; (3) the awarding of merit pay, or promotion to the status of master teacher; and (4) the allocation of resources to schools. In all of these examples, the perception that test results are linked to a high-stakes decision is accurate. In many school districts, local policymakers have mandated that the results be used *automatically* to make such decisions.

Three typical examples of school-district testing programs involving high stakes should suffice. The first is taken from a front-page story in the *Boston Globe* (October 4, 1986), entitled "Math, reading scores for city students down." In the article Superintendent Laval S. Wilson is quoted as saying:

> I am disappointed to report that this year for the first time in four years, our standardized test scores in reading and math have taken a down turn.

The article continues:

> Wilson said he has already stressed to teachers in all schools that increasing basic reading and math skills are among his priorities this year. He also said that he will hold school administrators accountable for low test scores when the test is next given.

The Boston example is simply a variation on a common theme across the country. A superintendent unhappy with newspaper stories about the district's standardized test results gets the message out to teachers and administrators that next year those scores had better go up; that they will be held accountable if improvement in the test scores—not necessarily in the skills, a distinction lost on many superintendents—is not forthcoming.[8] This situation did not prevail in the Irish study.

The second example comes from St. Louis. There the stakes for teachers are made more explicit than in the Boston example. Albert Shanker, admittedly not an unbiased observer, described the St. Louis situation:

---

[8] As a colleague, Joe Cronin, recently reminded me, the superintendent is also well aware that if the scores do not go up, the school committee, like the owners of a baseball team, will change the manager. Fortunately for superintendents, it is easier to raise test scores than it is to take a last-place team to pennant contention.

In St. Louis, Superintendent Jerome B. Jones last year announced that teachers in the district would be rated unsatisfactory and lose their jobs unless their students reached specific levels of achievement or improvement on standardized achievement tests (Shanker 1986).

Here is another theme that is unfortunately becoming more and more popular throughout the land.[9] The idea of linking teacher accountability to student test performance is an enduring concept, by no means unique to Superintendent Jones. He has merely reinvented a crooked wheel. The St. Louis plan is a throwback to the old payment by results concept, which first surfaced in Treviso in 1444, and which was an extremely popular administrative mechanism of accountability in the 19th century in the educational systems of Great Britain, Ireland, Jamaica, and parts of Australia (Madaus 1979; Madaus 1988). In the Irish study teachers were accountable for student test performance to no one but themselves.

Our final example is drawn from the recent work of the National Board of Inquiry formed by the National Coalition of Advocates for Students (NCAS), and chaired by Harold Howe II. This group assessed barriers to excellence in American education. One of their conclusions, based on extensive testimony of teachers and administrators, was that these newer uses of standardized test information by local educational authorities (LEAs) were fast becoming a barrier to excellence, and were being used as exclusionary devices, which had their heaviest impact on low-income, minority, and handicapped children (National Coalition of Advocates for Students 1985). More recently, NCAS reported mounting evidence that some teachers are finding ingenious ways to remove low-scoring students from the test pool because of fear that they will lose their jobs if they do not keep test scores up (First and Cardenas 1986). Teachers quickly adopt strategies to deal with this type of accountability, which was not necessary for the teachers to do in the Irish study.

There is a critical need to systematically evaluate LEA-sponsored high-stakes testing programs to learn more about the positive and negative aspects of such programs. For example, will the various "gates" programs, which use test results for grade-to-grade promotion, improve student learning or will they eventually increase the dropout rate? However, the difficulty with proposing such evaluations is that the policymakers who implement programs have a vested interest in them. They see their use of tests as a mechanism of power by which they can reform the system. Consequently, they are understandably reluctant to spend money to question the wisdom of their mandate.

---

[9] The idea of tying outcomes to accountability decisions is not limited to education. The principal agency accrediting the nation's hospitals will soon begin using surgical mortality rates, along with other measures of medical outcomes, as a central tool in accreditations (see Brinkley 1986).

Compared to the examples above, the Irish experiment can only be characterized as a low-stakes testing program. Consequently, the Irish results do not speak to the impact of high-stakes testing programs. However, we do know from experience with high-stakes external testing programs that certain undesirable side effects emerge when a testing program automatically associates important rewards, sanctions, or decisions with test performance. We should expect the same negative effects would attach to high-stakes local-district testing programs as well. I cannot review that literature here (see Madaus 1988; and Madaus and Greaney 1985 for reviews). However, Campbell has pointed to the essential problem associated with using any quantitative indicator for high-stakes decisions, namely, that the validity of the indicator eventually will be corrupted by those affected by it (Campbell 1975). More recently, in discussing the use of quantitative indicators in program evaluation, Campbell made two points relevant to high-stakes testing programs. First, he calls attention to the mistaken belief that quantitative *measures* can replace qualitative *knowing*. This is certainly a problem in many high-stakes testing programs; without reference to any other indicators, the scores are used automatically to make critical decisions about individuals or institutions. Campbell reminds us that without competence at the qualitative level, test scores can be misleading; to rule out plausible rival hypotheses to explain test performance we need situation-specific wisdom. Second, he points out that we too often have mistakenly bought into the logical positivist's definitional operationalism, specifying as program goals (or I might add individual goals) fallible measures open to bureaucratic (again I would add, teacher) manipulation (Campbell 1984). This happens because teachers, or bureaucrats, can manipulate those discretionary points in the process, and this distorts the validity of any inferences made from the quantitative score. As an example Campbell describes the Chicago public schools testing program:

> [in Chicago] they were spending millions of dollars on testing programs that used national norms for an annual humiliation of half of the grammar schools in the city. That testing program was destructive in its net effect. The annual humiliation did nothing to improve the schools, told them nothing about what they could do to make education better, and put tremendous corruption pressure on test administrations. (Rumored practices were to classify as many children as possible as abnormal ineligibles, and to manipulate the time schedules to optimize performance.) *This annual humiliation was destructive both of the validity of measurement and of the morale of the teacher* (Campbell 1984, 38; italics added). [10]

---

[10]For other examples of negative practices associated with high-stakes testing programs, including cheating, see Strenio (1981).

Elsewhere I have described seven general principles that can be used to predict the effects of any standardized testing program (Madaus, in press). Let me close by briefly describing them.

VI. GENERAL PRINCIPLES:
THE IMPACT OF STANDARDIZED TESTS

Principle 1:

The power of tests and examinations to affect individuals, institutions, curriculum, or instruction is a perceptual phenomenon: if students, teachers, or administrators believe that the results of an examination are important, it matters very little whether this is really true or false—the effect is produced by what individuals perceive to be the case.

Writing in the Sixty-eighth Yearbook of the National Society for the Study of Education, Ben Bloom coined this first principle: when people perceive a phenomenon to be true, their actions are guided by the importance perceived to be associated with it. The greater the stakes perceived to be linked to test results, the greater the impact on instruction and learning. The Irish study could have been expected to have a mild impact, and it did. A high-stakes program such as the one in St. Louis should have serious negative effects on teaching, learning, and the testing process itself.

Principle 2:

The more any quantitative social indicator is used for social decision making, the more likely it will be to distort and corrupt the social processes it is intended to monitor.

This principle comes directly from Donald Campbell's work on social indicators. Principle 2 is a social version of Heisenberg's uncertainty principle: you cannot measure either an electron's position or velocity without distorting one or the other. Any measurement of the status of an educational institution, no matter how well designed and well intentioned, inevitably changes its status.

This principle reminds us that while, historically, testing is seen as a relatively objective and impartial means of correcting abuses in the system, the negative effects eventually outweigh the early benefits. When test results are used for important social decisions, the changes in the system brought about by such a use tend to be both substantial and corrupting. How this comes to pass is described in the five remaining principles.

Principle 3:

*If important decisions are presumed to be related to test results, then teachers
will teach to the test.*

    This accommodation to the power of a high-stakes test can be a double-
edged sword. High-stakes tests can focus instruction, giving students and
teachers specific goals to attain. If the test is measuring basic skills, preparing
students for the skills measured by the test could, proponents argue, serve as a
powerful lever to improve basic skills. Unfortunately the only evidence to
support this position is that the scores on tests of basic skills rise, not that the
skill necessarily improves. People fail to distinguish between the skill and a
secondary indicator of it.

    If the test is specific to a more specialized curriculum area where higher
level cognitive outcomes are the goal—for example, college preparatory
physics—then the examination will eventually narrow instruction and learning,
focusing only on those things measured by the tests. Indeed, this narrowing of
the curriculum has been one of the enduring complaints leveled at external
certification examinations used for the important functions of certifying the
successful completion of elementary or secondary education, and admission to
third-level education or to certain jobs.

    Why does this happen? First, there is tremendous social pressure on
teachers to see to it that their students do well on the high-stakes tests. Second,
the results of the same tests are so important to students, teachers, and parents
that their own self-interest dictates that instructional time focus on test
preparation.

Principle 4:

*In every setting where a high-stakes test operates, a tradition of past tests
develops, which eventually* de facto *defines the curriculum.*

    Given Principle 3, the question remains: How do teachers cope with the
pressure of the testing program? The answer is relatively simple. Teachers see
the kind of intellectual activity required by previous test questions and prepare
the students to meet these demands. Some have argued strongly that if the
skills are well chosen, and if the tests truly measure them, then coaching is
perfectly acceptable (Popham 1981; Popham 1985; Millman 1981). This argument sounds reasonable, and, in the short term, it may even work. It ignores,
however, a fundamental fact of life: when the teacher's professional worth is
estimated in terms of test success, teachers will corrupt the skills measured by
reducing them to the level of strategies in which the examinee is drilled.
Further, the expectations and deep-seated primary agenda of students and
their parents for test success will further corrupt the process. The view that we
can coach for the skills apart from the tradition of test questions embodies a
staggeringly optimistic view of human nature that ignores the powerful pull of

self-interest. It simply does not consider the long-term effects of the sanctions associated with the test scores.

Principle 5:

Teachers pay particular attention to the form of the questions on a high-stakes test, for example, short answer, essay, multiple choice, and adjust their instruction accordingly.

The problem here is that the form of the test question can narrow instruction, study, and learning to the detriment of other skills. It is important to keep in mind that the form the questions most often take in high-stakes programs in our schools is that of the multiple-choice question; students are required to select, not supply, answers.[11] Given our free-enterprise system, publishers have begun to look at state-mandated minimum competency, or basic-skills tests in order to design materials to better train pupils to take them.[12] Children are apt, therefore, to find themselves spending more and more time filling out ditto answer sheets or workbooks.

Principle 6:

When test results are the sole or even partial arbiter of future educational or life choices, society tends to treat test results as the major goal of schooling rather than as a useful but fallible indicator of achievement.

Of all of the effects attributed to tests, those embodied in this principle may be the most damaging. The dangers here are best embodied in the Boston example described above. Will the yearly tests scores in Boston become the major goal of schooling for teachers, administrators, and pupils? It seems that this is happening around the country; test scores are becoming the principal criterion for evaluating systems, schools, teachers, and pupils.

Principle 7:

A high-stakes test transfers control over the curriculum to the agency which sets or controls the exam.

The agency responsible for a high-stakes test assumes a great deal of power or control over what is taught, how it is taught, what is learned, and how it is learned. And while this shift in power is also understood in this country by

---

[11]This is not to imply that supply-type questions cannot also be corrupted. For an example of how high-stakes writing exercises can be corrupted, see Madaus and Greaney (1985).

[12]These materials are currently being used in schools. Parents are also the target of such materials; for example, see the series entitled *Dr. Gary Gruber's Essential Guide to Test-Taking for Kids.*

policymakers who are mandating graduation and promotion tests, the implications of the shift from the local educational authority to the state department of education has not received sufficient attention and discussion; nor has the shift in power to the companies who sell tests for local districts to use in high-stakes situations.

VII. CONCLUSION

The picture that the Irish study findings suggest is one in which standardized testing seems to have been easily assimilated into the operating evaluative system of the classroom. The results of the Irish study also clearly indicate that an expectancy process is at work with or without the intrusion of test scores.

However, the type of testing program simulated in the Irish study is fast becoming extinct. Because today's school-district testing programs involve high stakes, we can expect the results to conform to the seven principles outlined above. Given the negative consequences flowing from these principles, we need to work toward two goals. First, we have to demand that well-designed independent evaluations of such programs be carried out, including evaluations of the tests themselves, their uses, and effects. Second, it is time we began to work toward lowering the stakes associated with test use. Test results can provide valuable information, but only one piece of information, and only when interpreted with wisdom, in conjunction with many other indicators and factors.

REFERENCES

Adams, G. S. 1964. *Measurement and evaluation in education, psychology, and guidance.* New York: Holt, Rinehart and Winston.

Bloom, B. S. 1969. Some theoretical issues relating to educational evaluation. In *Educational evaluation: New roles, new means,* ed. R. W. Tyler. Sixty-eighth Yearbook of the National Society for the Study of Education, Part II. Chicago: NSSE.

Brinkley, J. 1986. Key hospital accrediting agency to start weighing mortality rates. *New York Times,* 4 November, 1.

Campbell, D. T. 1975. Assessing the impact of planned social change. In *Social research and public policies: The Dartmouth/OECD conference.* Hanover, NH: Public Affairs Center, Dartmouth College.

Campbell, D. T. 1984. Can we be scientific in applied social science? In *Evaluation Studies Review Annual,* 9, ed. R. F. Conner, D. G. Altman, and C. Jackson, 26-48. Beverly Hills, CA: Sage Publications.

Carroll, P. T. 1986. American science transformed. *American Scientist* 74 (5): 466-85.

Clark, K. B. 1963. Educational stimulation of racially disadvantaged children. In *Education in depressed areas,* ed. A. H. Passow. New York: Bureau of Publications, Teachers College, Columbia University.

Cronbach, L. J. 1975. Five decades of public controversy over mental testing. *American Psychologist* 30:1-4.

Ebel, R. L. 1966. The social consequences of educational testing. In *Testing problems in perspective,* ed. A. Anastasi. Washington, DC: American Council on Education.

Educational Research Centre. 1978a. *Drumcondra Attainment Tests, Level I. Form A: Mathematics and English. Administration and technical manual.* Dublin: Educational Research Centre, St. Patrick's College.

Educational Research Centre. 1978b. *Drumcondra Attainment Tests, Level II. Form A: Mathematics, Irish, and English. Administration and technical manual.* Dublin: Educational Research Centre, St. Patrick's College.

Educational Research Centre. 1979a. *Drumcondra Attainment Tests, Level I. Form B: Mathematics, Irish, and English. Administration and technical manual.* Dublin: Educational Research Centre, St. Patrick's College.

Educational Research Centre. 1979b. *Drumcondra Attainment Tests, Level II. Form B: Mathematics, Irish, and English. Administration and technical manual.* Dublin: Educational Research Centre, St. Patrick's College.

Educational Research Centre. 1980a. *Drumcondra Attainment Tests, Level III. Form B: Mathematics, Irish, and English. Administration and technical manual.* Dublin: Educational Research Centre, St. Patrick's College.

Educational Research Centre. 1980b. *Drumcondra Criterion Referenced Mathematics Test, Level VI. Manual.* Dublin: Educational Research Centre, St. Patrick's College.

Findley, W. G. 1963. Purposes of school testing programs and their efficient development. In *The impact and improvement of school testing programs,* ed. W. G. Findley. Sixty-second Yearbook of the National Society for the Study of Education, Part II. Chicago: NSSE.

First, J. M., and J. Cardenas. 1986. A minority view on testing. *Educational Measurement: Issues and Practice* 5:6–11.

Goslin, D. A. 1967. *Teachers and testing.* New York: Russell Sage Foundation.

Gruber, G. R. 1986. *Dr. Gary Gruber's essential guide to test-taking for kids.* New York: Quill William Morrow.

Holt, J. 1968. *On testing.* Cambridge, MA: Pinck Leodas Association.

Houts, P. L. 1975a. A conversation with Banesh Hoffman. *National Elementary Principal* 54:30–39.

Ingenkamp, K. 1977. *Educational assessment.* Slough, Berkshire: NFER Publishing.

Jensen, A. R. 1980. *Bias in mental testing.* New York: Free Press.

Kellaghan, T., G. F. Madaus, and P. W. Airasian. 1982. *The effects of standardized testing.* Boston: Kluwer-Nijhoff.

Madaus, G. F. 1979. Testing and funding: Measurement and policy issues. *New Directions for Testing and Measurement* 1:52–62.

Madaus, G. F. 1988. Testing and the curriculum: From compliant servant to dictatorial master. In *National Society for the Study of Education 1988 Yearbook,* ed. L. Tanner. Chicago: University of Chicago Press.

Madaus, G. F., and V. Greaney. 1985. The Irish experience in competency testing: Implications for American education. *American Journal of Education* 93:268–94.

Madaus, G. F., and J. Macnamara. 1970. *Public examinations. A study of the Irish Leaving Certificate.* Dublin: Educational Research Centre.

Millman, J. 1981. Protesting the detesting of PRO testing. *NCME Measurement in Education* 12:1–6.

National Coalition of Advocates for Students. 1985. *Barriers to excellence.* Boston: National Coalition of Advocates for Students.

O'Meara, J. F. 1944. A critical study of external examinations and of their influence on secondary education. Master's dissertation. University College, Cork, Ireland.

Pidgeon, D. A. 1970. *Expectation and pupil performance.* Slough, Berkshire: NFER Publishing.

Popham, W. J. 1981. The case for minimum competency testing. *Phi Delta Kappan* 63:89–92.

Popham, W. J. 1985. Measurement-driven instruction: It's on the road. *Phi Delta Kappan* 66:628–35.

Rosenthal, R., and L. Jacobsen. 1968. *Pygmalion in the classroom*. New York: Holt, Rinehart and Winston.

Shanker, A. 1968. Power vs. knowledge in St. Louis: Professionals under fire. *New York Times*, 26 October, 5.

Strenio, A. J. 1981. *The testing trap*. New York: Rawson, Wade Publishers.

Travers, R. M. W. 1983. *How research has changed American schools: A history from 1840 to the present*. Kalamazoo, MI: Mythos Press.

Tyler, R. W. 1968. Critique of the issue on educational and psychological testing. *Review of Educational Research* 38:102–7.

Tyler, R. W., ed. 1969. *Educational evaluation: New roles, new means*. Sixty-eighth Yearbook of the National Society for the Study of Education, Part II. Chicago: NSSE.

Wilson, L. 1968. In Math, reading scores for city students down. *Boston Globe*, 4 October.

II

TESTS IN EDUCATIONAL DECISION MAKING:
PSYCHOMETRIC AND POLITICAL BOUNDARY
CONDITIONS

Using Test Scores for Decision Making

William A. Mehrens

Tests can provide information that facilitates and supports decision making, particularly in the domain of education. However, each type of decision, each type of inference from test data, and each model of decision making carries with it certain constraints and risks. In this chapter I will outline the principles of interaction between these aspects of test-supported decisions, detailing the risks, benefits, and limitations of each. In the first section I present a brief discussion of the various types of decisions in which test data can profitably be brought to bear. These include instructional decisions, guidance decisions, classification/placement decisions, educational selection decisions, licensure and employment decisions, and program evaluation decisions. The second section discusses the various types of validity evidence: content, criterion-related, construct, and instructional/curricular validity. The third section covers the relationship between the type of decision being made and the type of validity evidence required. For example, different evidence is required for guidance decisions than for program evaluation decisions; different evidence is required for selection decisions than for licensure decisions. The fourth section discusses the various models for combining data from different sources to make a single decision. The conjunctive, disjunctive, and compensatory models are described briefly and examples given where one model is more likely to function better than the other models. Finally, the chapter includes a short section on how test scores, if used correctly, will increase the quality of the decisions made.

A decision can be defined as the process of selecting one action from a number of alternative courses of action (Bross 1953). It is axiomatic that decisions should be based on as much accurate information as can be reasonably gathered. Policymakers, school administrators, teachers, parents, students, and taxpayers voting on educational issues need information prior to making decisions. In many cases, it is the responsibility of professional educators to determine what information should be gathered, to assure that the information gathered is of sufficiently high quality, and to impart that information to the decisionmakers in understandable terms.

TYPES OF EDUCATIONAL DECISIONS

Most people agree that decisions should be made based on some rational approach. However, just how this rational approach should operate has long been debated (see, for example, Bross 1953; Edwards 1961; Wald 1950). Two variables that influence any decision are the utility values and the probabilities of the various possible outcomes of any given course of action. The utilities are the possible reward values of an outcome and the probabilities are the chances of any outcome occurring. People actually make decisions based on what are termed *subjective* probabilities—what the decisionmaker perceives the chances are for a particular outcome. Unfortunately, many decisionmakers do not even think through all the possible outcomes, let alone determine their utility values. Neither do they consider whether the subjective probabilities are at all close to the objective (or true) probabilities. However, at times data exist or can be gathered that provide relevant information regarding the likelihood of an outcome. Bayesian theory suggests that if decisionmakers gather, understand, and use the data wisely, they will form a subjective probability that approximates the true (objective) probability. Thus, the primary use of data in decision making is to combine subjective and objective probabilities and thereby improve the decision made.

Occasionally the notions of measurement and decision making are misunderstood. Some people believe that if a decision leads to a poor outcome, then that indicates the data should not have been used to help make the decision. That belief seems particularly prevalent when tests are used in decision making. (For example, if the use of a selection test leads to a poor outcome, one should not have used the test.) Such a belief is faulty. In making decisions we are always taking risks because we cannot predict outcomes with complete certainty. A good decision is based on as much relevant data as can reasonably be obtained. Good data increase the chances of making a decision that will result in the predicted outcome, but it does not guarantee it. We need to keep this point constantly in mind when we consider the use of tests in educational decision making.

There are many ways to classify educational decisions. We could differentiate between *institutional* and *individual* decisions. Institutional decisions are those in which a large number of comparable decisions are made. For example, a university deciding which applicants to admit is making an institutional decision. A licensure agency determining which applicants to grant licensure to is making an institutional decision. We can think of institutional decisions as decisions made about people. Individual decisions are decisions where the choice confronting a particular decisionmaker will rarely or never recur. For example, a student deciding whether to take advanced algebra is making an individual decision. At times, institutional decision making will appropriately restrict individual decision making.

Another way to classify educational decisions is to differentiate between such decisions as instructional, guidance, classification, placement, selection, certification, licensure, employment, and program evaluation decisions. These types of decisions will be discussed briefly in the paragraphs below. (The classification is not exhaustive. The list could also include, for example, research decisions and policy decisions.)

Instructional Decisions

Instructional decisions are those that determine the methodology of instruction. The major role of an individual teacher is to facilitate certain types of student learning. In order to know what instructional techniques to employ, the teacher needs to have data available. As Parnell stated:

> Measurement is the hand-maiden of instruction. Without measurement there cannot be evaluation. Without evaluation, there cannot be feedback. Without feedback, there cannot be good knowledge of results. Without knowledge of results, there cannot be systematic improvement in learning (Parnell 1973, 2698).

Tests aid teachers in their instructional decision making by helping to (1) provide knowledge concerning the students' entry behaviors; (2) set, refine, and clarify realistic goals for each student; (3) determine the degree to which the objectives have been achieved; and (4) determine, evaluate, and refine the instructional techniques.

Tests aid students in their decision making by communicating teachers' objectives and by providing feedback to students that identifies their strengths and weaknesses. More details on the value of tests in instructional decision making can be found in Mehrens and Lehmann (1984, 7–11).

Guidance Decisions

Students need guidance to make individual decisions. They use tests, as indicated above, for instructional guidance. But the term *guidance*, as used here, applies to the decisions made concerning vocational choice, educational program choice, and personal problems. Tests of aptitude and achievement, and interest and personality inventories can all assist students in making better decisions. They provide students with data about significant individual characteristics and help them develop realistic self-concepts. Data from tests and inventories thus give students some information about the likelihood of success (or happiness) in various educational/vocational endeavors.

Classification/Placement Decisions

The remaining types of decisions to be discussed could be classified as administrative decisions. They are institutional decisions made about individuals or programs. The types of administrative decisions, however, differ from each other and need separate definitions.

In *classification* decisions we determine the type of program or treatment an individual should receive; in *placement* decisions we choose the level of treatment from among several alternatives. Classification and placement decisions are sometimes combined under one or the other heading, but as we shall see in a later section, they are actually different decisions and each requires different types of validity evidence to justify the use of the associated data that are collected.

Selection Decisions in Education

Selection decisions occur when an individual or institution decides whether to admit an applicant to a program or hire an applicant for a job. Selection decisions differ from classification and placement decisions in that the latter decisions do not reject an individual. Bloom et al. (1981) suggested that there was a trend in education to move away from the use of tests for selection decisions and to use them instead for instructional decisions. The notion was that educators should accept all individuals for treatment (instruction). This view is differentially accepted depending on the level of education and the particular decision being made. For example, in elementary school we do not and should not select individuals into (or out of) further public schooling. Our decisions about students tend to be instructional, guidance, placement, and classification. Looking at the decision at a more microscopic level, however, a band teacher must limit the number of students in a pep band and a basketball coach can only start five players. Anytime there is a numerical restriction, it is necessary to make selection decisions. At higher levels of education, many feel it is appropriate to make selection decisions. For example, not all applicants can or should be admitted to medical school. In spite of some individuals' beliefs about education being for everyone, there are some educational programs that by their very nature must restrict the number of individuals who participate. Thus, selection decisions must be made.

A distinction should be drawn between opposition to policies regarding decisions being made and opposition to the data used to make a decision. For example, some individuals are opposed to selection decisions regarding who should be admitted to colleges of education. They believe everyone who wishes to should be given the chance to attend. Others may believe it is more appropriate to select applicants who have the best predicted chances to succeed in college. Either position may be defended on philosophical grounds. If one believes, however, in open admissions, the philosophical stance should be argued directly. It is inappropriate to argue that tests are not useful for selecting those most likely to succeed (too much evidence opposes such an argument). Basic measurement textbooks (for example, Mehrens and Lehmann 1984) have long stressed the importance of differentiating between the decision being made and the tools used to assist in making the decision. Decisions are not always pleasant or in keeping with our philosophical stance, but we should not blame the unpleasantness on the tests that assist in the decision making. Unfortunately some individuals seem to assume that if we do away with tests we can avoid making decisions. That is not likely to be the case.

Selection Decisions in Certification, Licensure, and Employment

The terms *certification* and *licensure* are often used interchangeably, and it is not always clear to educators how employment exams differ from certification and licensure exams. But both the psychological and legal professions disinguish between the three terms, and some definitions and explanations are in order.

For professional or occupational exams, the United States Department of Health, Education and Welfare defines licensure and certification as follows:

> *Licensure:* The process by which an agency of government grants permission to persons to engage in a given profession or occupation by certifying that those licensed have attained the minimal degree of competence necessary to ensure that the public health, safety and welfare will be reasonably well protected.

> *Certification:* The process by which a nongovernmental agency or association grants recognition to an individual who has met certain predetermined qualifications specified by that agency or association (1971, 7).

The major distinction in the above definitions is whether the agency is governmental or nongovernmental. In educational decision making the term certification has frequently been used for high-school competency examinations. The term certification has also been used for the process that grants prospective teachers the right to teach. However, because a governmental agency grants that permission, teacher tests really are licensure examinations.

Employment tests usually have a different purpose from licensure tests. Employment tests are intended to help identify those job applicants who are likely to be the most successful. Whereas licensing exams are designed to further the states' interests, employment exams are intended to further the employers' interests. As stated in the *Standards for Educational and Psychological Testing*, issued jointly by the American Psychological Association (APA), the American Educational Research Association (AERA), and the National Council on Measurement in Education (NCME), "For licensure or certification the focus of test standards is on levels of knowledge and skills necessary to assure the public that a person is competent to practice, whereas an employer may use tests in order to maximize productivity" (APA 1985, 63).

The term "educational certification test" is often used "as a generic term that applies to many different uses of test results" (APA 1985, 49). Thus, some use this term for what we have called instructional, selection, or classification decisions. In recent years, however, more and more states and school districts have implemented a requirement that students must pass a test before being awarded a high school diploma. That test is frequently called an educational certification test. The only subsequent use of the term educational certification in this chapter will be for high school graduation decisions.

Program Evaluation

In program evaluation we are making a decision about how to improve an educational program and/or whether to continue it. Such decisions would include a range of decisions from a local school choosing specific curricular materials, to a governmental agency deciding whether or not to continue funding a mammoth federal program. Program evaluation is considerably broader than student evaluation. Knowledge of student achievement levels may be the most important aspect of program evaluation, but in program evaluation we also evaluate other variables such as the goals themselves, the impact of the program on others, unintended outcomes, and the cost-effectiveness of the program.

TYPES OF VALIDITY EVIDENCE

A test designed to be useful in assisting in one type of decision may not be useful for another type of decision. Different decisions call for different types of inferences. To use tests wisely we need information about what types of inferences can reasonably be made from the scores. This is a matter of validity, which "refers to the appropriateness, meaningfulness, and usefulness of the specific inferences made from test scores. Test validation is the process of accumulating evidence to support such inferences" (APA 1985, 9). Validity is a unitary concept, but the evidence for it may be accumulated in many ways. Traditionally, psychometricians have categorized the various types of validity evidence into content-related, criterion-related, and construct-related evidence of validity even though "rigorous distinctions between the categories are not possible" (APA 1985, 9). "In general, content-related evidence demonstrates the degree to which the sample of items, tasks, or questions on a test are representative of some defined universe or domain of content"(p. 10). "Criterion-related evidence demonstrates that test scores are systematically related to one or more outcome criteria" (p. 11). Construct-related validity evidence "focuses primarily on the test score as a measure of the psychological characteristic of interest. . . . Such characteristics are referred to as constructs because they are theoretical constructions about the nature of human behavior" (p. 9).

Content Validity Evidence

For some types of decisions, inferences about a characteristic or behavioral domain of a person are needed. A test serves as a sample of the domain if the items are drawn from a clearly defined universe. Content validity evidence is related to the adequacy of the test as a sample from the universe about which an inference is to be made. Content validity is particularly important for achievement tests where we wish to make an inference about what a person knows about a subject matter domain. We cannot test the total domain, so we test a sample from it and make an inference to the total domain. As Cronbach stated, "Content validity is established only in test construction, by specifying a domain of tasks and sampling rigorously. The inference back to the domain can then be purely deductive" (1980, 105).

Thus, in judging content validity we must first define the content domain. There has been some debate about how explicitly the content domain needs to be defined. It is probably desirable in most cases to define the domain as specifically as possible in terms of a complete, finite set of behavioral objectives or task statements.

Although content validity is established at the time of test construction, the adequacy of the validity can also be judged after the fact. There is no commonly used numerical expression for content validity. Rather, it is typically a subjective judgment based on the adequacy of the construction process. If the test construction process involved appropriate methods for defining the original domain and writing items that sample that domain in an appropriate fashion, then the test should have adequate content validity. If the individuals judging the content validity of a test are as expert in the domain being tested as the original test builders, they can judge the content validity by looking at the items and the domain definitions. They could judge the adequacy of the definition and whether each item did, in fact, sample the domain. Because the judgment is subjective, such after-the-fact judgments may not agree with the test builders' judgments. There is no way to determine whose judgment is correct. However, a single judge's after-the-fact opinion should not count as much as the opinion of a team of competent individuals who first constructed the test. Although it is sometimes done, it seems inappropriate for measurement experts to second-guess the decisions of the content experts who originally constructed the test regarding whether or not the test or the specific items measure appropriate content.

In addition to expert judgment, there are other procedures for estimating content validity. See Mehrens and Lehmann (1987) for a further discussion of these methods.

Criterion-Related Validity Evidence

Criterion-related validity evidence is necessary to make inferences about how well a person will perform on some independent external measure (a criterion). Such validity evidence is important for selection decisions where one is trying to select those who are apt to be the most successful. For example, in employment selection decisions, employers wish to hire those who will be most productive on the job. Graduate schools may wish to admit (select) those who will perform the best in graduate school (or perhaps who will be the most productive scholars after graduate school).

Thus, when we wish to infer from a test score to some other type of performance, it is helpful to have some evidence that the inference is correct. Logic should not be discounted, but empirical evidence is often useful. Thus, evidence showing that individuals who score higher on the Scholastic Aptitude Test typically do better in college would be useful if we wish to use the Scholastic Aptitude Test to select those who will be the best students in college.

There are frequently problems in obtaining good criterion-related validity data. The major problems center on obtaining a good conceptual definition of the criterion and good measurements of that definition. Are supervisor ratings really good measures of job productivity? Are grade-point averages really good measures of success in college? Even if we could agree on the conceptual definition of the criterion, it would not follow that we could measure the criterion accurately. Supervisor ratings, for example, could well be biased. Suppose the supervisor of a group of employees believed women were less capable of doing a task than men. That belief may bias the supervisor's ratings of how well the women were performing their job. (For further discussion of the problems in measuring the criterion, see Mehrens 1987, or Mehrens and Lehmann 1987.)

Construct Validity Evidence

If we wish to make an inference about a theoretical psychological construct, there should be some evidence suggesting that the inference is correct. We typically call that construct validity evidence. For example, if we wish to make an inference about the degree of assertiveness, compulsiveness, ego strength, paranoia, or such other construct a person may possess, we should have some evidence that a correct inference has been made from the data. Again, the evidence may be logical or empirical.

Some measurement experts contend that all validity evidence is construct validity evidence. Thus, what some would call content validity evidence, others would call construct validity evidence because the definition of the domain is a definition of a construct, and how adequately the domain was sampled tells us something about how well the construct was measured. Other measurement experts prefer to keep the distinction between content and construct, because construct validity is about a theoretical construct and this often implies the construct is hypothetical. For example, the notions of ego, id, and super ego are hypothetical. Such constructs do not have extensions in the world of experience independent of the theoretical framework of which they are primitives. They are quite different from the knowledge of basic addition facts, or knowledge about American history.

Another reason some measurement experts are concerned about calling all validity "construct validity" is that construct validation is viewed "as an ill defined and unending process" (Linn 1984, 7). Thus, a critic of test use could always argue that more evidence should be gathered about the validity of the inference before the test scores are used in decision making. (Of course, if the test scores were not used, decisions would be based on less information. Typically, other data have less validity evidence than do test data.)

The important thing to remember is that whether we call the evidence construct validity evidence or something else, there should be some evidence—or at least good logic—for the inference we wish to make. The term we give to the evidence (content or construct) is only a matter of semantics.

Instructional/Curricular Validity

Instructional validity refers to the degree to which the test content has actually been taught. *Curricular validity* refers to the question of whether the test content has been covered in the curricular materials. A test could have curricular validity without having instructional validity (or vice versa) if a teacher's instruction departed from the curricular materials for the class. The problems of obtaining evidence of instructional/curricular validity will not be discussed in this chapter. (Such evidence is not easy to gather.)

There has been some confusion between content and instructional/curricular validity. There is, however, a clear distinction. Recall that content validity refers to the degree to which the test samples a domain. That domain certainly does not have to be a domain that was in a school curriculum or taught by a particular teacher. If I wish to make an inference about the degree to which a set of students are knowledgeable about Spanish, I should give them a test on Spanish. (Of course, "knowledgeable about" would have to be defined more specifically.) If the test items adequately sampled the defined domain of Spanish, the test would have content validity. That is, the inference about Spanish knowledge would be valid. That is true whether or not the students had ever had instruction in Spanish. Actually, instructional/curricular validity issues should really not be termed validity issues at all. They are issues about the adequacy of preparation. As Yalow and Popham argue, "adequacy-of-preparation is not necessary for one to make sensible inferences about what scores signify" (1983, 13).

VALIDITY EVIDENCE REQUIRED FOR SPECIFIC DECISIONS

As has been mentioned, different decisions call for different types of inferences, which in turn require different types of validity evidence. This was discussed in the previous section as a necessary component of explaining the different types of validity evidence. In this section we take a more systematic look at the types of validity evidence needed for various decisions.

Validity Evidence for Instructional Decisions

In making instructional decisions based on achievement test data, the evidence considered most important is the content validity evidence of the test. We need to be sure we are making inferences about the student's knowledge in the correct domain. We would not, for example, wish to infer that a student did not know basic arithmetic skills based on a low score on a test measuring the student's ability to solve story problems.

If the instructional decision is to focus on the areas where the student has the greatest need, then we must also make decisions about the relative strengths and weaknesses of the student in a subject matter area. To correctly make such decisions requires evidence that the different scores in basic arithmetic and story problems are sufficiently reliable so that the observed differences would not likely have occurred by chance. While this evidence is typically called "reliability" evidence, it is important for such inferences. Educators do not always understand this adequately. Thus, a teacher may make an instructional decision about what to emphasize for a particular student when, in fact, the score in that sub-domain was only lower than the other scores due to chance factors.

If in instructional decision making a teacher is determining whether to allow a student to proceed to the next unit, it would probably be useful to have some criterion-related validity information. For example, in mastery learning the decision rule may be that students must repeat a unit until they have "mastered" it (usually a score such as 80% of the items correct). That decision should not be made unless there is evidence that a student who scores below a certain point is more likely to have difficulties learning the material in the next unit. Of course we should not reject the logic of the decision. If material is hierarchical, there is some logic in believing that a student who does not know the first unit cannot learn the material in the second. But it is best to test such a logical inference empirically.

If we were to infer that a student did not achieve well because of some psychological characteristic—such as lack of motivation or low academic ability—it would be well to have a measure of the psychological characteristic. For a test of a psychological characteristic it would be important to have some construct validity evidence that the test was really measuring that characteristic.

If one wishes to make an inference from the level of achievement to the adequacy of the instruction, then instructional validity evidence is needed. However, it seems more reasonable to think of inferences about the instructional or curricular adequacy as program evaluation decisions.

Validity Evidence for Guidance Decisions

Guidance decisions may depend upon information about levels of achievement as well as about measures of various psychological characteristics such as "level of aspiration" or "compulsivity." Thus, if the test is to inform the decisionmaker about achievement, it should have content validity—that is, the test should measure the domain about which an inference is made. The person who assists the individual in making a guidance decision (for example, the counselor) must make sure the individual understands what domain is being measured by the test so that the inference will be congruent to that domain. If one makes an inference about a trait such as compulsivity, it is important that there be construct validity evidence that the test measures such a trait.

If students are going to use test results to decide some future course of action—for example, whether to take Algebra II—it would be useful if there were some criterion-related validity evidence. Does the test score really predict success in Algebra II? Just as counselors must make sure that students understand the concept (construct) being measured, counselors must also help students understand the significance of a score in a certain area as it relates to the decision being made.

For other future courses of action, criterion-related validity may not be so important. For example, if a counselor is using the results of an interest inventory to encourage career exploration (not deciding on a specific job), it may not be important for the inventory to predict anything. It simply helps the student learn something about his/her own interests.

Validity Evidence for Classification/Placement Decisions

A classification decision determines which of several programs, classes, or treatments in which to place a person. To make such a decision, there should be evidence (or good logic) to support the inference that an individual will be better off in the assigned program. For example, if we use an aptitude test score to help determine that an individual should be placed in a remedial education program, there should be evidence that individuals with such a score are apt to be better served by the remedial program. Indeed, such evidence is useful in court cases considering the legality of such a placement. If we use the results of a personality inventory to assign clients to different therapists, there should be evidence that the classification is beneficial to the well-being of the clients. This type of validity evidence, which can be gathered from research studies, is typically called *discriminant validity evidence*. It is a subclassification of what is termed, in this chapter, criterion-related validity evidence.

A placement decision determines the level of treatment in which to place a person. Although classification and placement are sometimes used interchangeably, the assignment of a student to chemistry or to algebra is typically a classification decision, whereas the assignment of a student to basic algebra or to honors algebra is a placement decision. For placement decisions, as for classification decisions, there should be some evidence that the individuals will profit from the placement. Again, this should be based on criterion-related validity evidence.

Quite often the evidence does not support the classification or placement decision. For example, the research on aptitude/treatment interaction often suggests that there is no good evidence that different treatments work differentially well with students with different characteristics. If, for all different types of students, one of two treatments always resulted in better outcomes than the other treatment, it should be obvious that the better treatment is the one to be used. In this case, a differential classification or placement decision should not be made.

Validity Evidence for Selection Decisions in Education

If a selection decision is based in part on test scores, an inference is being made that the students selected are the ones likely to be most successful or likely to profit most from the program. When a selection occurs there is usually some outside criterion against which the determination is made. Once this criterion is specified (success, value to the student, or whatever), we should obtain some criterion-related validity evidence that those selected actually are more likely to have higher measures on the criterion variable.

If we are simply interested in choosing those most likely to do well on the criterion measure, it would not be necessary, strictly speaking, to have any construct validity evidence. If we wish to know, however, why those who scored higher on the test also did better on the criterion measure, it would be necessary to know what construct was being measured. For example, a test may help predict success in college. If we are only interested in making a technician's decision to admit those with the highest predicted criterion scores, it would not be necessary to know what construct the predictor test measured. If we wish, however, to understand why the test predicted as it did, it would be necessary to know what construct the test measured. Does it predict because it measures "intelligence" and that is a useful construct for college success? Does it predict because it measures "quality of previous schooling" or "level of aspiration" or "test-taking skills"? To answer these questions, we would have to understand what the test measured.

Validity Evidence for Certification, Licensure, and Employment Decisions

As mentioned earlier, in professional and occupational certification and licensure decisions, we wish to infer if a person has achieved a specified standard of competence. We are not making inferences about the likely degree of success among those deemed competent. In employment decisions, however, an employer wishes to select the very best applicant in order to maximize productivity.

As the *Standards* point out, for licensure and certification "primary reliance must usually be placed on content evidence that is supplemented by evidence of the appropriateness of the construct being measured" (APA 1985, 63). Other measurement leaders writing in the field of professional licensure/certification generally agree with the position taken in the *Standards* that content validity is the primary concern.

The content domain of a licensure test is limited to the "knowledge and skills necessary to protect the public" (APA 1985, 9). Note that "abilities" was left out of this statement. This suggests that the authors recognized that a theoretical construct was not to be measured. Rather the measurement was to focus on knowledge and skills. Further, "skills that may be important to job success but which are not necessary for competent performance and therefore are not needed to protect the public are appropriately excluded from consideration in a licensing examination" (Linn 1984, 9).

Those who attack licensure or certification tests sometimes claim that such tests do not guarantee who will be good at the job. That is true, but totally irrelevant. Certainly anyone who knows anything about either testing or the task of predicting future human behavior would know that a test score can offer no guarantees. But should not such tests have some predictive validity? A few writers would argue yes, but most, including myself, would submit that licensure or certification tests are not designed to be predictive among those labeled competent. They are designed to provide evidence on "an examinee's present competence on specific abilities that are needed for practice" (Kane 1984, 2). As Shimberg pointed out:

> Those who believe that it is the purpose of licensing boards to predict job success might think so, but to follow their lead would drastically change the nature and purpose of licensing. It is doubtful that many legislators would agree that predicting job success should be a function of licensing boards (1982, 60).

Further, for many licensure decisions it is extremely difficult, if not impossible, to develop the good criterion measures necessary even to investigate criterion-related validity evidence. Many individuals would rather trust the test scores than the criterion measures if a criterion validity study were completed and the test failed to predict. For example, suppose a test was designed to determine whether chemistry teachers knew enough about chemistry to teach it. If the test showed a person to have inadequate knowledge of chemistry, but an administrator rated the person a competent (or even very successful) teacher, most individuals would not believe the rating. Logic alone would tell us that a teacher cannot adequately teach what he or she does not know.

Because licensure exams are designed to protect the public, the appropriate judgment of validity should be on whether the tests cover the knowledge and skills that those licensed should possess. For the purpose of the licensure decision, it is irrelevant and inappropriate to consider curricular or instructional validity in judging the quality of the test.

Because an employment test is used to assist in selecting those who will be the most successful or the most productive, criterion-related validity should be obtained if a suitable criterion measure can be identified. At times it is appropriate to measure an individual's aptitude to learn a specific job. In such a case, one would not need content validity, but would wish to have evidence that those who scored higher on the aptitude test really did learn a specific job better or faster than those who scored lower on the test. A major problem in employment testing is that the criterion is frequently hard to measure. Also, the number of candidates hired may be too low to conduct a criterion-related study. When there is no direct criterion-related validity evidence, it is important to build a test with content validity. The content domain should be defined by a job analysis that determines what tasks are demanded on the job.

For an educational certification test required for a high school diploma, it is important that the test have adequate content validity, where the domain is composed of knowledge and skills that are deemed important prerequisites to the granting of a high school diploma. It is also important for the test to have instructional/curricular validity. It is considered inappropriate and illegal to deny students a high school diploma for failing a test if they have not been given the opportunity to learn the material in the public schools.

Validity Evidence for Program Evaluation Decisions

Program evaluation covers a broad area. In making decisions about a program one would usually want to have some information about the results of the program in terms of student performance. The domain of student performance measured should be the domain to which the decisionmaker wishes to infer. At times one only wants to make inferences to a domain that exactly matches the instructional/curricular domain. In those cases it is appropriate to have instructional/curricular validity. However, that is not always the case. As Cronbach pointed out over twenty years ago:

> In course evaluation, we need not be much concerned about making measuring instruments fit the curriculum. . . . An ideal

evaluation might include measures of all the types of proficiency that might reasonably be desired in the area in question, not just the selected outcomes to which this curriculum directs substantial attention. (Cronbach 1963, 254)

COMBINING DATA

Typically more than one piece of data is used to make any decision. When multiple sources of data are available for use in making a single decision, the data must be combined in some fashion. One approach is to treat the data clinically. The decisionmaker looks at the total set of data and, taking it as a gestalt, arrives at a conclusion regarding what decision should be made. This approach might be used, for example, in a vocational counseling setting where the decision involves what to do first in exploring information about careers. Here, a precise mathematical approach for combining the data makes little sense. Little, if any, harm is done if an individual decides to learn more about job opportunities in one field rather than another prior to the next vocational counseling session. If the clinical "decision rule" is not constant for students with the same pattern of data, it does not really matter.

If the decision involves a selection, licensure, or employment decision, however, it is generally considered wise to have a more precise decision rule. In the first place, abundant research suggests that statistical decision making produces better results than clinical decision making. Further, it seems wise to have a consistent rule for the sake of fairness and because of the potential for litigation.

When we wish to employ a statistical or mathematical rule for combining data, there are basically three models to choose from: the *compensatory* model, the *conjunctive* model, and the *disjunctive* model. In the compensatory model, a large amount of one characteristic is allowed to compensate for a small amount of another characteristic. If we had criterion data and wished to use a decision rule based on a criterion-related validity study, a common example of this type of approach would be to use a multiple regression equation. Even without criterion data we could establish a compensatory model rule. For example, we could allow great strength to compensate for slow speed (or vice versa) in making a decision about an offensive lineman.

In the conjunctive model, a high score on one characteristic does not compensate for a low score on another characteristic. Rather the decision rule is that an individual must "pass" both measures to be acceptable. This approach is frequently called a multiple-cutoff model.

In the disjunctive model, the decision rule is to accept individuals if they "pass" on any of the various pieces of data. Probably the only time the disjunctive model is used is when there are multiple measures of the same variable and we wish to allow the applicant to benefit from positive errors of measurement, but not to suffer from negative errors of measurement. It will not be discussed further in this section.

The major issues to be considered in choosing between the conjunctive and compensatory models are (1) whether there is a linear relationship between each predictor variable and the criterion variable and (2) whether an excess of one variable can compensate for a deficiency in another variable. (Because we may not have any valid or reliable measures of the criterion variable, these are frequently logical questions rather than empirical ones.) To drastically oversimplify the issue, the compensatory model of combining data is likely to be better for selection decisions and the conjunctive model better for licensure decisions. The reason for the distinction is that for selection decisions (as previously discussed) we are interested in selecting the very best (maximizing productivity in employment selection). However, for licensure decisions, we wish to license all those who are minimally qualified and to exclude all those who are not. The purpose of a licensure examination is not to predict degrees of success. Concerning minimal competence, we make the same inference about someone who scores far above the minimum on an examination as we do about someone who scores just above the minimum cutoff score.

An approach that has been implemented as a part of a consent decree regarding teacher licensure tests in one state is to allow those who failed the competency test to count their college GPA as 50% in a linear weighting approach. Thus, high grades are used to compensate positively for individuals whose test scores are below the cutoff, but low grades are not used to deny licensure to individuals who score just above the cutoff score on a licensure test. The reasons why this approach is unsound are not hard to understand. The public is concerned about false acceptances, not false rejections, and the purpose of a licensure exam is to protect the public against false acceptances. The decision rule just described, of course, increases the number of false acceptances. (For a more thorough discussion of why GPAs should not be used in a compensatory model with licensure tests, see Mehrens, Phillips, and Anderson 1987.)

Sometimes people get confused about the multiple-cutoff approach. The data may be gathered sequentially, and the individual being tested may score above the cutoff score on all variables except the final test (or interview, or whatever). Critics will look at this final decision point and argue that the decision was inappropriately made on the basis of a single piece of data. Not so: several pieces of data were used—but they were used sequentially in the decision making. In general, in sequential testing and decision making, we use already available data first, gather relevant data that are fairly moderate in cost for more decisions, and use expensive data-gathering techniques to make decisions about a smaller set of individuals who already "passed" the previous test. Actually, sequential decision making usually results in *more* data being collected; we can often afford to gather *more* types of data for the same cost because not all data are gathered for all individuals.

TEST SCORES INCREASE THE QUALITY OF DECISIONS

When deciding whether or not to use test data in decision making, we must consider the incremental validity of the decision. That is, can a better decision be made by using the other data alone or by adding the test information to the other data? Once this question has been answered, we must inquire if this increase in the quality of the decision is sufficiently great to justify the cost of gathering and using the test data. Theoretically, both of these questions can be answered in a quantitative manner, but in practice the answers must frequently be subjective.

First of all, there are different definitions of what constitutes a good decision. Decisions can be judged on the basis of two criteria: *process* and *outcome*. A good process is one in which all relevant information is gathered and weighted properly prior to the decision. A good outcome is one in which the result of the decision is desirable. Under either definition, the more relevant information a person has, the better the decision can be. In fact, according to the process definition of good decision making, it is essential to gather all relevant information prior to making the decision. Even when good decision making is defined in terms of the outcome, the more information we have, the better the chances of our making a good decision. It should be stressed that additional data, *if it is used wisely*, cannot result in poorer decision making. At the worst, the data would be irrelevant to the decision and therefore would not improve the quality of the decision. Of course if we misuse the test results by weighting them improperly or misinterpreting the data, we may end up making poorer decisions using the test information than we would have made had we not used the test results at all.

One of the problems of doing a cost analysis regarding the value of a test as a tool in decision making is that it is difficult to place cost values on false acceptances and false rejections. Consider, for example, using teacher competency examinations for licensure purposes. When licensure decisions are made, there are two possible errors that can be made. We may license someone who is incompetent (false acceptance), or we may fail to grant a license to someone who is competent (false rejection). Not everyone would agree about the relative costs of these two types of errors, let alone the actual dollar costs. Further, because there is no measure external to the test that is a better measure of competence, there is no way to know whether someone who is licensed is a false acceptance or whether someone who is rejected is a false rejection.

However, in the absence of truth, we must still make decisions. When making decisions, decisionmakers should specifically consider their values concerning the relative costs of the two kinds of errors. For example, licensure boards no doubt realize that they have a responsibility to protect the public from incompetents. Thus, they should be (in my opinion, at least) more concerned about false acceptances than false rejections.

If we have subjectively determined how many fewer faulty decisions we would make with test data than without and the costs of the faulty decisions, it would be possible to compare the savings in costs against the cost of gathering the test data. However, it should be stressed that in educational decision making the test data "is usually placed in the student's file and used for many later decisions: admission, choice of major, selection of courses, career planning, and so forth. A test with multiple uses can repay a cost that would be unreasonable if a test were to be used once and forgotten" (Cronbach 1971, 496).

Finally, it should be emphasized in reference to test validity and decision making that validity is always a matter of degree. No test will result in perfect decision making. Some errors are bound to occur. Our goal is to minimize errors in decision making, but one should *not* conclude that a test should not be used because it is possible to point to incorrect inferences made with the use of test data (for example, "I scored 88 on an intelligence test and a counselor told me I could not succeed in college, but now I have a PhD in education; therefore all intelligence tests are invalid"). The crucial question in validity is not whether errors will be made in individual cases—the answer is invariably "yes." The crucial question is whether fewer errors will be made by using a test in addition to other data than would be made using just the other data. If test data are used wisely, it is impossible to make a poorer decision with additional data than without it.

SUMMARY AND CONCLUSIONS

This chapter has presented a brief discussion of various types of educational decisions, various types of validity evidence, and the relationship between the type of decision being made and the type of validity evidence deemed desirable. The key points in any decision making are to consider just what inference is involved in the decision, what types of data would be helpful in making an accurate inference, and what types of evidence (or logic) would be helpful in judging the degree of confidence that should be placed on the accuracy of the inference. For some inferences it is necessary to have content validity evidence, for others we would like criterion-related validity evidence, and for still others we would like construct validity evidence. Ideally, we might want evidence of all types for some inferences.

Another section of the chapter briefly discussed models of combining data from different sources when making a single decision. Conjunctive and compensatory models are both frequently used. When the variables being used for making the decision are linearly related to a criterion measure, when an excess of one variable can compensate for a deficiency in another, and when we are interested in inferring degree of attainment of the criterion variable, the compensatory model is typically preferred. But if there is not a linear relationship, if an excess of one variable cannot compensate for a deficiency in another, and if we are interested only in inferring that a person has a minimum amount of a characteristic (rather than the degree of the characteristic), such as in a licensure decision, then the conjunctive model is likely to be more appropriate.

Finally, this chapter contained a short section on how we should consider the costs of the data gathering and the saving in faulty decisions that is likely if we use test information. Logically, if we use data wisely, we cannot make a poorer decision with test data than without it.

As a final point regarding testing and educational decision making, it should be noted that educational tests can be burdened with too much responsibility (Madaus 1985). Yet, we can also expect too little of testing. It seems to me that the critics both from within and outside the profession have tended to set (or project onto others) either very low aspirations or very high or unrealistic aspirations for what measurement can do. (For example, some critics say teacher licensure tests will not solve all the problems of incompetent teachers, other critics say they cannot solve any of the problems.) We should set intermediate levels of aspiration for test use. Tests can and do help us make better decisions. They do not allow us to make perfect decisions.

REFERENCES

American Educational Research Association, American Psychological Association, and National Council on Measurement in Education. 1985. *Standards for educational and psychological testing.* Washington, D.C.: American Psychological Association. (Known as APA *Standards.*)

Bloom, B. S., G. F. Madaus, and T. T. Hastings. 1981. *Evaluation to improve learning.* New York: McGraw-Hill.

Bross, I. D. 1953. *Design for decision.* New York: Macmillan.

Cronbach, L. J. 1963. Course improvement through evaluation. *Teacher's College Record* 64:672–83.

_____. 1971. Test validation. In *Educational masurement.* 2d ed., ed. R. L. Thorndike. Washington, D.C.: American Council on Education.

_____. 1980. Validity on parole: How can we go straight? In *Measuring achievement: Progress over a decade. New directions for testing and measurement.* ed. W. B. Schrader, no. 5, 99–108. San Francisco: Jossey-Bass.

Edwards, W. 1961. Behavioral decision theory. *Annual Review of Psychology* 12:473–99.

Kane, M. T. 1984. Strategies in validating licensure examinations. Paper presented at the annual meeting of the American Educational Research Association, New Orleans, LA.

Linn, R. L. 1984. Standards for validity in licensure testing. Paper presented at the Validity in Licensure Testing symposium at the annual meeting of the American Educational Research Association, New Orleans, LA.

Madaus, G. 1985. Public policy and the testing profession—You've never had it so good? *Educational Measurement: Issues and Practice* 4:4, 5–11.

Mehrens, W. A. 1987. Issues in teacher competency tests. Paper prepared for the National Commission on Testing and Public Policy, Graduate School of Education, University of California, Berkeley.

Mehrens, W. A. and I. J. Lehmann. 1984. *Measurement and evaluation in education and psychology.* 3d. ed. New York: Holt, Rinehart and Winston.

_____. 1987. *Using standardized tests in education.* 4th ed. New York: Longman.

Mehrens, W. A., S. E. Phillips, and A. E. Anderson. 1987. Conjunctive versus compensatory models for teacher licensure decisions: Monte Carlo and logical investigations. Paper presented at the annual meeting of the American Educational Research Association, Washington, D.C.

Parnell, D. 1973. In *Elementary and Secondary Education Amendment of 1973: Hearings before the General Subcommittee on Education of the Committee on Education and Labor, House of Representatives.* 93d.

Cong.,1st sess. (On H.R. 16, H.R. 5163 and H.R. 5823.) Part 3 and Appendix.

Shimberg, B. 1982. *Occupational licensing: A public perspective.* Princeton, N.J.: Educational Testing Service.

U.S. Department of Health, Education and Welfare. 1971. *Report on licensure and related health personnel credentialing.* Department of Health, Education and Welfare Publication 72-11. Washington, D.C.: Author.

Wald, A. 1950. *Statistical decision functions.* New York: Wiley.

Yalow, E. S., and W. J. Popham. 1983. Content validity at the crossroads. *Educational Researcher* 128:10–14, 21.

If Not Tests, Then What?

CONFERENCE REMARKS

Christopher Jencks

I think that there are two big questions that we might want to ask about tests in the present political climate. One is whether we should restrict their use and consider alternatives to testing, and the other is whether we can improve the tests that we are using.

I do not think it is too profitable to focus on alternative types of tests. I doubt that alternative tests will take us very far toward meeting any of the political objections that have surfaced in the last ten years to the ways we are using tests at the present.

As I understand them, those objections are three. First, the tests are unfair to various disadvantaged groups. Tests exclude disadvantaged groups from opportunities which we would like to see them get and to which we believe they are entitled. Second, the tests are incompatible with efficient selection procedures. They keep out people who could actually do a good job in one context or another. (Tests are bad for the institutions that use them, if you will). And third, tests violate our sense of fairness in society as a whole because the outcomes of testing are not what we want.

Now all of those objections seem to apply with equal force to the range of tests that are currently being seriously considered either in the college admissions process or in the employment process. I do not want to say that all tests are indistinguishable and interchangeable—that is not true. But I think it is fair to say that there are no prospective changes in the kinds of tests that we use that would take us very far toward solving any of these three problems. Minor incremental improvements can be made. But I do not think that there are major differences between, let us say, aptitude tests and achievement tests as they might be used in the admissions process, or between different types of achievement tests, in terms of what they do to the prospects of disadvantaged individuals or in terms of their efficiency in selection.

Today, I would like to urge that we concentrate as much as we can, not just on the defects of tests as they now exist, but on whether the alternatives which would be likely to emerge in place of tests would be better or worse than the system that we already have. In a sense, that is an uncontroversial way to formulate the question, but it is not the way arguments about tests usually take place. Most of the discussion of tests focuses on their limitations and drawbacks. Relatively little of it asks what are the likely alternatives.

I start with an assumption that I suspect most people in this room would agree to, namely that all societies have elites. Some positions are more desirable than others and somehow or other people have to be selected for those roles. No society admits everyone who wants to attend to every educational program in the society. Very few societies even admit everyone who wants to attend a university. We come closer to that than most societies. Certainly no society randomly selects people for professional or managerial or even craft and clerical jobs. So if we are not going to use tests, what might we use instead to select people for these positions?

In trying to assess these alternatives, I will use three distinct criteria. The first criterion is, what does it do to the life chances of different demographic groups? If we give up tests and do something else, how does it affect the prospects of blacks compared to whites, males compared to females, poor people compared to rich people, the highly educated compared to the poorly educated?

The second criterion is, how does it affect the institutions? We can think about that in two different ways. First, does it select individuals who are more competent or less competent than the ones selected under the present system? And second, what does it do to the structure of motivation and morale and the character of the community into which those individuals come? Does it create a climate in an institution in which people feel that the right people have been chosen or that the process is fair? Almost all of our assessments of these issues focus on the first question—do we get competent people using one or another criterion? But it is also important to think about whether the different selection procedures affect the overall climate of an organization.

My third criterion is the one that comes most naturally to all of us. Will the new system make the society as a whole feel it is allocating privilege more fairly or less fairly?

If you think about the college admissions process as it now stands, the first thing that is striking is that the tests do not count very much. The college admissions process depends very heavily on self-selection and on grades and rather less on tests of any kind. But it could be argued, and I think correctly, that test scores play an important role in self-selection; and it can certainly also be argued that test scores, even if they are not the single most important criterion or even the second most important criterion, are not a negligible criterion in the way people think about what the allocation of educational opportunity looks like in the United States.

Now, suppose tomorrow morning it became illegal to use standardized tests in college admissions; how might the world look? Since it was not that long ago when we did not use such tests, and many institutions still do not, at least in any significant sense, it is not difficult to make some predictions.

There are four alternatives to the use of tests in college admissions. The first alternative is to rely on high school grades. This was the usual public university strategy before the advent of standardized testing. The second alternative is to rely on grades plus some measure of high school quality. That was the usual private college option before we had standardized tests. Before the advent of the College Board, private colleges in effect let secondary schools rank their graduates. Then the colleges adjusted these ratings on the basis of whether they thought this was a good, a not so good, or a terrible secondary school.

The third alternative is open admissions with a "big back door." That is, you let in everybody and then you have a relatively stringent grading procedure and kick out a lot of people or at least encourage them to depart in haste. For some generations, that was the Big Ten strategy. Everybody in the state could go to the state university, but almost everybody in the state also had the privilege of flunking out.

The fourth alternative is to have open admissions and not flunk out lots of people. That is the community college strategy, and in many ways increasingly approximates the city university strategy in New York. It is also, of course, the strategy of the American high school. Anyone can attend and almost anyone can finish.

Now, if we go through those alternatives, the most striking thing to me is how little we know about their consequences. Consider the "grades alone" option. Every college admits students on the basis of their high school grade-point average or their class rank, and perhaps modifies these criteria slightly using letters of recommendation. Now, notice what you are doing here. You are simply substituting tests designed by high school teachers for tests designed by the Educational Testing Service (ETS). If you use grades rather than class rank, you are also allowing high schools to set whatever distribution of grades they find appealing. They can give all As or all Cs or all Bs or whatever they like. A class ranking system "solves" that problem by requiring all schools to use the same mean, regardless of how good their students are.

That procedure works better for disadvantaged students. The correlation between grades and socioeconomic background or race is lower than the correlation between test scores and socioeconomic background or race. But what we do not know, at least what I do not know, is exactly why that comes about. It is easier to get an A in a low-income neighborhood school or in an all-black school than in a high-income neighborhood school or an all-white school. You could, in principle, just fix this up by adjusting the grades from different schools up or down so they meant the same thing. I do not know the extent to which the apparent advantage for disadvantaged students of using grades rather than test scores in the admissions process disappears if you do this. Is it the case, *within* any given school, that grades are less highly correlated with race and class than test scores are? Is it simply because there are different tracks in the same school, and a C in the general track has a different meaning than a C in the college track? Or is it the case that even within Mrs. Jones's classroom, her grades are less related to class background and less related to race than are Scholastic Aptitude Test (SAT) scores, or achievement test scores, or other standardized test scores?

Now if the last is the case, it seems to me we are on to something. That is, if it is true that test scores are really more biased against disadvantaged students than the grades that individual teachers give in their classrooms, it is worth trying to figure out why and it may well be the case that we can then use that fact to build a more persuasive argument against testing than many of the arguments I have seen.

Nonetheless, a grades-only system is clearly worse for the colleges. It may not be much worse, but it is a little worse. It formally precludes colleges from adjusting the qualifications of applicants for the quality of secondary schools. It simply says that you have to admit everybody who has a B average, or an A average, or a B- average, or whatever. This is a less efficient selection system than one that allows admissions officers to adjust for high school quality.

I do not know whether a system that allows admissions officers to adjust for school quality is less efficient than one that uses the SAT. I suspect that there is little difference between the two systems. That is, if we took high school grades for different schools, adjusted the grades for the quality of the schools, and then used those numbers to predict freshman grades or cumulative college grades, I think we would do just about as well as we do when we use high school grades and SAT scores. But I have not seen that piece of research done.

In the long run, nonetheless, such a system could not survive because it invites corruption. If you do not have some kind of system for certifying school quality and you do not build that into a college admissions process, then Gresham's Law takes over and you get competitive grade inflation.

In the absence of a universal testing system, students who apply to universities from institutions about which the university knows very little are going to be at a disadvantage. If a student applies to Harvard from Pocatello, and nobody in Pocatello has gone to Harvard for the last ten years, Harvard has no idea what a B+ or an A- means in Pocatello. Harvard will reject the student unless it has some way to evaluate the student's high school record.

That was what happened before the advent of standardized testing. The problem was not primarily, as ETS was fond of claiming, that kids from Pocatello were rejected by a selective university because they had not studied Latin in Pocatello. (That *was* a problem, but not a serious one.) The primary problem was that the old-boy network was substituted for the SAT as a way of ranking schools. Admissions officers trusted the judgments of schools that had sent them lots of applicants in the past. They did not trust the schools about which they did not know much. The standardized test is a device for allowing a student to prove that his or her A really means something.

If we got rid of standardized testing for individuals, small high schools would have a great incentive to bring it back as a school-level form of certification. Small high schools need a device for telling colleges what their grades mean. If colleges knew the *mean* test score of all the kids in Pocatello, plus the class rank of the student, they would probably know about all they needed (or wanted) to know for admitting him to college. Whether that would satisfy any of the people who are opposed to testing, I am less sure, but it would suspend the use of individual test scores.

The "big back door" open-admissions strategy could be either good or bad for disadvantaged students. If we took the top half of the grade distribution in an open-admissions college, I would expect it to contain more black students than the top half of the SAT distribution in the same school. But I have not seen such an analysis. We could do the same thing with income or any other measure of class background.

I should emphasize that this analysis is *not* the same as an analysis of whether test scores overpredict or underpredict the freshman grades of minority students or low-income students. SAT scores *over*estimate the mean grades of black students in many colleges. Yet even in these colleges, more black students might graduate, if the college had open admissions and flunked out half its freshmen, than would graduate if the college used only the SAT for admissions. That is counterintuitive. The arithmetic is a little obscure, but if somebody wants me to demonstrate it, I will. The great virtue of open admissions and a "big back door" is that it *looks* fair, and it may be good for minorities. It looks fair for the simpleminded reason that the criterion for kicking people out of colleges is actual performance instead of predicted performance.

Open admissions plus a "big back door" also improves the quality of a college's graduates. If you admit all the students who apply and kick out the bottom half, the students who remain will inevitably have a higher sophomore grade-point average or senior grade-point average than a group admitted on the basis of good SAT scores or high school grades.

The problem with this system is cost. If you admit a lot of people and then kick out a lot of them, you spend a lot of money instructing those who will not finish. It is also expensive in a less obvious way, because it creates a completely different climate in the institution. An institution set up on the assumption that you are going to kick out half of the students has a different relationship to its students than one set up like an elite university on the assumption that everybody we let in here will surely graduate. You move from a "we're all on the same side and you're going to get through here" state of mind to "we're on opposite sides and the question is whether you deserve to get through here" state of mind. If you are a good student, and you have a choice between institutions operating on these two systems, you should choose an institution that assumes you will get through, not one in which you have to prove that you deserve to get through.

The last thing to be said about the "big back door" is that it is impractical. We used to have it. We had it in a day when instructors did not worry too much about giving Fs. Professors do not like to do that anymore. So today, open admissions means comparatively open graduation as well. Not everyone will get through. But the old system of flunking half the freshmen is just not politically viable.

One thing that modifies all the observations I have made is the problem of self-selection. In every system I have described, self-selection is an important determinant of who gets the goodies. We know remarkably little about what influences the way people select themselves into institutions. But clearly there is a complicated feedback process. People will not apply to institutions where they expect to fail. Almost nobody likes to fail. Students do not want to go to colleges where they think the other students will be a lot smarter than themselves. Nor do they like to go to places where they are humiliated because they are not able to do the work. So there are all kinds of self-selection processes working here. The extent to which getting rid of test scores would change those mechanisms is hard to predict, but very important.

Now, let me say a couple of things about employment, where I think that the logic of the situation is much the same but some of the options are different. In employment we have essentially the same range of alternatives as in college admissions. We could start off by setting no requirements and then firing lots of people who do not do a good job. Just as flunking students out of college is difficult, firing people is not easy either. Perhaps assistant professors and fruit pickers are the only groups of people who still get fired.

You could also hire large numbers of employees and not fire them, if your operation has many low-level jobs and few opportunities for promotion. Then you promote the few, you keep the many, and you do not have to fire many people. I sometimes think of this as the "McDonald's option." Most organizations are not set up with that kind of a pyramid. They do not have many low-level jobs that "everybody" can do. So they want to do a little screening beforehand in order to avoid having to fire people.

Some of those organizations use something that is analogous to the "grades only" option; that is, they hire people on the basis of their performance in a similar previous job. Or they hire someone right out of school on the basis of their performance in school, which is essentially the "grades only" option in a less efficient format (since school grades are not a terribly good predictor of performance in most jobs).

Some firms use the "grades only" option modified by school quality. That is, they say okay, I'll hire the top 10% of the Harvard graduating class for my law firm; but I'll only hire the top 5% from Michigan.

With one vital exception, the problems posed by those options are about the same for employment as for colleges. The exception is that in the case of education, if you have an open-admissions system with no "big back door," all you need is additional resources to run the system. The fact that some students are incompetent does not impose any large costs on society, except for the cost of supporting faculty members who pretend to teach them. Incompetent workers can do real harm. Incompetent students cannot.

These observations lead me to two general conclusions about the goal of the National Commission on Testing and Public Policy. First, if this commission is to make useful or convincing judgments about merits and demerits of using tests for various purposes, it needs to be both explicit and realistic about the likely alternatives. If we abolish or restrict the use of tests, those who now use tests to select people for privileged positions will have to invent other ways to select these people. We must ask who will gain and who will lose from substituting these alternatives for existing tests.

My second general conclusion is that we do not know enough about different selection systems to answer questions of this kind reliably. We might be able to piece together fairly reliable answers from thorough reviews of existing research, but, for the most part, I doubt that this will be feasible. This means that if the commission is to make pronouncements based on evidence, it will have to be prepared to invest in research as well as airfares and tape recorders.

Advice to the Commission

CONFERENCE REMARKS

George Hanford[1]

Today, in the spirit of the Christmas season, I have one request, two comments, three observations, four plus one generalizations, five messages, and one conclusion, but no partridges or pear trees—seventeen points that I will try to cover, on the average, at the rate of less than one minute each. Are you ready?

First, the request: On Thursday afternoon, James Crouse characterized the College Board and, by implication, me, as arrogant and not forthright. My request is that you read the report of the Wakefield Colloquium on *Measures in the College Admissions Process*. Read it, then make your own judgment.

Next, the two comments: First, the College Board is not a testing company. It is an association of twenty-five hundred schools and colleges, including the University of California and the San Francisco public schools. We try to help students move from secondary to higher education. To help with the testing part of that process, we contract with a testing company, ETS. But we do a lot of other things besides sponsor the SAT.

Second comment: Do not tar all tests with accounts of the misdesign and misuse of tests by the New York Police Department. The head of the highly selective nursing program at El Paso Community College does not! She knows that the best way to predict performance on the Texas licensing examination in nursing is to use the SAT or ACT. But she makes her tough admissions decisions based on multiple criteria, not test scores alone.

Now, the three observations: First, the recent reports of the National Governors' Association and the Carnegie Foundation for the Advancement of Teaching have put the spotlight on assessment *in* and *of* higher education. As I noted to John Fremer yesterday, and as he has pointed out in passing this morning, the agenda for this meeting has not addressed it. The proposed commission should. There is no more prominent topic on the public political agenda today.

Second observation: I would note now, as I did in accepting Bernard Gifford's invitation, the absence here of two important parties to the testing process: the direct users and the regulators of tests—admissions officers or employment directors in the first instance and legislators or statewide

---

1 These comments were composed during the planning conference for the National Commission on Testing and Public Policy and delivered at the end of that conference.

authorities in the second. They should be represented in the commission's deliberations.

Third observation: The emphasis in the call to this meeting stressed the allocative function of tests. The commissioners could be misled into forgetting the educative, diagnostic, counseling, and distributive (for which read "self-selective") functions of tests. I hope they do not!

And now to my generalizations and messages via the outline of John Fremer's presentation. Because his outline contains a number of references to College Board tests, it is not surprising that the trends he identifies generally as operating across education, the economy, and our society are mirrored in the experience of the College Board. This brings me to my first generalization: Those trends historically reflect the continuing tension in our society between egalitarianism and meritocracy—in the lexicon of the College Board, the tension between quality and equality as reflected in our Educational EQuality Project. Bernard Gifford's letter of invitation reflects one view of that tension when it speaks of tests as "previously seen by many as tools for achieving a more democratic society" now "come to be seen by many as one of the major obstacles to equal opportunity."

By contrast, let me share a quite different perspective. Consider "truth-in-testing legislation" espoused by FairTest. I understand that this legislative approach was generated by disappointed majority law-school applicants who saw their places being "given" (in quotes) to minority students who had apparently scored lower. They blamed the tests for causing their disappointment, enlisted in Ralph Nader's consumer movement, and devised so-called "truth-in-testing," a trend or movement that has received little attention here. Do not forget, this movement is out "to get the testers" and do away with tests—or at least to so cripple their effectiveness that, in my world, selective colleges would have to go back to relying on the "old-boy network" of schools to which Christopher Jencks referred.

At the same time, a message explicit in the data surrounding the SAT score decline was that minority students, for reasons of educational disadvantage, were not doing as well as the majority. One of the first battles I fought as president of the College Board was for the release of ethnic data in relation to SAT performance. Opposed by black leaders then, the results of that move are now applauded, for instance, by Benjamin Hooks of the NAACP. The Urban League is promoting special preparation for the SAT. And the Hispanic Higher Education Coalition has succeeded in getting us to publish a Hispanic Test-taking Kit. Minority leaders are not out to shoot the messenger; they are out to change the message.

In terms of the tension between quality and equality, they have joined the quality movement and are seeking to use it to improve the educational lot of the students they represent, which brings me to my first message. It is that, as Carolyn Webber observed, the uses of tests reflect societal conditions; they do not drive them. They are not responsible for social change. What I came here to hear discussed is the responsible adaptation of the use of tests to changing social conditions and needs, not how to use tests to foster change, to promote your agenda or mine. This is an attitude I urge the commission to adopt.

This leads to my second generalization: Educators take pride in their civil-rights record, in having integrated higher education. They forget that they did so in response to *Brown v. Board of Education*. My second generalization, therefore, is that externally mandated change "ain't all bad." And it is a generalization that applies to testing.

When I joined the College Board staff in 1955, students were not allowed to know their SAT scores. By 1957, they were. And, when our older daughter took the test in 1962, she was given half an SAT to practice on. What truth-in-testing did was to greatly accelerate that healthy but gradual opening up of the testing process, an opening up that the commission should foster, which is my second message.

That brings me to my third generalization and third message: While testing is subject to the influence of social change, it is also subject to the influence of technological change. As John Fremer's outline suggests, "There is ample evidence of the impact of technology on testing." As George Madaus suggested at the 1985 ETS Invitational Conference in his paper on the perils and promises of new tests and new technologies, there is the promise of relating tests more closely to instruction, the interactive teaching identified by Donald Schwartz and espoused by John Goodlad in his assault on "frontal teaching," the cramming of man's ever-expanding knowledge into young heads without the opportunity either to think or talk about it. I see more promise than peril, but urge the commission to encourage the pursuit of the former without overlooking the dangers of the latter, which is my third message.

And my fourth generalization and message are like the third, and moreover are related to the stated topic of this session, "the political economy of the testing industry." The generalization is that just as testing is subject to the influence of technological change, so also it is subject to political and economic change. I tend to bracket the two. The reform movements that overtook secondary education in 1983 and higher education this past year are driven by motives that are both political and economic, inextricably so. Proof? The movement has been inspired in part by governors in the South seeking to upgrade the skills of their labor forces to which industry from the North fled in the early years of the century and away from which it has fled in recent years to cheaper labor overseas. Edward Potter's concern about international competition, the need to respond to the demands of the service and information industries identified by Robert Gelerter yesterday, and political reality have all put the spotlight on education and the need to provide accountability for the dollars spent by taxpayers and industry. And, recalling

Henry Levin's observations on employability, what better way to demonstrate accountability than through tests? As a result, one can find in the halls of state legislatures an interesting tension between those who would legislate to control testing and those who would use testing to control education and employment. But given that tension, please tell me one thing: Who is for quality and who is for equality? Whatever your answer, my fourth message is this: Do not sell out to either side!

This brings me to my fifth generalization and message: The generalization is that the field of psychometrics is not wholly the pawn of external forces. It has a large measure of control over its own destiny. And there are three trends in this area that excite me. One is the move to integrate assessment more closely with instruction, a possibility first raised here by Walter Haney, urged by Robert Taggart, and implicitly suggested in Norman Chachkin's final comment. A second is the use of tests for purposes of diagnosis and prescription. And the third is the work Howard Gardner and Robert Sternberg are doing in exploring new dimensions of intellect. I see these attempts to broaden the use of tests and our bases of human assessment as developments I believe the National Commission on Testing and Public Policy should foster, which, you will have realized, is my fifth message.

In conclusion: In all that we have been talking about, there is an implicit assumption that meritocracy and egalitarianism cannot be simultaneously served, that tests either open up access or obstruct it. The easiest thing in society, I have found, is to be an advocate. You are for equality and therefore against anything that gets in its way, such as quality. Or you are for quality and against anything that gets in its way, such as equality. You are for tests or you are against them. You are for teacher testing or you are against it. You are for the Golden Rule settlement or you are against it. You like the SAT or you do not. That kind of posture makes the cause clearer and the rhetoric easier. The harder task is to be a moderate, to be, as I am, for both quality and equality. The cause is less clear; the rhetoric harder. But I believe that the causes both of meritocracy and egalitarianism can be served by testing and the National Commission on Testing and Public Policy will, if it chooses the harder road, have the opportunity to advance both causes.

III

LANGUAGE, CULTURE, ETHNICITY, AND TESTING

Aspects of Differential Performance by Minorities on Standardized Tests: Linguistic and Sociocultural Factors

Mary Catherine O'Connor

I. INTRODUCTION

Since the earliest attempts to construct and administer standardized intelligence and aptitude tests, there have been those who questioned the wisdom of using these tests, normed on white middle-class populations, in testing ethnic and linguistic minorities. As standardized testing has become more and more central to the goals of educators, administrators, and, more recently, legislative bodies at state and federal levels, the number of concerned individuals has grown.[1]

In this chapter, I will review some of the literature on standardized tests and ethnolinguistic minorities. The purpose of the first section is to present the issues, conceptual and policy-oriented, that figure in current debates over the use of such tests in the United States, principally in education. The focus will be on linguistic and sociocultural factors that influence test performance of minorities—a vast topic in itself—and many aspects of the problems will only be touched on briefly.

The problem to be addressed is the observed differential performance by minorities on standardized paper-and-pencil tests. On average, black and Hispanic background students perform at about one standard deviation below the mean on standardized tests of intelligence, aptitude, and achievement (Samuda 1975; Padilla 1979; Olmedo 1981; Green 1981). Of course, many of the dimensions of language, thought, and behavior discussed herein are relevant to the larger question of school success and failure. For the purposes of this chapter, however, the focus will be narrowed to performance on standardized measures of aptitude and achievement.

---

[1] There are many excellent reviews of the large literature on the problem of standardized testing and ethnic and linguistic minorities. Among these are Durán (in press); Padilla (1979); Green (1981); Olmedo (1981); Samuda (1975); and Williams (1983). Bersoff (1981) presents a useful review of the legal aspects of testing in the case of minorities.

Research Perspectives

At least three general categories of explanation are given for the differential performance by minority populations on standardized measures. The first of these is held by proponents of the heritability model, which assumes that scores on standardized measures reliably reflect innate abilities and aptitudes. The heritability theorists (for example, Jensen 1969) point out that educators and researchers have failed to find ways to substantially raise test scores of some minorities, and to explain the higher-than-expected scores of others. They interpret this failure as evidence for their position that extrinsic factors play an insignificant role in differential performance. I will not review the works of members of this school of thought. The social and intellectual responses to this position are reviewed in Samuda (1975); see also the papers collected in Block and Dworkin (1976).

The second position views performance on tests as merely one of a number of measures of school success or failure, including grades and teacher evaluations, retention, and the acquisition of degrees. All such measures are assumed, in this model, to be determined by macrolevel social factors, and the individual's and community's response to them. Ogbu (1978), Labov (1982b), Ogbu and Matute-Bianchi (1986), and others have pointed out that among these factors are the minority's status within the matrix society with respect to conditions of entry, whether through immigration or enslavement; the source of cultural differences between the minority and the mainstream population (that is, did the differences arise before the groups came into contact, or are they a reaction to the subordination experienced by the minority after contact?); and the constraints on the economic future of the minority. Proponents of this perspective assume that the failure to ameliorate high rates of failure on standardized tests simply reflects society's failure to address the basic economic and social structural factors that reproduce and maintain relations of inequality.

The third position maintains that, while these macrolevel factors certainly determine a large proportion of school failure and success, they are not the whole story. From this perspective, inequality is maintained and enacted in encounters between individuals. Members of minority groups share systems of practices, beliefs, norms, and experiences that differ from those shared by members of the dominant culture of which the school is a central institution. Social and cultural differences are assumed to play a large role in school failure. (This position is elaborated in papers found in Gumperz 1982a, 1982b.) From this perspective, the failure of researchers and educators to change test scores is a function of many things; but at least one of them is the possibility that we do not yet understand the correct way to approach the sociocultural differences among groups in the schools with respect to the activity of taking tests, with all that implies.[2]

Most of the research reviewed here implicitly or explicitly assumes the last view. Many also support the second view, but have put their research efforts into investigating the more local sources of difficulty on standardized tests. This paper will not present an exhaustive review of any literature, but will provide an explication of some of the important conceptual (and to a lesser extent, methodological) issues confronting educators, researchers, testmakers, and policymakers who are concerned with the question of differential performance by minorities.

Much of the literature on standardized testing and minorities deals with the *aftermath* of differential performance, that is, with problems of selection and placement, or with the appropriate interpretation of scores. Mean test-score differentials raise a number of equity issues. Overrepresentation of minorities in remedial programs and underrepresentation of the same groups in institutions of higher learning are only two of the obvious examples.

Measurement specialists commonly define *bias* as the over- or underprediction of performance on a criterion (see Anastasi 1968). When challenged by parents, researchers, and legislators over the past several decades to explain or account for the large scoring gap, measurement specialists have responded by narrowing the focus of concern to the *methods* used to detect bias in particular tests. Using sophisticated correlational and regression analyses, they have established that, on purely statistical grounds, the predictions that standardized tests make for minorities are as accurate as the predictions regarding the criterion performance of mainstream individuals (where the criterion for future performance is usually GPA or a score on some other test). For further discussion on this point the reader is directed to the papers in Berk (1982); Reschly and Sabers (1979); and Goldman and Hewitt (1976).[3]

---

[2] This general perspective is implicitly held by many outside the social sciences as well.   Compare the following statement by a biologist: "The argument that compensatory education is hopeless is equivalent to saying that changing the form of the seventeenth-century gutter would not have a pronounced effect on public sanitation. What compensatory education will be able to accomplish when the study of human behavior finally emerges from its prescientific era is anyone's guess. It will be most extraordinary if it stands as the sole exception to the rule that technological progress exceeds by manyfold what even the most optimistic might have imagined" (Lewontin 1976, 92).

[3] Some researchers have argued that the standard of equal regression lines is not as useful as many assume, since even if the regression lines are equal for the different groups, the degree of correlation between the measurement and the criterion is not so high for either mainstream or minority students. It is generally below .5 (Lunemann 1974).

The proliferation of statistical methods for detecting bias resulted in a refocusing of interest. However, many concerned individuals turned their attention away from technical questions of measurement toward more global analyses of the problem. Test users (policymakers, teachers, and so on) demanded alternate definitions of bias, and the focus changed from the properties of tests to the *fair use* of tests. Measurement specialists and policymakers began to consider strategies that would ensure fair selection for whatever the goals of the test givers were: admission, access to training, and so forth. That is, instead of setting one cutoff point for selection by test score, test administrators and users began to implement selection procedures which would result in equal representation for different ethnic groups. The theory of selection of multiple cutoff points began to develop, as well as consideration of other measures to ensure equity. Other researchers suggested that tests be regarded as measures of performance relative only to the sociocultural group of which the test taker was a member (Mercer 1973, 1977).

Thus, much of the research literature views differential performance as a fact, and tries to derive fair methods for dealing with the results. The aftermath of test taking (scores and subgroup norm differences) also figures centrally in many areas of educational policy. For example, standardized achievement tests are the measure of differential school or program effectiveness in most studies intended to inform district- or state-level policy. In contrast, the research that forms the bulk of this chapter is concerned with the discovery and qualitative analysis of the *sources* of the differential performance. If progress can be made in understanding this issue, educators will have a deeper informational base from which to act, both in evaluating schools by aggregated test scores (see Baker, this volume) and in directing instructional policy. Clearly, the contemporaneous pursuit of both of these avenues of research is desirable and necessary. Tests will continue to affect students' lives while researchers are trying to discover the factors affecting the students' performance. If we are to develop clear understandings of what test scores really mean, then we must continue to pursue the question of sources of performance with the same intensity accorded to the question of the uses and aftermaths of testing.

In this chapter I will focus on two potential determinants of performance: language and sociocultural factors. The literature will be reviewed selectively. First, language as a structural entity will be considered, then sociocultural aspects of language use will be discussed, along with a few other sociocultural factors that play a role in test performance. Finally, I will briefly report on some preliminary research findings regarding characteristics of tests and test takers that may contribute to differential performance by minority children.

II. LANGUAGE STRUCTURE AS A FACTOR IN PERFORMANCE ON STANDARDIZED TESTS

Many researchers have noted that, with a few exceptions, every standardized test, whether of intelligence, aptitude, or achievement, relies on language, either spoken or written. This fact raises serious questions about whether there is really any difference in what is being measured by these tests. In spite of differences in content, it may be that for certain test takers language proficiency is the most important contributor to performance (Williams 1983; Padilla 1979; Williams and Mitchell 1977).

In this section, I will briefly discuss the minorities involved in regard to these questions, some policy issues that arise, and some research findings. I will consider ways to address some of the policy issues, and offer a few suggestions for further research and consideration.

Linguistic Minorities

While the scope of this paper does not allow a detailed consideration of any particular minority, it will be useful here to consider the general issues involved. The term *linguistic minorities* includes both the growing U.S. population of nonnative English speakers (NNESs), and other student populations who are native speakers of English, but who also are exposed from birth to some other language in the home. Hispanic background students are the largest such group, including those of Mexican origin (Chicanos or Mexican Americans), Cuban Americans, Puerto Ricans, and Spanish speakers from Central or South America. The United States census of 1980 reported 14.6 million "persons of Spanish origin" living in the U.S. In addition there were 3.5 million Asian and Pacific Islanders, and 1.4 million American Indians, Eskimos, and Aleuts (Olmedo 1981, 1078–79).

Some of these are newcomers and have no proficiency in English. On the other hand, the National Institute of Education and the National Center for Educational Statistics report that "there are over 3.5 million linguistic minority school age children who are 'limited English proficient' (LEP) and need some special language assistance to cope with the school curriculum. Most of these children. . . were born in this country" (Olmedo 1981).

Among the Hispanic background students alone, there is a tremendous amount of dialectal variation in both vocabulary and grammar. Moreover, there is an equally wide range of degrees of bilingualism—differences in relative proficiency in speaking Spanish and English (Matluck and Mace 1973). Both of these constitute obstacles to interpreting test scores and will be discussed further below.

The Southeast Asian population presents another type of linguistic challenge. Many of the recent immigrants are refugees from Laos, Vietnam, and Cambodia. Some speak the majority language of their country, such as

Vietnamese, Lao, or Cambodian, but many are minority groups within their own country of origin. These are members of hill-dwelling or lowland tribes who speak one or more languages that are very different from the majority languages. These include Hmong, Akha, Mien, and others. Some of these languages are poorly understood, even by linguists who specialize in that part of the world. Moreover, most of these minority languages have developed a written form of the language only recently, if at all.

Another minority group that has been the subject of a considerable amount of research in this area includes speakers of what has been called Black English Vernacular (BEV).[4] In order to place the research results in the proper perspective, it is important to briefly review the facts concerning the varieties of English spoken by black Americans. Linguistic divergence of Black English Vernacular from Standard English is a charged issue: reactions to BEV as a linguistic entity have been filtered through social and political attitudes that often served to obscure BEV's real role in educational processes. Early on, many white researchers viewed BEV as an ill-formed variety of English spoken by blacks as a result of verbal and cognitive deprivation. The differences in language structure and use were claimed to reflect an inability to engage in logical thought (Jensen 1969; Bereiter and Engelmann 1966). A strong empirically and theoretically grounded refutation of these ideas by scholars such as Labov (1969) and Baratz and Baratz (1969) set the tone for scientific research into the nature and origins of BEV.

In the late sixties and early seventies, some dialectologists and many prominent black leaders reacted to the study of Black English; they insisted that in fact BEV did not exist at all, and that the features identified with it were simply a dialect, not specific to blacks, originating in the "lowerclass life of the South" (see references in Labov 1982a, 178). These individuals opposed the acknowledgment of features of so-called Black English in educational curricula on the grounds that BEV was an invention of white liberals, and "was a conspiracy to teach imperfect English, and so impose a 'relic of Slavery' on black children" (Labov 1982a, 178).

A federal district-court case provided the opportunity to apply all the linguistic evidence regarding the nature of BEV as a distinct linguistic system to issues of equity in the classroom. A suit brought against the Ann Arbor school system asserted, among other things, that black children were being denied equal access to educational opportunities because of linguistic barriers in the

---

4 The term *Black English Vernacular* is conventionally used in the linguistic literature to refer to the "remarkably uniform grammar that is used by black children throughout the United States and by most black adults in intimate or vernacular settings" (Labov 1982, 174). The term *Black English* includes all varieties of English spoken by blacks in the United States, including Standard Black English, which differs from Standard English only in phonological variables, not in grammatical structure.

classroom and curriculum (Joiner 1979). In that trial, it was argued and accepted that Black English Vernacular is a variety of English with a distinct set of phonological and syntactic rules, incorporating many features of Southern phonology, morphology, and syntax, and showing evidence of derivation from an earlier Creole similar to the present-day Creoles of the Caribbean. One of its most striking differences from Standard English involves a highly developed aspect system, quite different from other dialects of English, which shows a continuing development of its semantic structure. (For a review of the comparative and historical evidence that produced consensus in the linguistic community on the status of Black English as a linguistic entity, see Labov 1982a and the papers in Chambers 1983.)

The work of Labov and his colleagues has shown that the relationship between BEV and Standard English is complex and subtle; because of this complex relationship, and also because much of BEV is like Standard English, it has been difficult for educators to isolate systematic sources of difficulty in language comprehension, both spoken and written.

One such source of difficulty is the negative interactional consequences that tend to result when teachers are not informed about the structural discrepancies between BEV and Standard English. I will not discuss these here; the reader is referred to Labov (1972), and Baratz and Shuy (1969). It is important to understand, however, that their effects in the classroom may have an impact on test performance. For example, when black children are put in remedial reading because of dialect differences, they must often spend large amounts of time on the decoding aspects of reading. This restricts the amount of time spent on the "top-down" aspects of reading, or comprehension-related activities. Moreover, the gradual accrual of negative self-image and the loss of self-esteem stemming from continual frustrating encounters with Standard English in school do not facilitate the task that black children face: becoming bidialectal in their home language and in Standard English.

This brief description of some of the relevant minority populations should give a sense of the linguistic and cultural diversity facing educators, policymakers, and testmakers concerned with the problems of bias and fairness in testing.

Language Proficiency and Performance on Standardized Tests

The most obvious problem presented to nonnative English speakers (NNES) or to those who speak a nonstandard variety of English is familiarity with or knowledge of the words and linguistic structures of Standard English. This obstacle to comprehension presumably lessens as speakers become more proficient in English.

Even after NNESs do master many words and grammatical constructions, it takes them longer to access this knowledge in the second language. MacNamara (1976) has found that second-language learners take longer to recognize words they do know, and hypothesizes that this imposes an extra load on short-term memory, which serves to further lower the level of comprehension. In timed situations such as tests, this is particularly relevant.

Another factor, which may be more difficult to detect, involves the role of expectation in reading. Current models of reading (Just and Carpenter 1980; Stanovich 1980; Spiro, Bruce, and Brewer 1980) are *interactive*. That is, data-driven, bottom-up processes proceed at the same time that higher level top-down processes generate expectations about what will come next in the text. While the data-driven processes are slowed down by the NNES's lack of familiarity with particular words and constructions, the top-down processes are also affected. When a native speaker sees a word in a text, a wide range of semantic associations are triggered. These help the reader to predict what will come next, and thus facilitate interpretation of what does come next. When a reader is not very familiar with a word, the network of semantic associates of the word will be only partially available and text comprehension will be made more difficult. Automatized access to knowledge of syntactic, semantic, and discourse constraints may help readers to anticipate what is coming next in the text, and thus aid in constructing interpretations as the reading progresses. If access to these types of knowledge is not highly automatized, readers will not be able to generate expectations about text characteristics. There is some evidence that nonnative speakers suffer from just such deficits (Cziko 1978).

Finally, some researchers feel that there is evidence that in the early years of schooling, cognitive deficits may result from the gradual loss of the child's first language as English is acquired, if the child has not reached a particular level of linguistic competence in that first language. This "threshold" effect means that a child acquiring English in a mainstream American school that does not provide any supporting instruction in the child's home language is at risk for generally lower performance in the areas tested by various standardized measures.[5]

---

[5] The issue of the possible cognitive benefits and detriments associated with bilingualism is an extremely complex one. In general, bilingualism itself is considered a cognitive and linguistic advantage. However, certain sociopolitical and educational configurations can result in difficulties for the young child who is trying to learn a second language. Lambert (1984) reviews studies showing that majority children in Canada (anglophones) who enter immersion programs in French benefit cognitively and socially from becoming bilingual. For them, bilingualism is additive. On the other hand, other studies he cites show that, for a host of largely sociocultural reasons, when minority children enter an English-only "submersion" program, they show cognitive deficits accompanied by the gradual loss of proficiency in their home language. For them, bilingualism is subtractive. Cummins (1979) hypothesizes that this may be due to an interaction of social and cognitive factors: the social and cultural pressure to give up the home language creates a situation in which the young nonnative English speaker never quite attains the "threshold" level of competence in the home language to attain the cognitive gains shown by monolingual peers.

Thus, language proficiency plays a role at several levels of performance tapped by standardized tests.

Policy Issues

Virtually all reviewers of the literature on standardized testing and minority test takers conclude that language is a major factor in the observed differential performance under discussion. From that point of consensus onward, however, little else is clear. Policy considerations regarding this fact depend on the purposes of testing. Similarly, avenues of research and educational innovation to avoid the problem or to factor out its effects depend on the goals of the test consumer.

Briefly, we can isolate two important concerns. First, if the results of standardized tests are used for funding purposes, either as a source of information on which to make decisions regarding funding of remedial programs or as a basis for deciding which school districts to close down (Education Week 1985), or if they are used for teacher evaluation, then an important goal is to be able to make reasonable decisions concerning the use of test scores of students who do not have complete proficiency in Standard English.[6] Should a district or state include such test scores in their evaluation of schools and programs? For example, a large influx of refugee families into a school district would have clear consequences for the test-based evaluation of that district. If the scores of all students serve as input to district decisions, unmediated by information about each test taker's English proficiency, then the general depression of test scores due to language problems of immigrant children will obscure important information about changes in the performance of native English speakers from year to year. Moreover, a mean score derived from all students will provide no information about the needs of students who specifically require training in English proficiency.

Second, if selection for academic programs and access to remedial programs is to be determined by test scores, then a clear picture of the student's proficiency in English is required to interpret the results of tests in other subject areas. It is in this domain that equity issues come to the fore. As Airasian and Madaus point out (1983, 115), the more likely a policy decision is to harm individual test takers (through labeling or denial of access to resources of any kind), the more assiduously we must seek to verify the link between the test and the curriculum.

With these background issues in mind, let us review some of the findings on language as a factor in standardized testing of minority students.

---

[6] For excellent discussions of some of the general problems inherent in linking standardized test results with various state and federal funding schemes, see the papers by Berke, Burke, and Madaus in Schrader 1979.

Studies of Language Structure as a Factor in Test Performance

The assumption that language plays a significant role in test performance is plausible, and is widely held to be true. However, the literature purporting to show this is sometimes difficult to interpret. Many early studies did not control for socioeconomic differences between populations, and it is difficult (if not impossible) to control for cultural variables. In addition, since many of the published studies of the interaction of language and performance on standardized tests do not examine the actual test items or verbal/written directions, but instead compute various statistical relationships between language variables (for example, language spoken by parents) and test scores, we cannot tell how language difficulty is instantiated in any particular study. We can assume, however, that in all standardized tests administered in written form, any lack of proficiency in Standard English will have diffuse effects throughout the test. Sensitive educators and researchers have been aware of these problems since the beginning of the use of standardized tests. Paschal and Sullivan (1925) and Sanchez (1934) presented cogent arguments regarding the obstacles that confront children taking a test in a language other than their native language. (They also pointed out the problems implicit in attempts to create simple translations of standardized tests into Spanish. We will return to this topic below.)

Types of Studies

Many types of studies show that lack of native proficiency in English affects performance on many standardized tests. One type shows that on nonverbal measures, such as the Draw-a-Man test, black, white, and Hispanic-American children do not differ significantly (Samuda 1975). Another type of study demonstrates that the patterns of performance on *verbal* versus *performance* scales for minorities differ from those of whites, implying that language proficiency is a significant factor for these subjects, whereas it is not for white subjects (Meeker and Meeker 1973; Valencia 1983; Laosa 1984). Many studies simply compare the scores of mainstream and minority groups, controlling to a greater or lesser extent for social and economic variables (Anastasi and Cordova 1953; Padilla 1979). Some studies do factor analyses of language variables, and find that child and parental language proficiencies are one of the strongest predictors of intellectual ability (Valencia, Henderson, and Rankin 1981). Moreover, language status and proficiency is associated with observed differences in predictive validity coefficients of tests at a number of educational levels (Valencia 1983; Valencia and Rankin 1983; Durán, in press). Durán (in press) reviews the findings of a number of large, national surveys which assessed language background of respondents as well as a number of measures of achievement and educational outcomes. These surveys have allowed researchers to use regression techniques in the investigation of the importance of language characteristics in achievement of various kinds. When other variables are controlled for, it is found that language factors are a consistent and powerful predictor of performance on several measures (see especially So and Chan 1984, cited in Durán).

In attempting to determine the importance of language as a factor, some researchers designed experiments in which the test was administered in the language of the minority child. In general, improvement in scores did not result. However, interpretation of such a result is not straightforward. Other factors may play a role in the lack of improvement.

For example, Quay (1971, 1972) demonstrated that black preschoolers, whether or not they are "severely disadvantaged," do not significantly improve in their performance on the Stanford-Binet Intelligence test when it is administered in Black English. She interprets this to mean that these children are already bidialectal in the dimension of oral language comprehension.

Studies of older students often involve translations of tests. A few of these will be described below. In these cases, lack of improvement may be a consequence of a poor translation of the test. Early attempts to translate various psychological and educational tests into Spanish relied on Castilian translators. This form of Spanish may have been even more difficult than English for some children (Padilla 1979; Durán, in press).

Sources of Difficulty in the Test

Perhaps the easiest issue to address is the use of tests that seek to establish whether a child has a perceptual deficit. It is well known that the sounds of a speaker's native language determine which sounds he or she can easily discriminate. Early school testing for auditory problems must be adapted to speakers of different dialects and languages, and it has been in recent years, to some extent (see Samuda 1975). There remain problems with immigrants and refugees who speak languages not previously well studied in the United States, however.

Another problem remains in that other tests in the primary grades frequently require either production or comprehension of Standard English. Green and Griffore (1980) found that linguistic sources contributed to bias in the reading test scores of black, American Indian, and Mexican-American children. For example, one analysis reported that 46 percent of the errors made on Gray's oral reading test were due to dialect differences. Bartel, Grill, and Bryen (1973) review certain studies of Black English and black children's interaction with tests, and conclude that testmakers must become more sensitive to problems arising out of linguistic differences at the phonological level.

Many of the achievement tests used in elementary school require the child to listen to the teacher pronounce a word, and then to find that word in the list of available options. Conflicting pronunciations of a word, based on home language or dialect, may complicate both the recognition of the correct choice, and the grapheme to phoneme decoding process that the child must engage in to eliminate other choices. Ulibarra (1985) suggests that this problem is not sufficiently controlled for in standardized tests.

Much of the earliest research on sources of difficulty for black children centered on reading and the differences between BEV and Standard English that presented obstacles for the BEV speaker and the teacher. These differences present problems in several ways. First, in tests of oral reading, if teachers are not aware of the systematic nature of these differences, they will result in consistent frustration and negative feedback. More importantly, these differences are so complex that teachers may not be able to systematically make the sound translations from the child's output to the Standard English target. Thus they may believe that the child is not succeeding in the task of decoding, when in fact the child has successfully translated the symbols into a sound representation in his or her own dialect.

For example, one of the most salient differences between BEV and Standard English involves the reduction of final consonant clusters. This results in a large number of homonyms for BEV speakers, such as *miss, mist*, and *missed*, all of which are pronounced as *miss*. While this in itself may, at some stages, result in additional complexity in spelling and reading for the BEV speaker, a more serious difficulty results from the fact that much of the derivational and inflectional morphology in English consists of word-final consonants. Thus teachers may hear the child neutralize the sound difference between *miss* and *missed*, and draw incorrect inferences about the child's comprehension.

Labov (1972) shows that the relationships between the child's *pronunciation* of grammatical morphemes like the past tense suffix, his or her *perception* of the sounds, and his or her *comprehension* of those markers are by no means straightforward. He shows by a converging set of tests that the *-ed* suffix does not function as a marker of the past tense for a number of young black BEV speakers, although the same speakers do use the irregular past tense forms (such as *kept* and *told*). They usually do not pronounce the suffix either. On the other hand, some of his subjects do recognize the *-ed* suffix as a past tense marker, although they do not pronounce it. In this case the student must have learned a relationship between a purely orthographic symbol and a grammatical category.

This example demonstrates the complexity of the mapping between phonemes, graphemes, and grammatical categories. The relevance of this in the classroom, and in the acquisition of reading, is obvious. By extension, we can see that the task of taking a standardized test at any point past the first grade (that is, a test presented in written form) may have a number of levels of complexity for the BEV speaker engaged in the acquisition of Standard English.

A related problem concerns ungrammatical items used as distractors. For example, the following question contains a distractor which is semantically acceptable, given the content of the passage, but which can only be ruled out by sensitivity to the grammatical marginality that results from its use in the stem (the question containing the blank to be filled in):

> If a bronco buster wants to win a rodeo contest, he must observe the contest rules. One of these rules is that the rider must keep one hand in the air. A rider who does not do this is disqualified.

> In a rodeo contest, a bronco buster must keep one hand _____ (under, still, free, hold)

One might argue that sensitivity to such facts is a good measure of English proficiency. However, performance in such contexts must be viewed as part of a larger process of language acquisition. The child who is in the process of acquiring English hears a number of new expressions and words every day. Language learners cannot assume that any slightly unfamiliar expression is ungrammatical; it may be that they simply have not heard that particular usage. This openness to new forms and usages reflects a desirable flexibility in the language learner. Use of grammaticality judgments as cues to the correct answer during the period when the child is acquiring the language seems at best uninformative, and at worst, unfair. For further discussion of the example above, as well as others, see Fillmore and Kay (1983).

Finally, one structural aspect of tests may be unfairly distracting to students with low English proficiency. Evidence suggests that the multiple-choice test format fosters a strategy of simply choosing the answer that matches some aspect of the passage (at least in the case of linguistic minorities who may have difficulty with comprehension). A study by Freedle and Fellbaum (1987) shows that difficulty of listening comprehension items on TOEFL (Test of English as a Foreign Language) exams can be predicted by the amount of lexical repetition between stems and response options. If the correct response contains a repetition of one of the lexical items in the stem, the test item is relatively easier. If it contains distractors with lexical repetitions of stem elements, it is more difficult. Ammon (in press) has also found that a matching strategy was frequently relied on by Chinese- and Spanish-speaking children taking written tests of reading comprehension.

Test Translation: A Remedy?

As stated previously, standardized tests serve a number of different purposes. Each of these purposes, from evaluation of districts to evaluation of individuals, suffers when test results are influenced by undetected linguistic factors in the tested population. One obvious way to avoid such a confound is to translate the standardized test into the language of the minority. There are problems with this strategy, each problem being more or less salient, depending on the type of test being administered, the goals of testing, and the age and the ethnic background of the test taker.

Construct Validity

It is useful to cite the experiences of the measurement specialists who participated in the translation of tests in various developing nations, used for selection of employees or for allocation of limited places in institutions of higher education. Many of these researchers reported that real problems with construct validity arose upon translation, and a conference on the topic of cross-cultural uses of standardized tests concluded that testmakers should be free to make up their own tests of aptitude, since so much construct indeterminacy resulted from translation (Cronbach and Drenth 1972).

We might expect that translation of common words would not present much of a problem, particularly in languages that are fairly closely related, such as English, Spanish, and French. Yet even here the construct validity of the test is subtly changed. Words with the same origin and spelling may vary widely in frequency in the source and target languages: for example, the word *moral* is in the first thousand most frequent words in Spanish, the second thousand in French, and the third thousand in English (Cortada de Kohan 1972, 122).

Valencia and Rankin (1985) present a good example of the subtlety of language/task interactions that can occur, seriously affecting equatability. In this case, the McCarthy Scales of Childrens' Abilities (MSCA) were carefully translated into Spanish appropriate for Mexican-American children. The test-taking sample consisted of 304 Mexican-American children of "very low" socioeconomic status. The children took the MSCA in English or Spanish depending on their dominant language as determined by five factors. Of the 157 MSCA items, 17 were found to be biased against the Spanish test group. (Here Thorndike's definition of bias was used; that is, the items presented more difficulty for one group, with general abilities held constant and no clear theoretical reason why the two groups should perform differently.) Surprisingly, the items that presented unexplained difficulty for the Spanish-dominant children were simple associative memory tasks, serial order short-term memory of digits.

Upon examination of the linguistic aspects of the items, it was found that when the digits were translated into Spanish, the task became substantially more difficult. Even though the children spoke Spanish natively, the structural features of Spanish imposed an additional load on their short-term memory. When the single-digit numbers were translated into Spanish, they resulted in nearly twice as many syllables. Thus for the same number of digits, the short-term memories of the children had to contain twice as many units of sound.

Not only were the words longer, but they sounded more similar to each other than the English number words did because Spanish has fewer vowels and consonants than English. Consequently, each phoneme occurs more frequently in the sample than each English phoneme does. Both of these effects, acoustic similarity and length of stimulus item, have been shown to significantly affect the results of memory tasks. This careful study shows the subtle ways that even a very good translation can change the nature of the task.

When and How Should Translated Tests Be Used?

If we assume that valid translations can be constructed for particular tests, other questions arise. These concern the appropriate use of the translated tests: for example, who should be given a translated test? How can we decide when a student has enough English proficiency to be included in the population of native English speakers? During the time when the student has not reached full proficiency in English, should all academic subjects be tested in the student's first language, or only some?

It is impossible to separate the issue of differential performance by linguistic minorities on standardized tests (particularly achievement tests), and the policy decisions regarding this differential performance, from the issues of teaching, curriculum concerns, and questions regarding the evaluation of language proficiency itself. Those who wish to make policy decisions about program, district, or teacher evaluations based on test scores will have to address questions such as the following ones.

If it is decided that the scores of NNES students on standardized tests should not be included in quantitative evaluations by district- and state-level investigators, then how are we to decide how to delimit the set of NNES students? Should we exclude from district means only students who are not at all proficient in English? Should all students whose home language is not English be excluded independently of how well they currently speak English?

If it is decided that the scores of NNES students *should* be included in such evaluations, similar questions arise. A sensible *interpretation* of such scores must be informed by knowledge about the general level of English proficiency in the tested population. For example, a plan in which some constant factor is added to the test scores of nonnative speakers would also be faced with the problem of how to determine language proficiency, in order to decide who should receive the normalizing factor, and what the size of the factor should be. Clearly, many children who speak languages other than English in the home do quite well in English, while others are essentially monolingual in their home language.

When test scores are used for selection or remediation purposes the same obstacle is encountered. To determine what a score on an achievement test given in English to a NNES truly means, a test-score evaluator should have independent evidence of the tested student's English proficiency level.

Unfortunately, the key tools for all of these decisions—reliable, objective measures of language proficiency—are largely unavailable. Durán (in press) discusses two sources of problems in the area of language proficiency testing. One is inconsistencies in existing measures of language proficiency now being used to classify children. Ulibarri, Spencer, and Rivas (1981) compared the classifications derived from three language proficiency tests used in California to determine whether children were non-English speaking, limited English proficient, or fluent English speakers. They found significant discrepancies in the results.

The other problem Durán discusses is perhaps more serious. It involves the lack of a theoretical consensus about what language proficiency is, and the failure of current instruments to indicate the entire range of competencies associated with being a proficient speaker of a language. The problem here can be broken down in several ways. First, a child may be quite competent in using English in face-to-face interaction and have virtually no success in reading and using written English. Cummins (1982) points out that use of English in conversational settings is usually supported by a number of cues, both physical and social. Because of this contextual support, relatively fewer demands are made of the child cognitively and in terms of language proficiency. On the other hand, use of English in the school setting is "context reduced"; the supporting cues and information are largely absent, and far more depends on knowledge of the language alone. Thus, a teacher's estimation of a child's English proficiency, based on classroom observation of social interaction, will frequently overpredict the child's performance on written measures. Second, besides knowledge of words and grammar, language proficiency includes knowledge of discourse conventions and strategic uses of language. The latter two are not tested for in most current measures of language proficiency.

Finally, many tests of language proficiency lack norming studies of performance, and "internal consistency and test retest reliability and validity research is sparse or non-existent for most tests" (Durán, in press, 12).

Thus, any school district or policymaker wishing to determine inclusion of nonnative English speakers in testing populations on the basis of their objectively determined proficiency in English would encounter problems in finding objective measures, for all of the above reasons.

Coordinating testing and teaching of English. Let us imagine that this problem did not exist. If we had perfectly translated standardized tests for all populations, and if we had reliable objective measures of English proficiency, yet another problem arises. This concerns the range of local policies regarding the best way to teach students who are not native speakers of English. The choice of instructional technique for students in the process of acquiring English will determine how translated tests and English language tests may most informatively be used.

Unfortunately, no consensus exists on the most effective way to maximize English proficiency while at the same time making sure that students keep pace with academic subjects. The following is a representative opinion on the state of the field of teaching bilingual learners.[7]

> It is clear that there is no shortage of explanatory variables to account for the different outcomes of immersion and submersion programs. However, what is lacking is a coherent framework within which the relative importance of different variables and the possible interactions between them can be conceptualized. While sociocultural variables are important, we do not know what are the links in the causal chain through which their effects are translated into academic outcomes. To take the obvious example, despite ten years of widespread bilingual education, there is no consensus as to the relative merits of ESL-only, transitional bilingual or maintenance bilingual programs in promoting academic and cognitive skills. There are, in fact, very few interpretable data which are directly related to the central issue. (Cummins 1979, 225)

The questions concerning the testing of bilingual learners cannot be any less complex. With this degree of disagreement within the field of bilingual pedagogy (see also Wong-Fillmore and Valadez 1986), not to mention within the legislature and general population, it is difficult to see how a standard approach can develop without a great deal more in the way of study and discussion.

It is clear to at least some bilingual researchers and educators that optimal development of linguistic minorities' cognitive and academic potential requires the acquisition of literacy both in the child's first language (L1) and the child's second language (L2) (Cummins 1979; Wong-Fillmore 1983). Comparative studies of bilinguals and monolinguals have found a clear positive relationship between bilingual proficiency and intellectual functioning. Scores on measures of cognitive functioning of monolinguals

---

7 "Immersion" and "submersion" programs are conducted in one language only. In the former case, speakers of the majority language are immersed in a minority language teaching situation. Most such studies have been conducted in Canada (Lambert 1984). In the latter case, linguistic minority students are "submerged" in the language of the majority. "ESL" (English as a Second Language) programs are those which teach English to nonnative speakers as an extra subject: these students attend regular classes in English, and spend part of each day in classes that focus on the study of English per se. "Bilingual" programs are those which provide instruction both in the student's home language, and in English (although programs differ widely in the way the first and second languages are used and in the amount of time spent using each.) These programs may have as their aim aiding the student in making the transition to English, or maintaining the home language of the student as a linguistic and cultural resource.

acquiring a second language increase as their bilingual proficiency increases. A number of studies have shown that there is a positive relationship between bilingualism and increased verbal skills. (For these and other references, see Cummins 1979; Wong-Fillmore and Valadez 1986; and Durán 1986.) If these researchers are right, then it is clearly desirable to have the means to monitor these students' progress while they acquire literacy skills in their first language.

However, programs that feature instruction in both languages take longer to pay off. The existing evidence shows that, contrary to popular opinion, it can take a number of years (up to six or seven) for a child to become truly proficient in English (Wong-Fillmore 1983; Cummins 1982). The apparent proficiency of some children after a year or two is often limited to face-to-face situations in which social and pragmatic context offer a great deal of support (Cummins 1982). Unless policymakers, legislators, and the public appreciate this fact, the issue of testing and language minority students may be seen as peripheral, as a symptom of a system which caters to minorities, instead of as a serious problem in the overall goals of accurate needs diagnosis and evaluation of educational progress.

These larger issues aside, the decision about what language to test in is locally complicated in other ways. Opinion differs over the preferability of bilingual education or ESL. The former would seem to require at least some testing in the first language of the student, whereas the latter may not. Even within programs that teach (at least part of the time) in the native language of the minority students, opinions differ as to the optimal way to teach different subjects. Some subject areas seem to lend themselves to use of English, for others the most sensible approach seems to be to start off with the native language of the NNESs. Thus teachers and districts may face complicated decisions regarding the congruence of the language used for different subjects in the classroom with the language used in achievement tests of the same subjects.

Wong-Fillmore and Valadez (1986) present an overview of findings concerning the efficacy of using either the child's first or second language in various subject areas. It seems clear that students who first learn to read in their stronger language have an advantage in learning to read in their second language over students who first learn to read in their second language. Mathematics is more difficult to evaluate. Although actual mathematical operations can be done with a fairly small number of vocabulary items, the actual content of the mathematics curriculum contains a great deal of language—word problems present obstacles for many students, and they are doubly difficult when encountered in a language the student is currently acquiring. Research in the U.S. seems to indicate that students who are taught mathematics at least partially in their native language do better than students who are taught wholly in English. However, the students who receive mathematics training in their first language do more poorly when tested in

English (Wong-Fillmore and Valadez 1986, 662). Mestre, Gerace, and Lochhead (1980, unpublished paper, cited in Durán, 1985) found that in translating simple verbal problems into equations, Hispanic engineering students who were balanced bilinguals could convert words into equations equally well in either language. However, they did not perform as well as English monolinguals. Moreover, their success in this task was significantly predicted by their reading comprehension facility in the relevant language. The same was true for English monolinguals, but to a lower degree.

Wong-Fillmore and Valadez review findings that suggest students perform significantly better in science and social studies when these are taught in their native language. They reason that "while science and social studies are subjects that lend themselves to being taught through activities and demonstrations, they involve many abstract ideas and concepts that would be difficult to deal with in the weaker language. The terminological precision that is required for talking about scientific concepts may be a particular problem." (1986, 662). However, Cazden (1979) argues that science is best taught to low English-proficiency students directly in the second language. Since students develop language proficiency most effectively in real communicative contexts, and since science education involves group activities and discussions and interaction with concrete objects, she sees it as an ideal place for developing proficiency in the second language.

For any state or federal program of evaluative testing to succeed, these and other complex issues must be addressed. Achievement testing for purposes of direct evaluation of students, in order to determine appropriate placement in educational programs, will necessarily be varied according to the complex circumstances of the locality.

Language Attitudes

When considering the translation of tests as a policy option, we must keep in mind the attitudes of the test users and the public toward the languages of translation.

In the case of black children, there is very little likelihood that anyone would consider translating a standardized test into BEV. With the exception of the "culture-specific movement" (see Wright and Isenstein 1975), there have been no major attempts to render standardized tests in BEV. The problems that arose with the use of BEV materials in early reading instruction (principally parental and community opposition) would certainly arise again (for a review of these, see Wolfram and Fasold 1979).

In general, negative attitudes in white mainstream populations toward the maintenance of other languages and cultures (for example, the state-level English-only ballot initiatives) would surely extend to the creation of tests in BEV; negative attitudes probably extend in some communities to development of tests in languages other than English as well.

Nevertheless, some large school districts are of necessity beginning to move into test development in languages other than English in order to serve their large nonnative English speaking populations. For example, the Los Angeles Unified School District serves a student population of six hundred thousand. Eighty-two languages are spoken in the district. Of those students who are native speakers of foreign languages, about 83 percent are speakers of Spanish, Korean, Cantonese, Vietnamese, and Armenian. Recently, the criteria for Chapter I funding changed, and to qualify for Chapter I funds, school districts are required to demonstrate the relative ranking of students by use of standardized tests. Los Angeles Unified School District is now poised to begin developing translations of standardized tests into the five languages mentioned above.[8] It remains to be seen how they will deal with the problems of validity discussed in this section.

Practical Obstacles

An obvious practical difficulty for translation is presented by the tremendous linguistic diversity discussed above. The states with the greatest linguistic diversity will be forced to face this problem eventually. The fiscal outlay required for translating and renorming tests would likely be quite significant. Only when faced with loss of Chapter I funds did Los Angeles Unified School District begin to consider translated tests on such a large scale.

Even when we consider a linguistically homogeneous population, the obstacles to translation of tests are not easy to overcome. Although a number of tests have been translated into Spanish (see compendium of tests for minority adolescents and adults in Samuda 1975), the difficulties described above concerning construct validity and assessment of proficiency of test takers still pertain. This situation has led some test consumers to call for a "consumers' reports" of standardized tests. At present the variety of instruments available is nowhere presented in standard form; neither are there cautionary or advisory analyses regarding their best use or limitations.

One might expect that a school district with a single linguistic minority might present the most hospitable setting for the introduction of translated tests. For example, the Fresno Unified School District in Northern California has the largest population of Hmong speakers in the state. The influx largely took place in the late seventies and early eighties. Here, however, the language itself presents a problem to translation. Hmong was not a written language until several decades ago. Many Hmong refugees were not literate in Hmong. Thus, even if it were possible to avoid problems of validity, translation of standardized tests into written Hmong would not serve the entire Hmong

---

[8] Personal communication, Floraleen Stevens, Los Angeles Unified School District Research and Evaluation Department.

population anyway. Currently, students in the Fresno Unified School District are administered CAP tests only when they have received at least one semester of instruction in an English reading program within the school district. However, even students who have passed this mark and are being tested in English are tested at a lower grade level than their classmates.[9]

Suggestions

The range of factors discussed above clearly rules out any hope for easy answers. Particularly difficult is determining a sensible approach to the use of test results of NNESs with respect to the wide range of purposes that testing serves. Policymakers concerned about accountability must collaborate closely with school administrators concerned about effective teaching of linguistic minorities. Both must draw on continuing research about effective instructional programs for bilingual learners. Collecting a comprehensive set of informed decisions to serve as a uniform policy base will not be easy.

In light of this task, it may seem trivial to suggest changes in tests to minimize the effects of linguistic difficulties for those who are not native speakers of Standard English. However, the frequently made observation that certain design characteristics of standardized tests present obvious difficulties does bear repeating.

The studies reported here suggest that in multiple-choice tests the use of distractors requiring a native speaker's confidence about judgments of grammaticality are of dubious value in the case of linguistic minorities. The same may be said of answer choices which assume a native speaker's knowledge of pronunciation (and possibly also those which contain lexical items that match a lexical item in the passage or stem, as discussed above).

This is not to say that such items do not have a use: they clearly indicate something, however indirectly, about proficiency in Standard English. However, they should be clearly marked as such and test users should be fully informed about their meaning. The current situation in which such items are often sprinkled randomly throughout a test does not contribute to the teacher's information about students' proficiency in English in any way. If testmakers wish to isolate the effects of language proficiency as much as possible, they must think carefully about the use of items such as those described above.

---

[9] Personal communication, Fresno Unified School District Office of Planning and Evaluation.

III. SOCIAL AND CULTURAL FACTORS IN TEST PERFORMANCE

Since the earliest uses of standardized tests, some educators and researchers have been aware that the discrepancies in background between the norming population (middle-class white children) and the population being tested (particularly black and Hispanic background children) called the validity of the tests into question. Throughout the intervening years, various individuals have tried to factor out the most significant environmental and background variables. First, I will review some approaches that treat social and cultural factors as variables to be investigated and, to a limited extent, manipulated in experimental contexts. I will then review some research that explicitly tries to link sociocultural factors and the cognitive demands of particular test-like problems, a theoretical move that may allow us to look more closely at the sources of differential performance among minorities. Finally, I will briefly review studies that take an ethnographic approach to the investigation of cultural differences in language and work socialization, and will show how these can illuminate our understanding of test performance.

Experimental and Measurement Approaches

Ogbu (1977) sees test scores as simply another sort of educational failure. He explicitly rejects the view that interactional mismatches in classrooms based on different cultural patterns of communication or linguistic/sociolinguistic incompatibilities between test takers and tests play a major role in school failure. Instead, macrolevel social factors determine individuals' chances for success or failure. For him, other factors—community attitudes toward schooling, job ceilings for certain minorities, and so forth—are the important determinants of success or failure. They are not subject to intervention at the level of the individual, but rather must be addressed at the level of the community or the larger society.

On the other hand, many researchers, particularly measurement specialists, have tried to determine experimentally the importance of different social and cultural factors in determining school success. It has been apparent from the earliest days of testing that more than language was involved. As mentioned earlier, socioeconomic status variables have been a robust predictor of success of most criterion measures. Researchers and measurement specialists have attempted to break down the monolithic variable "environment" in ways that will reveal the source of success and failure of measurement instruments.

In some of these attempts, the investigator treats social and cultural factors as sources of performance that can be treated and manipulated; in others, social and cultural variables are large-scale objects of study, which can inform our interpretation of test scores, but are not generally subject to manipulation.

An example of the first type is research focusing on cultural differences in attitudes toward time. These differences have long been hypothesized to be important determinants of test performance. Test speededness is seen as directly in conflict with the cultural norms of some groups. In 1935 Klineberg observed that "the attitude toward speed varies greatly in different cultures and not all people will work on the tests with equal interest in getting them done in the shortest time possible. Peterson and his associates (1925) have noted this relative indifference to speed among Negroes and the writer found the injunction to 'do this as quickly as you can' seemed to make no impression whatsoever on the American Indian children on the Yakima reservation in the state of Washington" (1935, 159).

An obvious experimental treatment suggests itself: allow test takers more time. The results of such experiments are variable. Some, like Knapp (1960), found that Mexican Americans gained significantly more than Anglos when the Cattell Culture Free Intelligence Test was administered without time limits (Padilla 1979, 228). Others have found that simply supplying extra time does not help. Wild, Durso, and Rubin (1979) found no differential score gains by sex, membership in minority or majority group, or years out of school, in administering the verbal and quantitative sections of the GRE. They conclude that extension of testing time does not reduce intergroup differences.

Another appealingly straightforward hypothesis has been suggested: the ethnic and language background of the experimenter or test giver should be the same as the test taker. When this is extensively investigated, results are equivocal. Quay (1971, 1972) found no difference in performance of black preschoolers on the Stanford-Binet whether the test was administered by a black or white examiner, in BEV or Standard English. She also found no effect associated with type of motivator, candy or verbal praise. Pryzwansky et al. (1974) also found that examiner race did not affect the performance of urban and rural second-grade girls. However, Samuda (1975) reports a number of studies where an effect was observed. Very young black children do more poorly on tests of oral-language behavior when the examiner is white, probably because of learned social-interactional constraints (for a discussion of the "non-verbal" behavior of young black children in hostile settings, and its effects on interpretation of such tests, see also Labov 1969).

Katz, Roberts, and Robinson (1965) present more complex results. In a test with a white examiner, black male college students performed better when the task was presented to them as a hand-eye coordination task, and more poorly when the task was presented as an intelligence test. The complexity of the social relationships and self-concepts involved are shown in a study by Katz et al. (1964), who demonstrated that black male junior high and high school students showed no difference in hostility to either black or white examiners when the test was presented as a research instrument, but showed hostility when the *black* examiner presented the test as a measure of intellectual ability.

They showed significantly less hostility toward a *white* examiner in the same situation.

It seems safe to assume that in both cases (studies of time and studies of race of examiner) these confusing results stand for a complex package of relationships: the perceived nature of the outcome, the test takers' beliefs about their own abilities, past experiences with superordinate whites judging them, personality variables, and so forth. Although the effects of time and of examiner race can be demonstrated in some settings, their practical implications are not clear.

A more unified approach was taken by researchers who sought to explain observed group differences in scores by way of factor analyses of sociocultural variables. Since many of these researchers believed that standardized tests "predict one and only one thing—the probability of a child's success in operating within an undeniably Euro-American institution: the American school system" (Gay and Abrahams 1973, 330), they set out to measure the distance of the minority child from that Euro-American norm. Acculturation, the "complex processes that take place when diverse cultural groups come into contact with one another. . . involves the acquisition of language, values, customs, and cognitive styles of the majority culture—all factors that may substantially affect performance on tests that have been standardized according to majority norms" (Olmedo 1981, 1082). Performance on standardized tests can then derivatively be seen as a measure of acculturation.

Using a model of cultural diffusion, Sanday (1972) suggested that a minority group's psychological, social, and geographical distances from the mainstream culture are the main determinants of performance on IQ tests, and may be measurable. Cultural isolation from the mainstream results in lack of exposure to the cultural elements related to the expression of mental ability (Cohen 1969), but exactly what these cultural elements consist of was not addressed.

Mercer (1973, 1977) developed scales of sociocultural variables in an attempt to factor acculturation effects into educational testing. She has shown that group differences in IQ among Anglo, black, and Chicano children can be explained in terms of variables such as urban acculturation, socioeconomic status, family structure, and family size. Using these scales, results of standardized tests may be used with the child being ranked within his/her own sociocultural group. Padilla (1979), Samuda (1975), and Hilliard (1979) have discussed this approach to test interpretation.

All of these results flow logically from a larger picture in which the acculturated minority child with educated parents has gained access not just to material resources (good nutrition, books, and so forth) but to expectations regarding possible success in the middle-class milieu.

Yet some researchers were dissatisfied with the lack of explication of the predictive value of large sociocultural variables. Within the measurement literature we can find a few studies that attempt to describe environmental variables in sufficient detail to generate qualitative hypotheses about *how* these variables generate success or failure on tests. Wolf (1964), frustrated with the partial information provided by standard measures of social status and economic resources, attempted to develop a psychometric approach to measurement of the environment that would indicate exactly what aspects of the environment fostered intellectual growth and academic achievement. Using interviewing techniques, he tried to gauge the kinds of activities found in the environment of children. Among the thirteen variables found to be most determinative of 'general intelligence' were (a) measures of the child's and parents' expectations for the child's future academic achievement, and (b) measures of the "Press for Language Development," including emphasis on use of language in a variety of situations, opportunities provided for enlarging vocabulary, and quality of language models available. These results were then correlated with achievement on tests of intelligence and academic achievement. Wolf found that they accounted for far more of the variance in measured intelligence than measures of social status did. He was able to raise the correlation coefficient to +0.87, close to the limit of reliability of such measures.

Laosa's (1982, 1984) detailed studies of performance by Mexican-American children on a variety of measures took a similar tack, but involved closer observation. He identified actual strategies of interaction that varied as a function of level of maternal education. He presents these as variables that are powerful predictors of performance, but does not give detailed explications of why these should be effective. Among the most powerful predictors of performance on intelligence tests *before three years of age* are the mothers' use of either (a) a verbal querying behavior associated with instructing the child in various tasks or (b) a nonverbal modeling strategy in such settings (physically mediated demonstrations of the task and physical guiding of the child through the task).

In order to begin to understand *why* these variables of behavior (which correlate highly with maternal level of education) predict performance on standardized tests, it will be useful to discuss work from two different traditions—anthropology and psychology—which has come into prominence in the last two to three decades.

Cross-cultural Research on Cognition

Two sources of research now enter our discussion of test performance. One is again the cross-cultural work on test adaptation. The other is work by cognitive anthropologists and psychologists seeking to extend our theoretical understanding of cognition through comparative work in other cultures.

Work of the first kind is useful for its focus on the untranslatable and pervasive cultural content of test items. The content of tests, whether to measure achievement or aptitude, may be differentially familiar to various minority populations.

Item Content

The most accessible examples of cross-cultural mismatch in tests involve the actual content of items. Irvine and Sanders (1972, 434) provide the example of test-sophisticated Nigerian children responding to an item on a reading test that was expected to be easy for them. They overwhelmingly avoided choosing a (correct) response containing the word *pig*. These children were all Moslem, and Irvine and Sanders suggest that an affective, ideological response determined their choice.

Cortada de Kohan gives an example from research in Argentina: "Some years ago, using the 1937 Stanford-Binet, we found that to the statement: 'The judge said to the prisoner, "You are to be hanged, and I hope it will be a warning to you" ' (Verbal Absurdities, XI) many children answered: 'Oh! This is silly!' But when we inquired why they found it 'foolish' or 'silly' they said proudly: 'Of course it is foolish: no judge could give anybody the death punishment in Argentina, this would be against the law' " (Cortada de Kohan 1972, 124).

This is not to imply that sensitive measurement specialists did not develop a large picture of the effects of culture and society on skills and abilities. In a polite reproach of fellow measurement specialists, Irvine and Sanders reason that "Whereas mankind's ability to adapt to almost every climate leaves little doubt that he will learn what he has to learn in order to survive, it is also a fact that he will sharpen specific skills in order to succeed better than his peers, within a socially sanctioned set of criteria for success. Society will value and devalue skills as they satisfy individual and group needs, which may be dictated by cultural, as well as biological, propensities" (1972, 437). That is, a broader theory about the sources of motivation and skills is needed to understand performance of non-Western peoples on Western testing instruments. While they wistfully acknowledge that the task of constructing a "theory of intellect that embraces affective and cognitive constructs in an interactive model is a technical task of some size" (p. 439), nevertheless, they do propose a psychometric technique for establishing the construct validity of a test in different populations. They suggest that the calculation of item difficulties within each group, and then a comparison of the rankings across groups, may provide a basis for reasonable doubt about the construct validity of the test in question.

This approach, the search for differential difficulty on an item-by-item basis, developed also in work on bias in testing in the United States. There are two branches to this approach. One focuses on quantitative methods of detecting item bias, the other features qualitative analysis.

Veale and Foreman (1983) suggest an interesting quantitative approach to isolating culturally biased items, although their method does not provide insight into the sources of bias. It does not require an unbiased external criterion, or a culturally valid test. It is based on the idea that different populations will be differentially attracted to (or repelled by) members of the set of distractors in a test item. It has the advantage that a particular distractor may be changed and the item retested, thus saving the item. Although Veale and Foreman do not suggest any methods of post hoc analysis of the biased distractors, their technique would probably be useful in gathering instances of differential patterns to build such methods. Other quantitative methods of determining item bias are reviewed in Berk (1982).

One of the first responses to the controversy over testing of ethnic and linguistic minorities was the establishment of minority panels to judge the content and language of test items (Shepard 1981; Tittle 1982; Scheuneman 1982). It was thought that adult members of minority panels could look at items before they were included in standardized tests and help obviate the sources of differential performance by detecting aspects of content or language that would be difficult for minority children. Unfortunately, these methods have by and large not worked (Sandoval and Miille, 1980). Moreover, their failure has been construed by those who support a heritability theory of test results as proof that there is no substance to the claim of cultural bias.

This has led to the current situation, in which sophisticated statistical methods of detecting item bias are followed by post hoc review by judgment panels containing members of the relevant minority groups. Frequently, there is a large 'dross rate' (Shepard 1982) of items that elicit significantly worse performance by minorities, but which are not visibly objectionable on any sociocultural or linguistic parameter.

By nature, post hoc analyses of item bias are sporadic and piecemeal, arising out of encounters with test items that show statistical bias, one by one. The few examples given above suggest that it might be quite difficult to develop a general qualitative theory about types of cultural interference in the content matter of test items. Nevertheless, it is clearly desirable that resources be brought to bear on this problem.

In the next section, I will review some literature suggesting that another locus of cross-cultural mismatch inheres in tests. This literature considers the type of cognitive task implicit in different types of items.

Culturally Specific Construals of Cognitive Tasks

The perspective we will consider here is represented well in the following statement, frequently encountered in the literature on cross-cultural differences in cognition:

Cultural differences reside more in differences in situations to which different cultural groups apply their skills than in differences in the skills possessed by the groups in questions . . . . The problem is to identify the range of capacities readily manifested in different groups and then to inquire whether the range is adequate to individual's needs in the various cultural settings. From this point of view, cultural *deprivation* represents a special case of cultural *difference* that arises when an individual is faced with demands to perform in a manner inconsistent with his past (cultural) experiences. In the present social context in the United States, the great power of the middle class has rendered differences into deficits because middle class behavior is the yardstick of success (Cole and Bruner 1971, 874).

In studies of literacy and reasoning in cultures remote from their own, Cole, Bruner, Scribner, and their colleagues have encountered responses to cognitive tasks on different types of tests and verbal activities that many researchers had believed were independent of culture. In doing this research they have uncovered dimensions of task complexity that are clearly culture-bound, in which success is determined by previous exposure to isomorphic tasks.

D'Andrade (1973) showed that even a test whose content requires no cultural knowledge, such as the Kohs Block Test, implicitly requires cultural knowledge of the activity itself, via precursory experiences of various kinds. Hausa children performed particularly poorly in this test, administered as part of the Wechsler IQ battery. They were presented with a graphic depiction of block patterns, which they were to reproduce with actual blocks. They were largely unable to match the patterns of dark and light, and the direction of diagonals. After extensive investigation, D'Andrade concluded that "it seems most probable that it is not a deficit in intelligence which makes for poor performance on the Kohs Block Test, but instead a lack of experience in or special methods by which reality can be symbolized" (p. 119). According to D'Andrade, two-dimensional graphic representations of designs are rare in this part of West Africa. The symbolic relation between the drawing of the blocks and the design the children were supposed to copy with an actual set of blocks was uninterpretable to them. When presented with a set of blocks to copy instead of a picture, their discrimination problems disappeared after brief training sessions.

In a number of cross-cultural studies designed to investigate the effects of cultural influences on reasoning and literacy (reported in Cole et al. 1971; Scribner 1977; Cole and Scribner 1974), syllogisms were presented to members of the Kpelle and Vai tribes in Liberia, West Africa. To a large extent, the individuals who had not been to school evinced modes of response to the problems that may be said to display an *empiric bias*: If they answered the problem, they based their conclusion on their own experiences, and did not limit themselves to the material in the problem. Those who had had three or more years of schooling displayed *theoretical* approaches to the problem: They reasoned based on the information presented in the problem.

Some examples will demonstrate the two types of responses:

(1) All women who live in Monrovia are married. Kemu is not married. Does she live in Monrovia?

Yes. Monrovia is not for any one kind of person, so Kemu came to live there. (denial of first premise)

(2) All schools in Vai land are in a town. I know a school in Vai land. Is it in a town?

Yes. All schools are in a town. A school *should* be for the *fact human beings are attending it so it can't be built in the bush.* (corroboration by common sense)

(3) All people who own houses pay a house tax. Boima does not pay a house tax. Does Boima own a house?

If you say Boima does not pay a house tax, he cannot own a house. (Scribner 1977, 489, 91–92)

The first two examples are cases of empiric bias. Notice that the answer to (1) is wrong, but the answer to (2) is right, even though the "logical" reasoning usually associated with syllogisms was not in evidence. The third example is a case of theoretical justification.

The importance of this work to the current topic is that it enables us to see that "people learn cultural readings of task types" (Hawkins et al. 1984, 585). The reasoning strategies associated with a task are not always obvious or given. They are products of the participant's interpretation of the task, an interpretation which itself is bound by the participant's previous experience. These notions will be returned to below.

Ethnographic Research: Sociocultural Determinants of School Success

Complementary to these somewhat experimental approaches to cross-cultural differences in reasoning are the ethnographic accounts of socialization practices described below. Ethnography is a method of research central to the traditional practice of anthropology. Recently it has become a useful research method in education. This research strategy is characterized by long-term observation and participation in the settings being described. The ethnographer is immersed in everyday life, as opposed to experimental settings (which often introduce tasks and objects not found in the everyday environment of the subjects). The ethnographer's goal is to describe the ways people in a particular social unit live and work. (For two historically grounded discussions of the nature of ethnography, see Hymes 1982 and Heath 1982.)

In the last several decades, a number of researchers have compiled ethnographic accounts of the contexts of learning, working, playing, and going to school of several minorities in the United States. In the following descriptions of these works, I will focus on only a small portion of the ethnographic detail. First, I will discuss one aspect of interaction, ethnographically observed, that has consequences for a child's motivation in taking a test. This is the dimension of collaboration versus competition. Second, I will discuss the importance of certain aspects of language use between parent and child that emerge in ethnographic studies. I will return to some of the issues presented in the section on the cross-cultural study of cognition, and tie these in with the findings on language socialization.

Sociocultural Bases of Motivation: Affiliation and Competition

Consider the child's experience of standardized tests as literacy events. The taking of a test is an isolated and isolating venture. It is not a collaborative activity, it is solitary and competitive. A child whose sociocultural background has fostered cooperative activity, in which individual achievement motivation is tied to group outcomes, will be at a loss when presented with a long series of decontextualized items in a competitive, individual, solitary situation. And yet, as the child continues on in school, more and more situations will be individualized and competitive.

We can briefly consider the sociocultural precursors that, when present, motivate children to perform on standardized tests as isolated, individualistic, competitive tasks. The following review, like those preceding it, is necessarily sketchy. It is intended to introduce the conceptual issues involved, and to suggest how a test score may be a partial product of interactional practices that are socioculturally transmitted to individuals as they grow up in their communities.

It has long been recognized that different cultural groups show different levels of motivation and directed effort in school-related tasks, including standardized tests (Anastasi 1958). As Samuda (1975) and many others have pointed out, parental demands and intervention are considered the principal determinant of achievement behavior and motivations; however, parents' goals for their children reflect the practices of the wider sociocultural unit. Thus it is not surprising that historical, economic, cultural, and social factors help to shape individuals' attitudes toward motivation and achievement.

Those who believe that differential performance on tests is completely determined by large-scale social and economic variables, such as Ogbu and his colleagues, would not envision a direct link between culturally specific ways of interacting and performance on tests. Rather, they would see the important effects as coming from group attitudes toward education, group sense of self-identity, and so forth. Academic failure is seen as proceeding from these large-scale factors, rather than from specific mismatches in culturally based practices or expectations. In this brief section, I will not pursue this very important perspective, but instead will concentrate on the effects of specific group differences in attitudes toward group collaboration, and the relative importance of achievement as a group or as an individual.

Many researchers have pointed to a striking difference between some minority group members and the white mainstream on the dimension of individual competitiveness versus group collaboration and affiliation-orientation.

Gallimore and Howard (1968) have made the ethnographically based generalization that Hawaiians are motivated to achieve in order to affiliate with others. This "affiliation orientation" pervades work, play, and school activities. The following statement by an ethnographer involved in the Kamehameha Early Education Project specifically concerns Hawaiian children, but similar observations have been made regarding other Pacific Islands cultures.

> Motivation for the (Hawaiian) individual comes from par-
> ticipation in group-directed collective activities, in which rewards
> for completion and success are inherent and shared. . . . To work
> alone and to be alone is a foreign situation. . . . A task is
> meaningful if its outcome is similar to previously experienced,
> valued outcomes even though the actual operations may be quite
> different. (Tharp et al. 1984, 104–5)

School settings, and especially standardized testing situations, contrast markedly to the ways in which such children are accustomed to learning and interacting. Commenting on this discontinuity in the case of black students, William Labov notes that "school learning is, on the whole, a matter of individual study and competitive display before the group. The skills that are highly developed in vernacular culture depend on a different strategy. Sports, formal and informal, depend on close cooperation of groups. The same holds for music" (Labov 1982b, 169).

Gay and Abrahams's (1973) formulation of the problem succinctly sums up the thinking of many researchers about the mismatch between activities that motivate children within their own home culture, and the school-based activity of test taking. They point out that "for Blacks [as opposed to other ethnic minorities with largely agrarian cultural heritages], as society continues to remain closed to them, many of their agrarian characteristics become further entrenched and combine with other behavioral patterns which constitute the normative structure of a complex, unique cultural entity" (p. 334). In this postagrarian sociocultural milieu, work is seen as cooperative. All children are incorporated into the "cooperative structure of the household," and are given responsibility for a wide range of household tasks from an early age. Their remarks about the relation between home culture and testing in schools are worth repeating at length.

> Learning generally takes place by observing, attempting, making mistakes, and receiving help. . . . One learns when confronted with a task in such a situation to observe others carrying out the task, to imitate them, and if need be, to ask for help. But if a Black child in a school setting, and especially a testing situation, attempts to operate on these norms—consulting one of his peers for help—he is all too often accused of cheating.

> Frustration in such a case is all the more profound because there is little in the home-learning situation which identifies work with individual initiative. (p. 335)

> Thus, testing violates the learned interactional practices of the Black child in a number of ways. First, he is given a written test when he is accustomed to demonstrating his abilities verbally. Second, he is asked to function individually, isolated from his compatriots, when his culture background sanctions cooperative efforts. Third, the environment is rigidly structured and formalized, while, within the Black community, he learns in an informal, social setting. All of these interferences operate on the child before he has the opportunity to address himself adequately to the task itself. (p. 339)

From these examples of two different ethnocultural groups, it is clear that many different factors can motivate a child to succeed. In some groups, the child is socialized to care about the success of the group, and the success of the individual is tied to group achievement. In other groups, the individual child is the locus of achievement, and the motivation to succeed is thus located in the individual. Thus, affiliation motivation and desire to collaborate may play a role in diminished performance on a wide array of academic tasks. The ethnographic approach to cultural description provides the kind of detailed information we will need to further our understanding of how achievement motivation works in the case of tests and other academic situations.

Socialization of Language Use

The extensive ethnographic research of Heath and others has yielded the following important findings: Different sociocultural groups vary tremendously in the ways they use language, both spoken and written. Different kinds of interactions are mediated in very different ways from group to group. Mainstream, educated families tend to mediate many of their transactions through the use of language, language used directively, in querying, in teaching, and so forth. The locus of verbal skills varies from group to group. Even within groups, there is a wide range of variation in the contact children will have with different uses of language, depending in part on the family's interactions with the surrounding community, and the status of that community within the wider cultural mainstream.

Perhaps the most striking finding about performance on standardized tests concerns the ways parents in each community use language in teaching—instructing their children in how to carry out tasks that they will then perform in the future. A number of studies have shown that mainstream care-givers rely heavily on language in directing children's accomplishment of a task. They mediate their interactions through use of language that monitors and corrects their child's actions, and guides the child in seeing the task in a particular way.

The isomorphism between this type of behavior and the language of the classroom is obvious. It is only one more step to see the relevance of such facts in written language, and in tests in particular. This relationship will be discussed below.

In contrast, many minority groups use an array of strategies that do not rely on language in the same way. For example, in Mexican-American families of relatively recent arrival in the U.S., researchers found that parents and other adult care-givers "do not usually accompany their actions with step-by-step directions, nor do they monitor children's actions by giving sequential orders or asking children to verbalize what they are doing as they work. They seldom ask questions that require children to repeat facts, rehearse the sequence of events, or foretell what they will do" (Heath 1986, 161).

Briggs (1984), in a study of communication in a rural Mexicano community in New Mexico (whose inhabitants are culturally Hispanic, Spanish speaking, with a significant Native American element in their ancestry), observes that adults elicit repetitions of their own utterances from children from an early age, and that later, when the child is interacting appropriately with an adult, his utterances to that adult may consist largely of repetitions of what another adult wishes to communicate to the first adult. The intensive, interview-like questioning that is characteristic of Anglo-Americans is quite inappropriate, even between adults.

Gay and Abrahams (1973) give ethnographic details of communicative norms in families where BEV is the home language. As described above, they assert that learning takes place by observing. "Questions are seldom encountered between adults and children, because there simply is little verbal interaction between the generations. When questions are asked, they generally arise from Mamma seeking quick information because of some failure in the smooth operation of the household. Thus, direct querying from adults to children tends to be associated, by Black children, with prospective threat in some accusation of wrongdoing" (Gay and Abrahams 1973, 335).

Based on a five-year ethnographic study of Hawaiian culture, Jordan (1983) reports that the socialization of children in that culture is quite different from that of mainland children. "The basic values of the family are *inter*dependence (rather than independence). . . sharing of work and resources, cooperation. . . . Direct confrontation with adults or negotiation between children and adult authorities is rare" (p. 285). As a complement to the ethnographic data, Jordan reports that behavior of Hawaiian mothers in an experimental setting (a joint task between child and mother) differed significantly from that of the mainland mothers. Hawaiian mothers relied heavily on co-participation and modeling/demonstration, while mainland mothers used verbal controlling strategies.

Moreover, children learn from each other by modeling and intervention. "Modelling occurs when one child performs a behavior which is, in that situation, appropriate for a second child (but not necessarily for the first), thus showing the second child what to do. Intervention occurs when a child partially or completely performs the correct behavior *for* another child, or physically causes the other child to do it" (Jordan 1983, 288).

Philips (1972) observes that young Warm Springs Sahaptin Indians, like many other Native Americans, learn skills differently from white mainstream children. A long period of silent watching and listening is the first step in learning any complex skill. "The use of speech in the process is notably minimal. Verbal directions or instructions are few, being confined to corrections and question-answering" (p. 387).

In great contrast to these is the socialization of the children of Chinese Americans: "In conversational exchanges, parents control topics, length of time for talk by children, and the direction of the conversation. Parents initiate conversations with children, ask them factual questions, talk about steps they are following as they go about tasks, and monitor their children's talk and activities through verbal correction, explication, and evaluation" (Heath 1986, 158). Notice that the parental control of discourse is isomorphic to what the student encounters in a typical test.

Recall that Laosa (1982, 1984) found that a strong predictor of Hispanic background children's performance on intelligence tests was the mother's use of verbal querying strategies, as opposed to physical modeling strategies, in instructing children in how to accomplish a task. The ethnographic work carried out by these researchers may tell us something about the actual mechanisms behind the findings of quantitative measurement and survey research. It may explain how education, acculturation to mainstream ways, and exposure to a certain type of language use prepares a child for the culture of school, and, not insignificantly, for taking standardized tests. If we consider how important verbal (oral or written) directions are in a testing context, and the wide range of language-mediated demands within a test, we might conclude that these are far more accessible to the child whose early background contained a comparably wide range of genres of language use.

This work provides alternative ways of thinking about how language might be a factor in test performance—it suggests that language enters into test performance in ways that are far more subtle than are problems arising from linguistic structure. An astute ethnographer of an American Indian group cautions those who would reduce the problem to proficiency in grammar and vocabulary. "Educators cannot assume that because Indian children (or any children from cultural backgrounds other than those that are implicit in American classrooms) speak English, or are taught it in the schools, that they have assimilated all of the sociolinguistic rules underlying interaction in classrooms and other non-Indian social situations where English is spoken" (Philips 1972, 392).

The Unifying Notion of Genre

How can we tie together this ethnographic research on language socialization and the work discussed earlier on cross-cultural cognition to develop ways to approach the interaction of test and test taker? The notion of *discourse genre* may provide the basis for such an approach. Through a number of recent works in sociolinguistics and sociocultural aspects of language use, the term discourse genre has gained a wide currency. Although it is frequently associated with written language, in these uses it means a map, plan, or schema for a longer stretch of discourse. The term was introduced into the field of sociolinguistics by Hymes (1974, 442–43):

> [Genres] have, so to speak, a beginning and an end, and a pattern to what comes between. . . . Genres, whether minimal or complex, are not in themselves the "doing" of a genre, that is, are not in themselves acts, events, performances. They can occur as whole events, or in various relationships to whole events. The structure of an event may encompass preliminaries and aftermaths, may allow only for partial use of a genre, or even just allusion to it, and so forth. And I want to consider performances as relationships to genres, such that one can say of a performance that its materials (genres) were reported, described, run through, illustrated, quoted, enacted. Full performance I want to consider as involving the acceptance of responsibility to perform, to do the thing with acceptance of being evaluated.

Scribner (1977) has pointed out the significance of this notion for a cross-culturally grounded theory of verbal problem solving. For Scribner, experience with a genre, "a socially evolved language structure" (p. 498), allows the development of cognitive schemata which serve as the basis for ever more complex instances of the genre. If we take the example of a verbal syllogism, as discussed previously, the social context in which an individual encounters this genre, although not well documented, is probably mostly in school contexts. Precursors to the genre, experience with its subparts, such as questions whose answers are limited to the information presented in the problem, may also be found in the talk of certain kinds of parents who themselves have a wide range of experience with this genre (compare Hawkins et al.'s 1984 study of syllogistic reasoning in Manhattan preschoolers).

For Heath, the notion is useful in the study of the acquisition of the socioculturally specific rules of language use. It denotes "the type or kind of organizing unit into which smaller units of language, such as conversations, sentences, lists or directives may fit. Each cultural group has fundamental genres that occur in recurrent situations; and each genre is so patterned as a whole that listeners can anticipate by the prosody or the opening formulae what is coming—a joke, a story, or a recounting of shared past experiences. Moreover, each sociocultural group recognizes and uses only a few of the total range of genres that humans are capable of producing" (Heath 1986, 166).

These notions, combined with the ethnographic results discussed above, provide us with new tools to address the original question: What are some of the linguistic and sociocultural sources of differential performance by minorities on standardized tests? I will present some preliminary results on this question centering on characteristics of the test taker, and characteristics of the test item.

Individual Styles in Interacting with Text

When we look at a child's test score, it tells us nothing about how that child construes the task of interacting with that test. Does the child see the task of reading and responding to a test as similar to reading and responding to a book? How similar are these to responding within conversational interaction? How does the child's early social experience with literacy-related tasks translate into an individual "style" or approach to particular literacy events such as standardized tests?

Heath's (1983) famous ethnographic study discussed earlier has provided a descriptive base for answers to these questions. Short of a lengthy ethnography, however, is there a way we can gain insight into these questions? In this section I will briefly review a preliminary attempt to do this.

The following are the preliminary findings in a study of interviews collected during an NIE-sponsored research project on reading comprehension tests (Fillmore and Kay 1983). The number of subjects discussed here is small, due to the nature of the investigation. Audio recordings were made of two different thirty- to fifty-minute sessions with third and fifth graders, during which time they were presented with reading comprehension items taken from standardized reading tests (for sources and items, see Fillmore and Kay 1983). The subjects read through the item as it was presented to them, a line at a time, responding to questions designed to reveal aspects of their understanding of the text as it unfolded.[10] For example, after reading the opening sentence of an item, "In 1848 a strange machine appeared which surprised many people," the child might be asked to guess what would come next in the text, or to describe the scene they imagined upon reading those words.

By looking at responses to standardized test items in this microanalytic mode, qualitative information not available from test scores or from item-by-item answers may be obtained. My analysis of these data was intended to discover whether a qualitative, observational investigation would reveal differences in the approaches of various students to the task of interpreting a test item.[11]

What does it mean to say that an individual has a particular "style" or "approach" to a text? Based on my reading of these transcripts, I began with a notion of *interactional frames*: predetermined attitudes toward the activity of reading the text, or tacit assumptions about how the text should be approached. This construct has been developed in the work of Deborah Tannen (1984, 24), following the insights of Gregory Bateson and Erving Goffman. (In that work her concern is with the stance individuals take toward the task of constructing an oral narrative about a film.)

A qualitative analytic scheme such as this can be developed only after many cases have been reviewed. At this stage the categories of analysis are provisional and idealized. One interactional frame can be characterized as follows: the reader sees the text as simply *a source of information*. This implies that the role of the reader is that of a reporter. Other readers, however, seem to take a different approach to the text. They see it as an *opportunity for interaction*. In this framing of reading a text, the reader has the role of interactant, with the license to bring in experience and information not strictly

---

[10] Although the scope of this paper precludes discussion of them, a few other researchers have used the clinical interview or extended verbal protocol as a technique for investigating the processes of comprehension that go on while young readers answer test questions. Among these are Haney and Scott (1980). Clifford Hill's work with Robert Aronowitz influenced the development of the Fillmore-Kay project within which these data were collected.

[11] Obviously no strong claims can be made for the relation that this setting bears to actual testing situations. In this setting each child was engaged in a dialogue with the experimenter. In an actual test the reading process is solitary. The inclusion of another individual in the task may completely change the nature of the cognitive processes involved. However, when we considered the fact that current research strategies that rely on products (scores, answers, and so forth) do not reveal anything about the process of comprehension, the tradeoff seemed worth the possible loss of comparability. These methods may provide a closer look at the constructive process of comprehension involving test items.

relevant to the text. In what follows I will draw some inferences about these two frames for test performance. [12]

My conclusions about these two idealized ways of approaching a text are based on observations about behavior on four different dimensions:[13]

1. *Source of information:*

A) Reader uses own experience to support comprehension.

B) Reader uses only text to support comprehension.

2. *Role of reader:*

A) Interpreting stance (reader judges, adds to text).

B) Reporting stance (reader reports on text content).

3. *Content expectations:*

A) Expectations about suitable themes, points.

B) No preference about points or themes.

4. *Sense of author as interlocutor:*

A) Active sense of author as intentional interactor.

B) No evidence for active sense of author.

These categories are idealizations; a few children were central exemplars of one of the two categories, while the rest showed some tendencies in one or the other direction.

Source of information is the dimension that encodes the source of evidence for the child's interpretation, as indicated by her answer to comprehension probes such as "why do you think Fritz felt that way?" Does support for the interpretation come strictly from the text or does the reader bring in his or her own experiences and inventions? Of course an expert reader uses both strategies, but with these beginning readers we find that often a child will tend toward one end of the continuum. (This dimension might also be thought of as a form of Scribner's empiric versus theoretical bias.)

The following transcript fragment shows a child who consistently drew on his own experience in choosing answers to every item with which he was presented:

---

[12] Of course, the positing of two types or categories in this fashion can be construed as implying a binary feature system. The problems with such approaches are well known, and I consider these categories to be best viewed as two poles on a continuum. For heuristic reasons, a focus on the ends of a continuum is obviously convenient. However, it is important to remember that the positing of two styles does not imply that all readers fall into one of the two, or even that there are only a few such styles.

[13] I cannot cover in detail here the findings of my study. Analysis of interview transcripts is a preliminary to the development of formal protocols. Moreover, no single transcript shows a complete array of evidence for any particular strategy or approach toward interpreting a test text. However, the transcripts I examined provided sufficient information to support a preliminary, qualitative descriptive account.

Popcorn is a special type of corn. It has small kernels that are harder than the kernels of other corn. When popcorn is heated, the moisture in the kernels expands, making the kernels explode or pop.

Child: Heated popcorn explodes because it contains
butter   moisture   powder   kernels

Researcher: Well, tell me why you picked this answer, butter.

Child: Well, my family always puts on butter, and I didn't know they put moisture in kernels.

The next dimension, *role of reader*, describes the way the reader construes her role relative to the text. This dimension bears a similarity to one Tannen describes in her work on spoken and written discourse—a dimension she calls interpreting. This dimension consists of the speaker or reader actively judging characters in the text, adding their own interpretive frames not suggested by the text. It is opposed to the strategy of simply "reporting" what is in the text. In her work, Tannen reports that her native Greek subjects are relatively more "interpreting" than her American subjects and that American-born Greek subjects whose parents are still speakers of the language are somewhere in the middle. The next reader is from just such a background. He is striking in that he is the only child in the whole third-grade sample of roughly ten children who actively added his own contribution to the "story" in the course of answering a test question, in spite of the fact that he seemed to know the answer was in the text.

If a bronco buster wants to win a rodeo contest, he must observe the contest rules. One of those rules is that the rider must keep one hand in the air. A rider who does not do this is disqualified.

A bronco buster who ignores a rodeo rule is ____

Child: (Reads aloud) skillful. . . disqualified.

Researcher: Is that a good answer?

Child: Yeah, it says that in the story. . . chosen. . . a winner. Yeah, that's a good answer. You cheat, you could be a winner.

Researcher: OK, now look at all four of these answers and which one do you think is the best answer?

Child: A winner.

In contrast, readers at the reporting end of the dimension, the style that limits itself to what is in the text, are reluctant to form opinions about what is not in the text. An Asian fifth-grade boy responded in a manner typical of a number of children:

> Fritz lived in a neighborhood with many interesting people. But he felt out of place.

> Researcher: What does it mean to feel out of place?

> Child: Like you don't belong.

> Researcher: Why did Fritz feel out of place?

> Child: I don't know.

It became clear upon further discussions that this child's "I don't know" did not reflect lack of understanding, but rather an unwillingness to hypothesize without evidence. His answers to the actual test questions revealed perfect understanding of what was presented explicitly in the text.

The third stylistic dimension that our transcripts revealed was that of a reader who has expectations about the point of a text or its content. This can be seen as a social interactional norm. What is an appropriate or noteworthy topic? The following example shows that to this girl, a black fifth grader, the topic of this story was obviously the relationship between Fritz and his neighbors.

> Fritz lived in a neighborhood with many interesting people but Fritz felt out of place. He felt that he was ordinary. In fact, he felt so ordinary that he thought nobody noticed him. "Today I'll be different" he thought. "I'll wear an extra hat." Then he went for a walk. People smiled at him. But no one spoke. At last he asked a neighbor, "Don't you see anything unusual about me today?" "Yes," the neighbor said. "You're wearing three hats instead of your usual two."

> Child: Friska [sic], he felt that he was ordinary.

> Researcher: Yeah, so what do you think they mean by "ordinary"?

> Child: Like, he was plain and had no feelings and when he was around people, like if he tell a joke and they don't laugh and he think he's ordinary and he can't do nothin' and they can laugh.

> Researcher: Have you ever tried to be different?

Child: Like when every, like. . . like when everybody gets. . . like well, like there's a lot of big people that live around me and they can skate better than me, and I try to pretend I skate better like them and then I say I can skate better now cause my sister teach me and I try to be different. . . ACT different.

Researcher: Can you read the answers they give?

Child: Friska takes a walk, Friska asks a question, Friska and his neighbors, Friska and his hat. . . wait. Friska and his neighbors.

Researcher: OK, that's what you think it is, huh. How come you don't think it's this one, Fritz takes a walk?

Child: Because, it was all about his neighbor wasn't noticing him, so that's why I. . .

Researcher: Ohh, so what about Fritz and his hats?

Child: It wasn't really nothin' bout the hats, it's about the neighbors.

In this and other parts of the transcript this reader showed a tremendous ability to reason about social phenomena; her discussions of what she is reading are full of observations about her family and friends, relating what is in the text to (sometimes somewhat peripheral) events or situations regarding her social world. In contrast, the answers of the Asian boy mentioned above are very terse. However, his pattern of never going outside the text serves him well in this particular literacy event. Standardized reading tests are sometimes almost syllogistic in their requirement that reasoning be limited to the text itself.

These performances highlight a paradox of the search for cultural bias in tests: by attempting to make each item completely dependent on the information presented within it, so that no child will be caught without the relevant background knowledge, testmakers may have imported a significant difficulty for some readers.

Finally, a few readers show evidence of having an active sense of the text's *author as an intentional being*. In data like these, not every child will give evidence along every dimension of preferred styles or strategies. However, some clear examples of each category emerged.

To summarize, this qualitative and preliminary investigation of styles of interaction with texts hypothesizes the existence of (at least) two strategies or styles. In one the reader sees the text as an interactional opportunity. This reader is characterized by a desire to fully participate in the text by means of bringing his or her own experience and expectations and beliefs to bear. The other type of reader sees the text as an independent source of information. The text is not to be changed or collaborated with in any active way. The text is there; it contains the answers; one need not look elsewhere. Of course, an expert reader will be able to switch frames depending on the text type and purpose, but remember that this sample consists of young able readers who have many pitfalls ahead in the road to expert readership.

In our sample of about twenty students, there was at least one trend. The Chinese students, all of whom spoke fluent English but whose parents and grandparents spoke Chinese to them at home at least some of the time, were the best examples of the "text as information source" frame. All our Chinese background students used this general style at least some of the time, and the best exemplars of this type were all Chinese. The best examples of the "text as interactional opportunity" frame were two black girls, one in third grade and one in fifth grade.

Some readers may find these categories disquietingly compatible with certain pronouncements that can be found in the social science literature of the last quarter century, regarding the hypothesized sources of academic failure of black children. Researchers on the consequences of "cultural deprivation" (see for example Hess and Shipman 1965; and Bereiter and Englemann 1966) often suggested that language in the lower-class home is "primarily used to control behavior, to express sentiments and emotions, to permit the vicarious sharing of experiences, and to keep the social machinery of the home running smoothly. . . But what is lacking. . . is the use of language to describe, to instruct, to inquire, to hypothesize. . . . " (Bereiter and Englemann 1966, 31). In other words, language use is limited to social control and interaction functions, and does not support the development of cognitive abilities required for school success.

The analysis suggested here should not be construed as supporting this view or following from the same premises. Rather, it follows from a context-dependent view of the socialization of cognition, in which the task itself and the social context in which it is embedded provide the structure that supports cognitive development. For example, Heath's ethnographic description of literacy events in Trackton, a black working-class community, asserts that literacy is a group activity there, carried out jointly in small or large groups, and that solitary reading is anomalous. The social-interactional nature of literacy events constitutes a significant feature of language and literacy socialization. Such experiences might provide the basis for an individual's framing of the task of reading and understanding a text.

Preliminary findings such as these will not support much speculation. However, they are suggestive of further avenues of research. One interesting aspect is the observation of the interaction of these styles with particular types of texts. One can imagine that the "text as information source" schema would be ideal for the task of approaching mathematical or scientific problems. In reading tasks outside the testing setting, the "text as interactional opportunity" style has much to recommend it.

Genre in Test Items

Any written text may be said to be an instance of a particular genre. When we consider test items, an additional factor is format, or the precise way that the test item accomplishes its aims. I will not consider here the role of format in tests, although this is clearly an area that needs study (Shepard 1982; Scheuneman 1982). Tolfa, Scruggs, and Bennion (1985) examined the role of format in learning-disabled students' performance on reading tests. They cite two unpublished studies showing that performance varied widely depending upon the type of format. They do a quantitative comparison of several popular reading achievement tests, and find that these vary widely on the dimension of both number of different formats (for example, picture and word matching, passage with question, cloze items, and so forth) and number of times the format changed during the test. In a review of considerations surrounding coaching for college entrance exams, Pike (1979) shows that in some studies performance on more complex item formats is more susceptible to coaching effects than simpler item formats, with some gains of up to a full standard deviation.

Here I will consider one genre of text particular to standardized tests of reading comprehension. I will briefly consider its characteristics, and then its accessibility to certain kinds of readers.

In what does this accessibility originate? A simple answer is that when students become familiar with a particular genre through many exposures to its rules and conventions, they can easily understand its implicit demands. I want here, however, to go beyond the question of familiarity derived from exposure to the written texts of school, to address the issue of language use practices that provide practice in the cognitive demands of particular genres. Many researchers have suggested over the years that written narratives have their structural roots in spoken narrative. It may be a useful strategy to consider what other kinds of spoken activities share properties with various written genres. That is, what are the types of mappings we find from spoken genres into written genres?

Consider the following text, taken from a standardized reading test (SRA Level C/ Form 1):

> Here is a magic trick. Cut one sheet of paper in half. Draw a face on each piece. The pieces should look just alike. Now hide one piece in your pocket. Give the other piece to a friend. Tell your friend to tear it into small pieces. Put the small pieces in your own pocket. Say, "Go back together, pieces!" Then pull out the other piece of paper.

1. What should you draw on each piece of paper?
A tree   A hand   A face   A flower

2. Which of these comes first when you do the magic trick?

You draw on some paper.
You hide some paper in your pocket.
You show some paper to a friend.
You cut some paper in half.

We might call this type of test item the "directions" genre. Basically it is a list of verbal directions, with a set of questions that require a search through the text for answers regarding some aspect of the directions just given, or an envisionment of the product of the directions. This type of item is pervasive in middle-level reading comprehension tests, perhaps due to constraints on the makers of tests: they must have large numbers of questions to maximize reliability. Yet each item must be relatively short, so that the test as a whole will not become unwieldy. Thus item writers who do not wish to limit themselves to simple narrative or expository texts must construct items from other, perhaps artificial genres.

If we ask what spoken discourse genre this written genre has as its precursor, the answer is clear—temporally sequenced verbal directions. If we ask what types of experience would allow a child easy access to this written genre, it is clear that a necessary condition, if not a sufficient condition, is experience with the spoken genre that corresponds to the written genre.

We have a good deal of ethnographic information about how this activity of demonstrating or teaching ("giving directions") is accomplished in some minority communities, including some Hispanic, black, American Indian, and Pacific Island communities. Modeling and intervention are not enacted by verbal directions isolated from intervention, nor by decontextualized statements of rules or principles.

The ethnographic literature, and the cross-cultural investigations of verbal reasoning allow us to generate hypotheses about how certain groups may perform on certain types of items. This small text is only the bare beginnings of a study of the effects of genre in standardized tests. Those concerned about item bias might well find it a fruitful domain for study.

Summary

In this section I have discussed how the ethnographic and experimental literature on cross-cultural cognition and socialization can provide us with ways to gain a deeper understanding of the demands of standardized tests. For example, it was suggested that a collaborative, cooperative, group-motivated child may evince reluctance or lack of interest in the individualistic, competitive context of test taking. In the domain of language, the mismatch between culturally-determined patterns of language use, and the decontextualized genres of test items is a promising area of study for those interested in understanding in detail the interaction of test taker and test. A child's wide-ranging facility with various discourse genres, and their corresponding textual genres as represented in certain types of tests, will certainly facilitate that child's performance on standardized measures.

This chapter has presented a sample of the wide array of approaches to the problem of persistent differential performance on standardized tests by ethnolinguistic groups in our society. Clearly, much research remains to be done on how linguistic and sociocultural background interacts with performance on tests, both in a local sense, as discussed above, and more globally, as suggested by the work of Ogbu and others. Unless we develop ways to more clearly understand what happens when an individual test taker interacts with an individual test, we will remain limited in our understanding of how macrolevel factors are instantiated in educational settings. Moreover, we will be hobbled in our attempts to create fair, equitable, and effective test policy.

REFERENCES

Airasian, P. W. and G. F. Madaus. 1983. Linking testing and instruction: Policy issues. *Journal of Educational Measurement* 20 (2): 103–18.

Ammon, M. S. In press. Patterns of performance among bilingual children who score low in reading. In *Becoming literate in English as a second language*, ed. S. Goldman and H. Trueba. New York: Ablex.

Anastasi, A. 1958. *Differential psychology*. New York: Macmillan.

Anastasi, A. 1968. *Psychological testing*. 3d. ed. New York: Macmillan.

———. 1981. Diverse effects of training on tests of academic intelligence. In *New directions for testing and measurement*, 5–20. See Green, ed. 1981.

Anastasi, A., and F. Cordova. 1953. Some effects of bilingualism upon the intelligence test performance of Puerto Rican children in New York City. *Journal of Educational Psychology* 44 (1): 1–19.

Bakare, C. G. M. 1972. Social-class differences in the performance of Nigerian children on the Draw-a-Man test. In *Mental tests and cultural adaptation*, 355–63. See Cronbach and Drenth, eds. 1972.

Baratz, J. C., and S. Baratz. 1969. Early childhood intervention: The social science basis of institutional racism. *Harvard Educational Review* 40:29–50.

Baratz, J. C., and R. Shuy, eds. 1969. *Teaching black children to read*. Washington, DC: Center for Applied Linguistics.

Bartel, N. R., J. J. Grill, and D. N. Bryen. 1973. Language characteristics of black children: Implications for assessment. *Journal of School Psychology* 11 (4): 351–63.

Bereiter, C. and S. Engelmann. 1966. *Teaching disadvantaged children in pre-school*. Englewood Cliffs, N.J.: Prentice-Hall.

Berk, R. A., ed. 1982. *Handbook of methods for detecting test bias*. Baltimore: Johns Hopkins University Press.

Bersoff, D. N. 1981. Testing and the law. *American Psychologist* 36 (10): 1047–56.

Block, N., and G. Dworkin, eds. 1970. *The IQ controversy*. London: Quartet Books.

Briggs, C. L. 1984. Learning how to ask: Native metacommunicative competence and the incompetence of fieldworkers. *Language in Society* 13:1–28.

Bruner, J. S., R. R. Olver, and P. M. Greenfield. 1966. *Studies in cognitive growth*. New York: Wiley.

Cazden, C. 1979. Curriculum language contexts for bilingual education. In *Language development in a bilingual setting*, 129–38. Los Angeles: National Dissemination and Assessment Center.

Chambers, J. W., ed. 1983. *Educational equity and the law*. Ann Arbor, Michigan: Karoma Publishers.

Clarke, M. 1980. The short circuit hypothesis of ESL reading—or when language competence interferes with reading performance. *Modern Language Journal* 64 (2):203-9.

Cohen, R. 1969. Conceptual styles, culture conflict and non-verbal tests of intelligence. *American Anthropologist* 71:828–56.

Cole, M., and J. Bruner. 1971. Cultural differences and inferences of psychological processes. *American Psychologist* 26:867–76.

Cole, M., J. Gay, J. A. Glick, and D. W. Sharp. 1971. *The cultural context of thinking and learning: An exploration in experimental psychology.* New York: Basic Books.

Cole, M., and S. Scribner. 1974. *Culture and thought.* New York: Wiley.

Cortada de Kohan, N. 1972. Test construction and standardization in different cultural settings. In *Mental tests and cultural adaptation*, 121–27. *See* Cronbach and Drenth, eds. 1972.

Crockenberg, S. 1983. Early mother and infant antecedents of Bayley Scale performance at 21 months. *Developmental Psychology* 19 (5): 727–30.

Cronbach, L. J., and P. J. D. Drenth, eds. 1972. *Mental tests and cultural adaptation.* The Hague: Mouton.

Cummins, J. 1982. Tests, achievement, and bilingual students. *Focus*, no. 9. National Clearinghouse for Bilingual Education.

Cummins, J. 1979. Linguistic interdependence and the educational development of bilingual children. *Review of Educational Research* 49 (2): 222–51.

Cziko, G. A. 1978. Differences in first- and second-language reading: The use of syntactic, semantic and discourse constraints. *Canadian Modern Language Review* 34:473–89.

D'Andrade, R. 1973. Cultural constructions of reality. In *Cultural illness and health: Essays in human adaptation*, ed. L. Nader and T. W. Maretzki, 115–29. Anthropological Studies no. 9. Washington, DC: American Anthropological Society.

Drew, C. J. 1973. Criterion-referenced and norm-referenced assessment of minority group children. *Journal of School Psychology* 11 (4): 323–29.

Dumont, R. V. Learning English and how to be silent: Studies in Sioux and Cherokee classrooms. In *Functions of language in the classroom*, ed. C. B. Cazden, V. P. John, D. Hymes. New York: Teachers College Press.

Durán, R. P. 1986. Validity and language skills assessment: Non-English background students. Paper presented at conference of the Eudcational Testing Service, Test Validity for the 1990s and Beyond, May, Princeton.

———. 1985. Influences of language skills on bilinguals' problem solving. In *Thinking and learning skills*. Vol. 2 of *Research and open questions*. Hillsdale, N.J.: L. Erlbaum Associates.

———. In press. Testing of linguistic minorities. In *Educational measurement*, 3d ed., ed. R. Linn. New York: Macmillan.

Education Week. 1985. Increased reliance on testing spurs Congressional review. Volume IV, 25:1,16. March 13.

Fillmore, C. J., and P. Kay. 1983. Final Report to NIE: Text semantic analysis of reading comprehension tests. NIE Grant No. G-790121 Rev. 1 IHL, University of California at Berkeley.

Freedle, R. O., and C. Fellbaum. 1987. An exploratory study of the relative difficulty of TOEFL's listening comprehension items. In *Linguistic and cognitive analysis of test performance*. ed. R. Freedle and R. Duran.

Gallimore, R., and A. Howard. 1968. The Hawaiian life style: Some qualitative considerations. In *Studies in a Hawaiian community: Na makamaka O nanakuli*. ed. R. Gallimore and A. Howard. Honolulu: Bernice P. Bishop Museum.

Gay, G., and R. D. Abrahams. 1973. Does the pot melt, boil, or brew? Black children and white assessment procedures. *Journal of School Psychology* 11 (4): 330–40

Goldman, R. D., and B. N. Hewitt. 1976. Predicting the success of Black, Chicano, Oriental and White college students. *Journal of Educational Measurement* 13 (2): 107–17.

Green, B. F., ed. 1981. Issues in testing: Coaching, disclosure, and ethnic bias. *New directions for testing and measurement*, no. 11. San Francisco: Jossey-Bass.

Green, R. L., and R. J. Griffore. 1980. The impact of standardized testing on minority students. *The Journal of Negro Education* 49:238–52.

Gumperz, J., ed. 1982a. *Language and social identity.* Cambridge: Cambridge University Press.

Gumperz, J. J. 1982b. *Discourse strategies.* Cambridge: Cambridge University Press.

Haney, W., and L. Scott. 1980. Talking with children about tests: A pilot study of test item ambiguity. National Consortium on Testing, Staff Circular no. 7.

Harrold-Stroebe, M. S. 1972. Cognitive development of children. In *Mental tests and cultural adaptation*, 317–27. *See* Cronbach and Drenth, eds. 1972.

Hawkins, J., R. D. Pea, J. Glick, and S. Scribner. 1984. "Merds that laugh don't like mushrooms": Evidence for deductive reasoning by preschoolers. *Developmental Psychology* 20 (4): 584–94.

Heath, S. B. 1983. *Ways with words: Language, life and work in communities and classrooms.* Cambridge: Cambridge University Press.

Heath, S. B. 1982a. What no bedtime story means: Narrative skills at home and school. *Language and Society* 2:77-104.

Heath, S. B. 1982b. Ethnography in education: defining the essentials. In *Children in and out of school*, eds. P. Gilmore and A. Glatthorn. Washington, DC: Center for Applied Linguistics.

Hess, R. D., and V. C. Shipman. 1965. Early experience and the socialization of cognitive modes in children. *Child Development* 36 (4): 869–86.

Hilliard, A. G. III. 1979. Cultural considerations: African-American. In *Testing, teaching and learning*, 204–18. *See* Tyler and White, eds. 1979.

Hymes, D. 1974. Ways of speaking. In *Explorations in the ethnography of speaking*, eds. R. Bauman and J. Scherzer. London: Cambridge University Press.

Hymes, D. 1982. What is ethnography? In *Children in and out of school*, eds. P. Gilmore and A. Glatthorn, 21-32. Washington, DC: Center for Applied Linguistics.

Irvine, S. H., and J. T. Sanders. 1972. Logic, language and method in construct identification across cultures. In *Mental tests and cultural adaptation*, 427–46. *See* Cronbach and Drenth, eds. 1972.

Jensen, A. R. 1969. How much can we boost IQ and scholastic achievement? *Harvard Educational Review* 39:1–123.

Joiner, C. W. 1979. Memorandum opinion and order on Civil Action 7-71861, *Martin Luther King Jr. Elementary School Children, et al. vs. Ann Arbor School District Board*.

Jordan, C. 1983. Cultural differences in communication patterns: Classroom adaptations and translation strategies. In *Pacific perspectives on language learning and teaching*, ed. M. Clarke and J. Handscombe, 285–94. Washington, DC: TESOL.

Just, M. A., and P. A. Carpenter. 1980. A theory of reading: From eye fixations to comprehension. *Psychological Review* 87:329–54.

Katz, I., S. D. Roberts, and J. M. Robinson. 1965. Effects of difficulty, race of administrator and instructions on Negro digit-symbol performance. *Journal of Personality and Social Psychology* 70:53–59.

Katz, I., J. M. Robinson, E. G. Epps, and P. Waly. 1964. The influence of race of the experimenter and instructions upon the expression of hostility by Negro boys. *Journal of Social Issues* 20:54–59.

Klineberg, O. 1935. *Race differences*. New York: Harper and Row.

Knapp, R. 1960. The effects of time limits on the intelligence test performance of Mexican and American subjects. *Journal of Educational Psychology* 51 (1): 14–20.

Kochman, T. 1970. Toward an ethnography of Black American speech behavior. In *Afro-American anthropology: Contemporary perspectives*, eds. N. E. Whitten, Jr. and J. F. Szwed. New York: Free Press.

Labov, W. 1969. *The logic of nonstandard English*. Georgetown monographs on language and linguistics, no. 22.

———. 1972. *Language in the inner city*. Philadelphia: University of Pennsylvania Press.

———. 1982a. Objectivity and commitment in linguistic science: The case of the Black English trial in Ann Arbor. *Language and Society* 10:165–201.

————. 1982b. Competing values in inner city schools. In *Children in and out of school*, ed. P. Gilmore and A. A. Glatthorn, 148–71. Washington, DC: Center for Applied Linguistics.

Lambert, W. E. 1984. An overview of issues in immersion education. *Studies in immersion education: A collection for United States educators.* Sacramento: California State Dept. of Education.

Laosa, L. M. 1982. School, occupation, culture and family: The impact of parental schooling on the parent-child relationship. *Journal of Educational Psychology* 74 (6): 791–827.

————. 1984. Ethnic, socioeconomic, and home language influences upon early performance on measures of abilities. *Journal of Educational Psychology* 76 (6): 1178–98.

Lewontin, R. C. 1976. Race and intelligence. In *The IQ controversy*, ed. N. Block and G. Dworkin, 78–92. London: Quartet Books.

Lunemann, A. 1974. The correlational validity of IQ as a function of ethnicity and desegregation. *Jounal of School Psychology* 12 (4): 263–68.

MacNamara, J. 1976. Comparative studies of reading and problem solving in two languages. In *English as a second language in bilingual education*, ed. J. E. Alatis and K. Twadell. Washington, DC: TESOL.

Madaus, G. F. 1979. Testing and funding: Measurement and policy issues. In *Measurement and educational policy*, ed. W. B. Schrader, 53–62. Proceedings of the 1978 Educational Testing Service Invitational Conference. San Francisco: Jossey-Bass.

Matluck, J. H., and B. J. Mace. 1973. Language characteristics of Mexican-American children: Implications for assessment. *Journal of School Psychology* 11:365–86.

Meeker, M. and R. Meeker. 1973. Strategies for assessing intellectual patterns in black, anglo and Mexican-American boys—or any other children—and implications for education. *Journal of School Psychology* 11 (4): 341–50.

Mercer, J. 1973. *Labeling the mentally retarded.* Berkeley and Los Angeles: University of California Press.

————. 1977. Identifying the gifted Chicano child. In *Chicano psychology*, ed. J. Martinez. New York: Academic Press.

Mitchell-Kernan, C., and K. T. Kernan. 1975. Children's insults: America and Samoa. In *Sociocultural dimensions of language use*, ed. M. Sanches and B. G. Blount, 307–15. New York: Academic Press.

Oakland, T. 1973. Assessing minority group children: Challenges for school psychologists. *Journal of School Psychology* 11 (4): 294–303.

Ogbu, J. 1978. *Minority education and caste: The American system in cross-cultural perspective.* New York: Academic Press.

Ogbu, J., and M. E. Matute-Bianchi. 1986. Understanding sociocultural factors: Knowledge, identity, and school adjustment. In *Beyond language: Social* and cultural factors in schooling language minority students. Bilingual Education Office. Evaluation, Dissemination and Assessment Center, California State University, Los Angeles.

Olmedo, E. L. 1981. Testing linguistic minorities. *American Psychologist* 36 (10): 1078–85.

Olson, D. R. and N. Torrance. 1981. Learning to meet the requirements of written text: Language development in the school years. In Vol. 2 of *Writing: The nature, development and teaching of written communication*, ed. C. Frederickson and J. F. Dominic. Hillsdale, N.J.: L. Erlbaum Associates.

Padilla, A. 1979. Cultural considerations: Hispanic-American. In *Testing, teaching and learning*, 219–43. *See* Tyler and White, eds. 1979.

Paschal, F. D., and L. R. Sullivan. 1925. Racial differences in the mental and physical development of Mexican children. *Comparative Psychology Monographs* 3(1): 1–76.

Philips, S. U. 1972. Participant structures and communicative competence: Warm Springs children in community and classroom. In *Functions of language in the classroom*, ed. C. B. Cazden, V. P. John, D. Hymes. New York: Teachers College Press.

Pike, L. W. 1979. *Short-term instruction, testwiseness, and the scholastic aptitude test: A literature review with research recommendations.* New York: College Entrance Examination Board.

Pryzwansky, W. B., C. L. Nicholson, and N. P. Uhl. 1974. The influence of examiner race on the cognitive functioning of urban and rural children of different races. *Journal of School Psychology* 12(1): 2.

Quay, L. C. 1971. Language dialect, reinforcement, and the intelligence-test performance of Negro children. *Child Development* 42:5–15.

———. 1972. Negro dialect and Binet performance in severely disadvantaged black four-year-olds. *Child Development* 43:245–50.

Reschly, D. J., and D. L. Sabers. 1979. Analysis of test bias in four groups with the regression definition. *Journal of Educational Measurement* 16 (1): 1–9.

Samuda, R. J. 1975. *Psychological testing of American minorities: issues and consequences.* New York: Dodd.

Sanchez, G. I. 1934. Bilingualism and mental measures. *Journal of Applied Psychology* 18 (6): 765–72.

Sanday, P. R. 1972. A model for the analysis of cultural determinants of between-group variation in measured intelligence. In *Mental tests and cultural adaptation*, 88–98. *See* Cronbach and Drenth, eds. 1972.

Sandoval, J., and M. P. W. Miille. 1980. Accuracy judgements of WISC-R item difficulty for minority groups. *Journal of Consulting and Clinical Psychology* 48:249–53.

Scheuneman, J. D. 1982. A posteriori analyses of biased items. In *Handbook of methods for detecting test bias*, 180–98. See Berk, Ed. 1982.

Schrader, W. B., ed. 1979. *Measurement and educational policy*, Proceedings of the 1978 Educational Testing Service Invitational Conference. San Francisco: Jossey-Bass.

Scribner, S. 1977. Modes of thinking and ways of speaking: Culture and logic reconsidered. In *Thinking: Readings in cognitive science*. ed. P. N Johnson-Laird and P. C. Wason, 483–500. Cambridge.

Shepard, L. A. 1981. Identifying bias in test items. In *New directions for testing and measurement*, no. 11, 79–104. See Green, ed. 1981.

———. 1982. Definitions of bias. In *Handbook of methods for detecting test bias*, 9–30. See Berk, ed. 1982.

Spiro, R. J., B. C. Bruce, and W. F. Brewer. 1980. Introduction and global issues. In *Theoretical issues in reading comprehension*, ed. R. J. Spiro, B. C. Bruce, and W. F. Brewer. Hillsdale, N.J.: L. Erlbaum Associates.

Stanovich, K. E. 1980. Toward an interactive-compensatory model of individual differences in the development of reading fluency. *Reading Research Quarterly* 16 (1): 32–71.

Tannen, D. 1984. Spoken and written narrative in Greek. In *Coherence in spoken and written discourse. Advances in discourse processes volume XII*. ed. D. Tannen, 21–41. Norwood, New Jersey: Ablex.

Tharp, R. et al. 1984. Product and process in applied developmental research: Education and the children of a minority. In *Advances in developmental psychology*. Hillsdale, J.J.: L. Erlbaum Associates.

Tittle, C. K. 1982. Use of judgmental methods in item bias studies. In *Handbook of methods for detecting test bias*. 31–63. See Berk, ed. 1982.

Tolfa, D., T. E. Scruggs, and K. Bennion. 1985. Format changes in reading achievement tests: implications for learning disabled students. *Psychology in the Schools* 22 (October): 387–91.

Tyler, R. W., and S. H. White. 1979. *Testing, teaching and learning. Report of a conference on research on testing*. National Institute of Education.

Ulibarri, D. M., M. L. Spencer, and G. A. Rivas. 1981. Language proficiency and academic achievement: A study of language proficiency tests and their relationship to school ratings as predictors of academic achievment. *NABE Journal* 5 (3): 47–80. Washington, DC: National Association for Bilingual Education.

Valencia, R. R. 1983. Stability of the McCarthy Scales of children's abilities over a one-year period for Mexican-American children. *Psychology in the Schools* 20:29–34.

Valencia, R. R., R. W. Henderson, and R. J. Rankin. 1981. Relationship of family constellation and schooling to intellectual performance of Mexican-American children. *Journal of Educational Psychology* 73:524–32.

Valencia, R. R., and R. J. Rankin. 1983. Concurrent validity and reliability of the Kaufman version of the McCarthy Scales for a sample of Mexican-American children. *Educational and Psychological Measurement* 43:915–25.

Valencia, R. R., and R. J. Rankin. 1985. Evidence of content bias on the McCarthy Scales with Mexican-American children: Implications for test translation and nonbiased assessment. *Journal of Educational Psychology* 77 (2): 197–207

Veale, J. R., and D. I. Foreman. 1983. Assessing cultural bias using foil response data: Cultural variation. *Journal of Educational Measurement* 20 (3): 251–58.

Wild, C. L., R. Durso, and D. B. Rubin. June, 1979. Effect of increased test-taking time on test scores by ethnic groups, age and sex. *Educational Testing Service Publication*. Princeton, NJ: ETS. (ERIC Accession number: ED241570)

Williams, T. S. 1983. Some issues in the standardized testing of minority students. *Boston University Journal of Education* 165 (2): 192–208.

Williams, R. L., and H. Mitchell. 1977. The testing game. *The Negro Educational Review* 28:172–82.

Wolf, R. 1964. The measure of environments. *Proceedings of the 1964 Invitational Conference on Testing Problems*. Princeton, N.J.: Educational Testing Service.

Wolfram, W., and R. Fasold. 1979. Social dialects and education. In *Sociolinguistic aspects of language learning and teaching*, ed. J. B. Pride. London: Oxford University Press.

Wong-Fillmore, L. 1983. The language learner as an individual. In *Pacific perspectives on language learning and teaching*, 157–73. ed. M. Clarke and J. Handscombe, Washington, DC: TESOL.

Wong-Fillmore, L., and C. Valadez. 1986. Teaching bilingual learners. In *Handbook of research on teaching*. 3d ed., ed. M. Wittrock. New York: MacMillan.

Wright, B. J., and V. R. Isenstein. 1975. *Psychological tests and minorities*. NIMH. U.S. Dept. of Health, Education and Welfare.

Yeates, K. O., D. MacPhee, F. A. Campbell, and C. T. Ramey. 1983. Maternal IQ and home environment as determinants of early childhood intellectual competence: A developmental analysis. *Developmental Psychology* 19 (5): 731–39.

Ethnic Group Differences in the Armed Services Vocational Aptitude Battery (ASVAB) Performance of American Youth: Implications for Career Prospects

Elsie G. J. Moore

The use of cognitive tests to select and classify individuals seeking higher educational placements, employment, career advancement, licensure, and certification is a prominent feature of our meritocratic system for distributing rewards and opportunities. It is therefore important to examine the advantages and disadvantages that are likely to accrue to various subpopulations of Americans when cognitive test scores are significant criteria for selection and/or placement in educational and career opportunities. Specifically, this paper will focus on the relative competitiveness of black youth, Hispanic youth, and white youth for these opportunities in view of their typical test performance.[1]

The projections of advantage and disadvantage for members of these three ethnic groups are based on test results from a 1980 large-scale research project called Profile of American Youth, sponsored by the Department of Defense and the military services in cooperation with the Department of Labor. The first part of this paper will focus on the purpose and scope of this research project, followed by a detailed description of the test battery administered in the Profile study—the Armed Services Vocational Aptitude Battery (ASVAB), including an examination of its psychometric properties (for example, reliability and validity). The ethnic group differences in ASVAB performance observed by the Profile study are subsequently presented, followed by a general discussion of the implications of the test results for black, Hispanic, and white youths' participation in our opportunity structure.

The Profile study provides an unprecedented opportunity to look at the "real life" significance of the scoring differences observed among black youth, Hispanic youth, and white youth. Both the scope of the study and its relationship to the military services allow for powerful inferences about the life

---

[1] By "competitiveness" we construe the author to mean "probability of succeeding relative to other individuals and groups" rather than the ability (inherent or otherwise) to compete.—Ed.

chances of members of these subgroups. Their performance on the ASVAB directly determines their success in gaining entrance to the four military services, and forms the basis for projections about success in entering other employment and educational contexts that use test scores as a major component of the selection and classification process.

I. THE U.S. MILITARY SERVICES' SEARCH FOR "QUALITY" RECRUITS AND THE PROFILE OF AMERICAN YOUTH STUDY

The United States military services' historical search for strategies to identify "those characteristics and attributes of military personnel that are considered desirable and that contribute to a more productive, capable, and better motivated force" (Doering, Eitelberg, and Sellman 1982, 2), that is, to determine "quality," has produced the current operational definition of the concept: educational attainment and standardized test scores. The emphasis placed on the possession of a high school diploma results from years of experience indicating that "a person who did not graduate high school is twice as likely to leave the military before completing the first three years of service as a high school diploma graduate" (Office of the Assistant Secretary of Defense, 1982, 2). Aptitude test scores are specifically used to index "trainability" in the military services. The first large-scale testing in the United States came during World War I to facilitate the military's mobilization planning. Since that time the military services have invested a considerable amount of resources in the development of reliable and valid tests to screen persons for trainability before they are permitted entry to the military services. Currently, the Armed Services Vocational Aptitude Battery (ASVAB), a broad-range battery of paper-and-pencil aptitude tests, is used to screen applicants for enlistment and to make military job-training assignments.

The Profile of American Youth Study

Since defense manpower analysts currently define "quality" in terms of educational and aptitude test score criteria, data on the distribution of these characteristics in the civilian youth population are necessary to determine the "representative quality" of new recruits. Prior to 1980, however, there existed no appropriate means for assessing the representative quality of military personnel on the aptitude criterion because aptitude test data had never been obtained for a nationally representative sample of military-age youth. Aptitude levels within the military services had been referenced to test results obtained for adult male recruits during World War II. Obviously, the continued use of this World War II reference population as the basis for making current military personnel decisions was, at best, a questionable policy.

In the summer of 1980, to establish contemporary normative data for the military entry tests, the ASVAB was administered to a sample of young

Americans selected to yield data that could be statistically projected (within known confidence limits) to represent the entire population born between January 1, 1957, and December 31, 1964 (Frankel and McWilliams 1981). As will become apparent later in this discussion, however, the unique data gathered in the Profile of American Youth study have value that extends far beyond the specialized technical objective of test standardization.

More about the Sample. The national probability sample to whom the ASVAB was administered consisted of 11,914 young men and women, aged 15 to 22 years, all of whom were participants in the ongoing Department of Labor project, National Longitudinal Study of Youth Labor Force Behavior (NLS). The NLS utilizes three independent samples: (a) a full probability sample of the noninstitutionalized civilian segment of the American population, aged 14 to 21 years as of January 1, 1979; (b) a supplemental oversample of civilian black, Hispanic, and economically disadvantaged white youth (that is, non-black, non-Hispanic) of the same age range; and (c) a probability sample of youth aged 17 to 21 years serving in the military as of September 30, 1978. The ethnic distribution of the sample tested is 7,043 white, 3,028 black, and 1,843 Hispanic. Of this sample, 5,969 are male, and 5,945 are female.

The Uniqueness of the Profile Data Set. The merger of the Profile study test data and the NLS interview data not only creates a data set unprecedented in its potential to inform present and future military manpower procurement policies, but it also affords a unique opportunity to assess the vocational potential of the contemporary youth population (as indexed by aptitude test performance) and to compare the performance of persons of varying social and educational backgrounds. Since the Profile study data come from persons of all segments of our society, sampled by direct home visits, they give a much broader picture of the assessed vocational potential of American young people than tests administered to schoolchildren (for example, the National Assessment of Educational Progress) or college-bound high school seniors (for example, Scholastic Aptitude Test [SAT] and American College Testing program [ACT] results reported annually).

The ASVAB, Form 8A. The tests used in the Profile study are those from the current operational ASVAB, Form 8A, which was introduced in the fall of 1980. It is a paper-and-pencil test, comprising ten independently timed and scored subtests. Bock and Mislevy's (1981) descriptions of each of the subtests (in order of administration) are as follows:

General Science (20 items, 11-minute time limit): Items are drawn from biology, medicine, chemistry, and physics. This subtest measures basic factual knowledge at a level appropriate to secondary general science courses.

Arithmetic Reasoning (30 items, 36-minute time limit): Often called "word problems," the items in this subtest require subjects to use arithmetic skills to solve problems described in short passages. Advanced mathematics is not required.

Word Knowledge (35 items, 11-minute time limit): This is essentially a vocabulary test. Subjects are given a word and asked to choose which of four other words is closest in meaning.

Paragraph Comprehension (50 items, 13-minute time limit): This subtest is designed to measure how well subjects can acquire information from written passages. Subjects are required to read short paragraphs and answer questions about them.

Numerical Operations (50 items, 3-minute time limit): This subtest covers basic arithmetic operations, which subjects are asked to solve as quickly as possible. Scores depend greatly on speed and accuracy.

Coding Speed (84 items, 7-minute time limit): Like Numerical Operations, this subtest emphasizes speed and accuracy. Given the code numbers for certain words at the top of the page in the test booklet, subjects are asked to mark the spaces on their answer sheet corresponding to the code numbers of the words.

Auto and Shop Information (25 items, 11-minute time limit): This subtest measures subjects' specific knowledge of the tools and the terms associated with the repair of vehicles.

Mathematics Knowledge (25 items, 24-minute time limit): This subtest covers material normally taught in high school classes, such as algebra, geometry, and trigonometry.

Mechanical Comprehension (25 items, 19-minute time limit): Items in this subtest show pictures related to basic machines, such as pulleys, levers, gears, and wedges; to answer the questions, subjects must visualize how the pictured objects would operate.

Electronics Information (20 items, 9-minute time limit): This subtest measures subjects' familiarity with electrical equipment, knowledge of electronics terminology, and ability to solve simple electrical problems.

The subtests included in the ASVAB are primarily power tests, that is, tests with time limits sufficient to allow examinees to attempt all items and in which the items become progressively more difficult from beginning to end. Differences in performance on power tests are due to the relative proportions of right and wrong answers, not the number of items attempted. In the case of Coding Speed and Numerical Operations, in which the items are about equal in difficulty, variation in scores is primarily due to differences in number of items attempted within the short time limit (for an expanded description of the ASVAB, Form 8A, see Bock and Moore 1986).

Reliability of the ASVAB. The reliabilities of the individual ASVAB subtests, defined as the ratio of non-error variance to the total score variance in the population tested, range from .87 (Arithmetic Reasoning) to .71 (Numeric Operations). These reliability estimates compare favorably to those observed for the Differential Aptitude Test (DAT). (The DAT is an aptitude test, originally developed in 1947, measuring the developed skills of young people in grades eight through twelve. This battery consists of eight subtests resembling those that appear in the ASVAB. However, the DAT was specifically designed for use with junior high and high school students to help them, in consultation with the school counselor and parents, plan their course of study in school and to make plans for future careers. The DAT is also sometimes used in educational and vocational counseling of young adults who are out of school and for employment selection.) The difference in DAT and ASVAB subtest reliabilities (favoring the DAT) is probably due in part to the fact that the ASVAB subtests are shorter, on the average, than those in the DAT, and longer tests are more reliable than shorter tests.

In actual practice, however, various ASVAB subtest composite scores are used by the military services to make job-training assignments, and these composites show very high reliabilities. The military services use the following common aptitude composites: Mechanical (derived from scores on the Mechanical Comprehension, Auto and Shop Information, and General Science subtests); Administrative (derived from scores on the Coding Speed, Numerical Operations, Paragraph Comprehension, and Word Knowledge subtests); General (derived from scores on the Arithmetic Reasoning, Paragraph Comprehension, and Word Knowledge subtests); and Electronics (derived from scores on the Arithmetic Reasoning, Electronics Information, General Science, and Mathematics Knowledge subtests). A composite score derived by combining individuals' scores on the Paragraph Comprehension, Word Knowledge, Numerical Operations, and Arithmetic Reasoning subtests, termed the Armed Forces Qualifying Test (AFQT), is the primary criterion for eligibility for enlistment into the military services. Reliabilities for these various composites are generally in excess of .90.

Validity of the ASVAB. Bock and Moore (1986) present a review of the validity data available for the ASVAB tests which indicate that, while somewhat shorter than standard aptitude batteries such as the DAT, they are roughly comparable in their ability to predict job success. Within the military context, ASVAB composite scores used to predict success in training schools show validity coefficients ranging from .86 to .21.

Studies of the differential validity of the ASVAB for black and white recruits, and males and females, have demonstrated some general limitations in the ASVAB composites to predict performance in various training schools. However, the available research does not indicate that the ASVAB provides more biased estimates of the criterion performance of blacks and women than is the case for whites and men (Valentine 1977).

II. ETHNIC GROUP DIFFERENCES IN ASVAB PERFORMANCE

The ethnic group differences in ASVAB performance observed in the Profile study are a strong indicator of the career prospects of ethnic minority youth when selection and classification decisions are made on the basis of cognitive test scores. This is because individuals who score high on the various ASVAB subtests are likely to score high on comparable tests, and, similarly, those who score low on the ASVAB will likely score low on other such tests. The reason for this prediction is that the widely used aptitude tests, such as the ASVAB, DAT, and the General Aptitude Test Battery (GATB—a test published by the federal government and used extensively by state employment services to guide people in their search for appropriate work), show considerable overlap in the types of skills assessed. In samples where two different aptitude test batteries have been administered (for example, the DAT and GATB), high correlations are observed between subtests that cover similar content. This means the relative standing of individuals' performance on one test is very similar to their standing on the comparable subtest of the other battery. Since this is the case, it is possible to make some reasonably accurate projections from Profile study ASVAB results about the relative competitiveness of black youth, Hispanic youth, and white youth for opportunities that use test results as a criterion for selection.

It should be noted at this point that although the Profile study provides ASVAB test results for young people between the ages of 15 and 22 at the time of testing, this analysis will focus on the performance of the 9,173 young men and women in the sample born between January 1, 1957, and December 31, 1962, that is, those who were from 18 to 23 years old at the time of testing. There are several reasons for circumscribing the analysis in this way. The older youth are more likely to be independent and trying to make their own way in life, and for them, test performance and its implications are already impinging upon their career prospects. Further, it is the older youth in the sample who have had full opportunity to benefit from the formal instruction in skills available in the public schools, whether they completed their secondary education or not, while the younger members of the sample may still have been in process. Also, the ASVAB tests are designed for the assessment of individuals who have completed high school, but have not attended college, the group that is at present the main source of recruits for the military services. (Analyses of the ASVAB performance of the 15- to 17-year-olds in the Profile sample have revealed essentially the same pattern of scoring differences between black, Hispanic, and white examinees as will be reported for the 18- to 22-year-olds [Bock and Moore 1986]). The ethnic distribution in the subpopulation of youth aged 18 to 23 years is white, 5,533; black, 2,298; and Hispanic, 1,342.

The average standard scores (set to a mean of 500 and a standard deviation of 100) observed for whites, blacks, and Hispanics, and males and females, in each of the ASVAB subtests are shown in table 1. The differences in average scores between the three ethnic groups are considerable in each of the subtests, with whites averaging the most favorable scores, and blacks and, to a lesser extent, Hispanics, averaging the least favorable scores.

TABLE 1
ASVAB Subtest Mean Standard Scores of
American Youth (18–23) by Ethnic Group and Sex

Subtest	General Science	Arithmetic Reasoning	Word Knowledge	Paragraph Comprehension	Numerical Operations
Number of questions	25	30	35	15	50
Male					
White	543	537	524	510	507
Black	405	413	386	399	408
Hispanic	438	450	429	427	442
Female					
White	501	504	525	530	528
Black	393	401	397	422	434
Hispanic	400	416	416	431	449
Total					
White[a]	522	521	525	520	518
Black	399	407	392	411	421
Hispanic[b]	419	433	423	429	446

(continued on next page)

TABLE 1—Continued

Subtest	Coding Speed	Auto & Shop Information	Mathematics Knowledge	Mechanical Comprehension	Electronics Information
Number of questions	84	25	25	25	20
Male					
White	494	603	524	572	529
Black	396	415	431	416	467
Hispanic	441	480	454	469	483
Female					
White	541	447	508	472	490
Black	442	345	430	378	445
Hispanic	468	361	430	387	451
Total					
White[a]	518	525	516	522	510
Black	419	380	431	397	456
Hispanic[b]	455	421	442	428	467

Source: M. J. Eitelberg and Z. D. Doering (1982).

[a] The average score of the total white sample on each of the subtests is significantly higher (p≤.05) than that observed for the total black sample and the total Hispanic sample.

[b] Although the total average score observed for the Hispanic sample is higher in each of the subtests than that observed for the total black sample, only the differences between these groups in Coding Speed and Auto and Shop Information are significant (p≤.05).

An examination of ethnic group differences in performance on subtests that assess scholastic skills—Arithmetic Reasoning, Word Knowledge, Numerical Operations, Paragraph Comprehension, and Mathematics Knowledge—shows differences in the average performance of blacks and whites that range from 133 points in Word Knowledge to 97 points in Numerical Operations. Since performance on these subtests is highly dependent upon formal instruction and facility in Standard English, the relative social isolation of blacks and Hispanics, and the quality of education they receive in the public schools are strongly implicated as factors in the ethnic group differences in performance.

Blacks and Hispanics show remarkable disadvantage, relative to their white peers, in their development of science, mathematics, and technical knowledge. Scores in the General Science, Arithmetic Reasoning, Auto and Shop Information, Mathematics Knowledge, Mechanical Comprehension, and Electronics Information subtests observed for the three ethnic groups attest to this point. We can infer that blacks and Hispanics will likely be less competitive for educational placements and job-training programs that lead to employment in the mathematics-related and technical fields, which offer excellent prospects for career placements currently and in the future.

Although gender differences in performance are not a particular focus of this analysis, the fact that white males show superior performance to their female counterparts in the science, mathematics, and technical subtests is noteworthy. As a matter of fact, within all the ethnic groups there is a pattern of higher male performance in the subtests that survey skills in these areas. The sex differentiation in performance in the ASVAB subtests indicates that females are likely to continue to be underrepresented in mathematics-related and technical professions. The scores presented in table 1 clearly show that whenever cognitive tests are used as a basis of selection for any context, proportionately more whites will qualify than blacks and Hispanics, and more Hispanics are likely to qualify than blacks. As noted earlier, one can make this assertion because the performance of an individual on other tests of the sort included in the ASVAB, particularly those surveying general verbal and quantitative skills, will tend to be similar to that observed in the ASVAB (that is, assuming there is no additional training in a particular skill area between examinations).

The Profile study reveals another significant ethnic group difference that has implications for the career prospects of minority youth. Among the 18- to 23-year-olds, there are considerable disparities in the proportions of those who have earned high school diplomas. The study estimates that while 16 percent of the white youth have not completed high school, 32 percent of black youth have not completed high school. Although Hispanic youth showed some advantage over blacks in their scoring in the ASVAB subtests, 42 percent of these young people have not completed high school. In view of the importance of the high school diploma for labor force entry, these differences in high school completion rates among the three ethnic groups are strong indicators of less than optimum career prospects for black youth and Hispanic youth.

In view of the ethnic group differences in aptitude test results observed in the Profile study, it is clear that testing for selection purposes is likely to contribute to continued higher unemployment rates for ethnic minority youth, particularly blacks. The use of test scores for educational placement will also result in the underrepresentation of blacks and Hispanics in training areas that are in demand in our expanding technical economy. It is therefore informative to consider the extent of testing in contemporary American society.

III. TESTING TODAY AND THE SIGNIFICANCE OF THE PROFILE DATA

The use of standardized tests (such as those included in the ASVAB) to select and classify individuals seeking higher educational placements, employment, career advancement, licensure, and certification has declined in the past decade in response to public concern about the fairness of such practices to ethnic minorities. Vulnerability to charges of discrimination from the legal system has also triggered some hesitancy to use standardized tests. However, test performance continues to have considerable impact on the educational and career opportunities available to young Americans.

Employment testing is widely used in those areas of the public sector where merit systems are in effect. Savas and Ginsburg (1978) project that the merit system "covers more than 95 percent of all permanent (civilian) federal employees, all state and county employees (particularly in the Northeastern states), most employees in more than three-fourths of America's cities, and almost all full-time policemen and firemen" (pp. 257–58). About three-fourths of these merit systems use tests of some sort to select and classify personnel (Tenopyr 1981).

In the private sector, available estimates indicate that about 60 percent of employers with more than twenty-five thousand employees do some testing, and about 39 percent with fewer than one hundred employees use employment tests in the selection process (Tenopyr 1981). It has been in the private sector that we have seen the sharpest decline in the use of employment tests. This decline is thought to be due, in large part, to the fact that private sector employers have been particularly vulnerable to formal charges of discrimination in their use of employment tests. There are indications, however, that we may see an increase in the use of employment tests in this sector of the labor market. Several investigators have hypothesized that there is a causal relationship between the abandonment of aptitude tests in employee selection and classification in the private sector and the decline in the growth in productivity observed in the U.S. economy in the past years (Schmidt and Hunter 1981; Tenopyr 1981). Another factor which may contribute to an increase in employment testing in the future is the accumulation of court-prescribed evidence of relevance (validity) of test scores for hiring decisions (for a review of this development, see Schmidt and Hunter 1981, but compare Levin, this volume).

Nearly all young people who choose to continue their education in colleges, universities, and specialized schools submit results from standardized entrance tests with their applications. It is estimated that 1.25 million persons each year take the Scholastic Aptitude Test (SAT), and in addition to, or in place of, the SAT, about one million persons take college entrance tests administered by the American College Testing Program (ACT). Although institutions vary in the emphasis placed on entrance tests in the selection process, test scores do affect admissions decisions at highly prestigious and selective institutions, college major options at less selective institutions, and are strong determinants of the allocation of noncollege-based scholarship funds (Hargadon 1981).

Young people who choose to continue their education in the military service academies and the Coast Guard Academy are also subject to entrance test requirements. Applicants to specialized federal training programs for offices such as Air Traffic Control, the Federal Bureau of Investigation, and the National Park Service are similarly assessed using test data.

Even among high school students, performance on cognitive tests such as appear in the ASVAB is a significant factor in their educational and career prospects because many high school counseling offices use ASVAB or DAT test results as tools in their educational and career counseling. In this context, it is not unusual for counselors to use low aptitude-test performance as a basis for encouraging future course-taking and educational and career planning that is inconsistent with the students' aspirations. This occurs because school counselors are charged with helping students, in collaboration with their parents, to understand their relative strengths and weaknesses in skill development, and the implications of these for their plans for subsequent course work in high school and advanced training beyond high school. In addition, although most counselor-training programs require course work in psychological testing, there is still a tendency to view aptitude test results as indicating some type of fixed capacity of the individual. Indeed, many test manuals encourage this type of interpretation of aptitude test scores. For example, the DAT manual defines the construct this test is designed to measure in various skill domains as "capacity to learn" (Bennett, Seashore, and Wesman 1974). This definition is repeated in the leaflet that accompanies students' score reports, with the additional explanation that "you take aptitude tests in order to be able to make better predictions of how you can expect to develop in school and in a job." The student is further informed that "this report will tell you how well you scored and will help you to use this information as you face the need to make many kinds of decisions: *What courses should I elect next year? What careers should I consider? How can I get ready for the careers that seem reasonable? Do my abilities jibe with my interests? With my opportunities?*" It is understandable that this type of information about what the scores of an aptitude test mean, combined with the test publisher's encouragement to use the test data to make such important educational decisions, would lead a counselor to discourage a poor inner-city student with average or below average grades, who scores very low on each of the aptitude subtests to continue to aspire to becoming a dentist and to take the college preparatory work in high school required to pursue this goal.

Even before young people are faced with career decisions, standardized test performance has had a considerable impact on their career prospects by determining the type and quality of curriculum placement they experience in the early school years. Many schoolchildren each year are relegated to inferior positions in the curriculum on the basis of cognitive test scores (Scarr 1981). These early school placements later translate into lower occupational assignments because the children have not had the opportunity to develop the skills that will allow them to compete for entry into the labor force at higher levels. The power of standardized tests administered by public schools to shape young people's vocational prospects continues to grow. This growth is evidenced by the rapid increase in the number of states adopting minimum competency testing programs to determine grade-to-grade promotions as well as who shall receive the most basic of educational credentials, the high school diploma (for a review of the minimum competency testing movement, see Lerner 1981).

Until this point in the discussion, projections of the relative advantage and disadvantage of the ethnic group differences in aptitude test performance observed in the Profile study have been rather general. To demonstrate more concretely the impact of these test performance differences between groups on their competitiveness for employment and educational placements that use test data for selection decisions, an examination of how the young people in the Profile study would fare in their application for military service is presented in the next section of this paper.

Ethnic Group Differences in Eligibility for Military Service: The Impact of ASVAB Performance

By far, the ASVAB is the most widely used employment test in the United States. Each year the ASVAB is administered to several hundred thousand young men and women applying for military service to determine eligibility for enlistment and training-school assignments. As Eitelberg and Doering have observed, for these young people, ASVAB performance is a "primary measure of 'excellence' and a visible determinant of 'success' or 'failure'" (1982, 4) in their bid for military service and desired training allocation. Since the use of the ASVAB tests for selection and classification in the military services is well established, this particular context can be used to demonstrate the significance of the Profile test data for the career prospects of ethnic minority youth .

AFQT Performance: Education Effects

The Armed Forces Qualifying Test (AFQT) score (a composite score based on the combination of scores on the Paragraph Comprehension, Word Knowledge, Numerical Operations, and Arithmetic Reasoning subtests of the ASVAB), as noted earlier, is used to determine eligibility for military service. The average AFQT scores of 18- to 23-year-olds in the Profile study by sex, ethnic group, and educational level are presented in table 2.

TABLE 2
Mean AFQT Standard Scores of American Youth (18-23) by Sex, Ethnic Group, and Educational Level

Ethnic Group and Sex	Non-High School Graduates	GED High School Equivalency	High School Diploma Graduate and Above
White[a]			
Male	468	518	550
Female	468	517	543
Total	468	517	547
Black			
Male	365	436	417
Female	346	441	456
Total	356	439	438
Hispanic[b]			
Male	388	470	505
Female	392	447	484
Total	392	460	494
Total			
Male	446	502	540
Female	446	500	529
Total	446	501	533

Source: M. J. Eitelberg and Z. D. Doering (1982).

[a] The average AFQT performance of the total white subsample is significantly higher (p≤.05) than that observed for the total black subsample and the total Hispanic subsample in each educational classification.

[b] The average AFQT performance of the total Hispanic subsample is significantly higher (p≤.05) than that observed for the total black subsample only in the High School Diploma Graduate and above classification.

In reviewing table 2, the unevenness of the effects of education on the demonstrated skill development of young people from various ethnic groups is apparent. It is obvious that the performance of individuals in all ethnic groups is improved by having more education. A substantial gap exists, however, in the test performance of whites, blacks, and Hispanics at each educational level, with whites scoring the highest. The scores shown in table 2 also make clear that whatever cutoff score the military services may use to select personnel, considerably more whites than blacks and Hispanics will qualify.

It is also noteworthy that the average AFQT score difference between white males and black males is smaller when the two groups have less than a high school diploma than when they have high school diplomas or more education. In all the other groups, including black females, the average difference in AFQT performance relative to their white educational counterparts tends to be smaller at the higher educational level.

The rather unusual effect of education on black males' AFQT performance is further indicated in the comparison of black males who have earned GED high school equivalency credentials and black males who have earned high school diplomas and more education. Those with GED credentials actually show higher average AFQT scores than black males who have high school diplomas or more education. Although this 19-point difference between black males with the GED and black males with a high school diploma or more education is not statistically significant, it is a rather curious finding in view of the fact that within none of the other ethnic/sex groups is this effect observed. Although why we see such education effects on black males' AFQT performance cannot be determined from these data, they warrant further consideration because of their uniqueness and the particular difficulty young black males experience in the competition for jobs.

Although we observe considerable differences in the AFQT performance of the three ethnic groups at each educational classification considered, these data make it clear that education does make a difference in the performance of all groups. Generally, the differences in average performance between whites, blacks, and Hispanics become smaller at higher educational classifications. These data indicate the prominent role education plays in preparing individuals from all ethnic groups to demonstrate the skills that will allow them to be competitive in situations that use such test results for selection and classification purposes.

In view of the differences in AFQT performance observed among the three ethnic groups under consideration here, it is obvious that many blacks and Hispanics will not qualify for military service. Analyses performed at the Brookings Institution in 1982 support this conclusion. Using separate service aptitude standards set in fiscal year 1981, estimates have been made of the proportion of American youth of military age (that is, 18- to 23-year-old segment of the Profile study sample) who would qualify for military service given their distribution of aptitude scores and educational attainment.

The results of the Brookings' analysis are presented in table 3. These projections make clear the substantial advantage enjoyed by white youth over black youth and Hispanic youth for enlistment in all the services, even when their educational attainment is comparable, because of their higher performance on the AFQT. For example, among white youth who have not completed high school, 41.7 percent would qualify for enlistment in the army, and 11.2 percent would qualify for enlistment in the air force, the most selective of the services. Among black youth who have not completed high school, only 7.1 percent would qualify for enlistment in the army, on the basis of AFQT scores, and less than 1 percent would qualify for enlistment in the air force. The prospects for enlistment of Hispanic youth who have not completed high school are better than those for blacks, but still much lower than that for similarly educated whites. Focusing on the overall eligibility potential for military service in the black and white segments of the youth population, the Brookings' estimates indicate that whites enjoy a 3-to-1 advantage for enlistment in the air force, a more than 2 -to-1 advantage for enlistment in the navy and marines, and slightly less than a 2-to-1 advantage for enlistment in the army.

TABLE 3

Estimated Percent of American Youth (18–23)
Who Would Qualify for Enlistment in the Military Service
by Racial/Ethnic Group and Educational Level[a]

Racial/Ethnic Group and Education	Army	Navy	Marine Corps	Air Force
White				
NHSG	41.7	19.9	22.5	11.2
GED	76.0	70.4	35.1	56.1
HSG	96.4	87.5	79.8	85.1
TOTAL	85.7	74.5	67.7	70.5
Black				
NHSG	7.1	3.8	3.0	0.8
GED	35.2	26.6	13.9	11.2
HSG	68.6	45.6	33.8	32.1
TOTAL	48.1	31.7	23.6	21.5
Hispanic				
NHSG	13.6	4.8	5.5	1.5
GED	40.0	35.7	18.8	16.8
HSG	85.7	64.8	54.7	56.7
TOTAL	54.6	39.2	33.3	32.7
TOTAL				
NHSG	31.6	15.0	16.8	8.0
GED	68.0	62.1	31.1	47.4
HSG	92.7	81.6	73.2	77.6
TOTAL	78.7	66.6	59.6	61.5

Sources: M. Binkin et al. (1982), 98; and special tabulations provided by the Office of the Assistant Secretary of Defense for Manpower, Reserve Affairs, and Logistics.

[a]Estimates of the percent of youth qualified for military service were calculated on the basis of results from the Profile of American Youth (administration of the Armed Services Vocational Aptitude Battery [ASVAB] to a national probability sample in 1980) and the 1981 education/aptitude standards used by the armed services. (It should be noted that eligibility for enlistment would also depend on other factors—including medical and moral requirements.)

The disparities in eligibility for various military services estimated for each of the three ethnic groups, controlling for educational attainment, demonstrate the importance of blacks' and Hispanics' lower average performance on each of the ASVAB subtests. Their lower average performance undermines their military enlistment potential even when they have high school diplomas or more education. That young people who have spent similar amounts of time in the educational process show such clearly defined differences in demonstrated skills by ethnicity raises an important question: Why? The answer is obviously quite complex, but clearly the education various ethnic groups experience is strongly implicated.

Ethnic Group Differences in Classification after Enlistment: Implications for Future Careers

In view of the average ASVAB test scores observed for blacks and Hispanics, it is not only apparent they will disproportionately *not* qualify for enlistment in the military services, but also that those who do will be relegated by their lower test scores to poorer training options. Support for this projection is presented in table 4, which displays the average composite scores of the three ethnic groups in the occupational areas typically used by the military services.

TABLE 4
Average Composite Standard Scores
for the Armed Services Vocational Aptitude Battery
1980 Youth Population by Ethnic Group

ASVAB Composite	White[a] (N=5,533)	Black (N=2,298)	Hispanic[b] (N=1,342)
Mechanical	522	401	431
Administrative	521	406	438
General	522	402	429
Electronics	521	407	428

Source: J. H. Laurence, M. J. Eitleberg, and B. K. Waters (1982).

[a]The average score of the white subsample on each of the composites is significantly higher ($p \leq .05$) than that observed for the black subsample and the Hispanic subsample.

[b]Although the average observed for the Hispanic subsample in each of the composites is higher than that observed for the black subsample, none of the differences between these groups are statistically significant.

Since high scores are generally required on the Mechanical and Electronics composites to qualify for technical skills training, it is clear that blacks and Hispanics are more likely to serve in "so-called soft, non-technical jobs where training is minimal and advancement is slow" (Binkin et al. 1982, 55). Black and Hispanic youths' lower aptitude test scores result in assignment to poorer training within the military services, which means that their civilian career prospects are not remarkably enhanced by their military experience. This may help to explain why the unemployment rates for black veterans, in particular, are consistently higher than those for white veterans, and as high, if not higher than, the rates for black males of the same age who have never been in the military services (*Employment and Training Report of the President* 1981). The high reenlistment rates of blacks, relative to other ethnic groups, may also be attributable to the poor job training they receive in the military service; that is, the relative lack of marketability in the civilian labor force of skills they develop in military service acts as an impetus to reenlistment.

The ASVAB test data that resulted from the Profile study make clear that inequalities persist in the life opportunities of young people from various ethnic groups in American society. These data show that large segments of the youth population do not demonstrate skills that will allow them to effectively compete for economic resources in our highly technical and literate society. The potential power of the differences in test performance observed for blacks, whites, and Hispanics to directly shape their career options has been demonstrated for the military services. In other contexts where test scores are used as a criterion for selection, placement, and classification, one can expect similar outcomes. Since the use of test scores for selection purposes is so widespread in American society, black and Hispanic youths' poorer average performance can be projected to have a profoundly negative effect on their career prospects. This observation is not new, and public and legal concerns about the "fairness" of the use of tests for selection and classification purposes have been expressed many times. To understand the continued use of tests for such purposes, in view of the profound effect they can have on the quality of life prospects of minority youth, I will present here a consideration of the rationale for aptitude testing in our society.

IV. THE RATIONALE FOR APTITUDE TESTING IN THE SELECTION AND CLASSIFICATION PROCESS

The extensive use of standardized tests in educational, industrial, and government settings to select individuals reflects the influence of the meritocratic ideal in the provision of educational and vocational opportunities in American society. In a meritocratic system, it is necessary to implement objective strategies to identify and reward individuals who "merit" special attention. This method of allocating educational resources is clearly documented in the National Defense Education Act (NDEA) of 1958, as is the prescribed procedure for identifying pupils for special treatment, "by establishing a program for testing the aptitudes and abilities of students in the public secondary schools" (for a discussion of testing requirements outlined in the NDEA, see Goslin 1963). Indeed, as observed by the National Research Council's Committee on ability testing, "The aim of testing is to identify those who are best prepared by nature and training to perform well in a given role" (Friedman and Williams 1982).

The practical value of standardized tests for the selection and classification of individuals in various educational and vocational contexts lies in their economy and efficiency. Compared to the available alternatives, such as subjective judgments based on interviews or even school grades (Bray and Moses 1972; Tenopyr 1981; Schmidt and Hunter 1981), tests are thought to be the most economical and efficient means of identifying individuals who are likely to be successful in a given role, In other words, test performance can be remarkably effective in predicting subsequent training success and job performance, particularly under highly favorable selection ratios (such as many applicants for a few placements). As a matter of fact, it is the predictive validity of standardized tests, even for individuals from demographic groups who typically achieve low average scores, that proponents of testing cite as evidence of tests' service to the meritocracy. Proponents of testing also argue that it is not the tests that cause adverse effects on individuals' competition for placements in the opportunity structure, but rather the failure of early training institutions—public education—to provide them with the skills they need to be competitive.

Aptitude Tests: What Do They Measure? The misconception that "aptitude tests" measure "innate capacity" and "achievement tests" measure the effects of learning was prevalent in the early days of the psychometric movement, even among professionals (Anastasi 1981). This misconception persists today among many professionals who use test data (for example, educators) and in the general public as well. However, both types of tests measure developed abilities and skills. The distinction between the two pertains primarily to how test results are used and the "degree of uniformity of relevant antecedent experience" (Anastasi 1982). Achievement tests are usually given to assess the individual's level of mastery after a uniform learning experience such as training in the second-grade reading curriculum. Aptitude tests, in contrast, are used to predict subsequent performance, and are assumed to reflect learning under relatively "uncontrolled and unknown conditions" (Anastasi 1982, 393), that is, the accumulated knowledge and skills from the totality of the individual's life experiences to the point of testing. The descriptions of the ASVAB subtests provided earlier in this paper attest to the experiential antecedents of performance in these tests. Most of the ASVAB subtests require very specific factual knowledge and skills of the sort typically learned in school. Clearly, the ASVAB and similar tests such as the DAT, NATB, GATB, SAT, and ACT primarily survey developed skills and knowledge.

Testing Policy and the Issue of Fairness. Some investigators believe there is a fundamental conflict between a so-called meritocratic approach to the allocation of educational and vocational opportunities and the attendant psychometric enterprise on the one hand, and the "assertion of a constitutional right to equal opportunity in education and employment" (Gordon and Terrell 1981, 1168) on the other. Gordon and Terrell argue that a commitment to the "democratization of opportunity or simply the optimal development of all human potential would mean that we move away from using tests to identify and reward a few who would most likely succeed." From the perspective of these investigators, the focus of testing would shift from assessment that seeks primarily to determine whether a given criterion of performance is likely to be met to questions of *how* it is met in some cases and *why* it has not been met in others. Answers to these questions would facilitate efforts to develop human potential, in general, and could serve the development of strategies to effectively democratize the opportunity structure. Such questions, however, are usually not addressed in establishing the predictive validity of tests like the ASVAB. The psychometric work on these tests is primarily focused on establishing their potential to predict criterion performance on measures such as training success or job performance in military or civilian life. There is usually little empirical analysis that addresses the questions of how and why the tests come to show significant relationships to the criteria.

In their review of the validity of the ASVAB, Bock and Moore (1986) conclude that the data confirm the important role that ethnic group differences in ASVAB performance will have on the success in job training and performance of young people in military and civilian life. They point out, however, that "we have not yet marshalled enough evidence to argue that the ASVAB is measuring the specific skills that are responsible for job success among the higher scores. All that we know is that, directly or indirectly, the test is able to identify those who will so perform" (p. 179). Important questions for future research in the testing area are why and how test performance and criterion performance are related. Efforts to address these questions are a logical next step in developing the knowledge base to recommend test use for purposes of selection and classification, and to consider viable alternatives to testing to achieve these goals.

While knowledge bases regarding the nature of correlations between test scores and criterion performance are being developed, more judicious use of test data may be in order. Users of test data for purposes of selection and classification should be reminded that no test is perfectly valid. As Sternberg has observed, "Tests work for some people some of the time, but they do not work for other people much of the time" (1984, 14). With this in mind, if evidence of excellent criterion performance in previous contexts is available (for example, scholastic achievement, job performance, and so forth), it should not be discounted as an indicator of future performance because test scores are low.

Although it is yet to be determined whether the level of specific skill development indexed by test performance is indeed the cause of its correlation with the criterion, basic literacy and numeracy skills are clearly essential to effective functioning in a highly literate and technical society such as ours. Since the public school system is invested with the responsibility to facilitate the development of such skills, testing in this context could serve a positive function in pupil development. The use of criterion-referenced tests or mastery tests in this context to assess pupils' progress toward the mastery of curriculum content and to identify the specific areas of weakness in skill development and cognitive processing could be very useful in tailoring instruction to individual needs. This approach to the use of tests, coupled with the facility in implementing such testing programs provided by the introduction of the computer into the classroom, could be particularly valuable in providing effective instruction to ethnic minority pupils at risk of low scholastic attainment. The current approach to testing in public schools involves, as Berlak describes, "mass administration of centrally produced objective tests," whose results are used as "the single most meaningful indicator of school quality, teacher competence, and student achievement" (1985, 17). This approach, in my view, is not particularly helpful to the individual pupil. Such norm-referenced testing does not indicate to the pupil, parents, or teachers why the child scored at the 30th percentile, or stanine 2 in reading. A more informative approach would be to use a testing procedure that permits specific analysis of the child's performance and allows for more precise identification of the problem areas in the pupil's skill development.

Similarly, standardized tests such as the ASVAB or PSAT could be administered to pupils at high school entry to help them plan a program of study. If the ninth-grade student wants to become an engineer, rather than using low aptitude-test scores to discourage that career ambition, as frequently happens, the school counselor could use low test scores to indicate the need for specific high school courses to improve skills in particular areas. In my view, the use of standardized aptitude and achievement test scores to chart plans to help young people to develop their potential and increase their career options is quite appropriate. All too often, however, test results are used to undermine the ambitions of lower scoring pupils, and to label and place them in segments of the curriculum that make it virtually impossible to develop the skills they need to be competitive for educational and employment placements once they complete their secondary school training.

In fairness to the publishers of the most widely used aptitude tests, it should be pointed out that they do emphasize to test users the need to take all relevant information about the individual into account, including his/her family and cultural background, interests and ambitions, and academic history in order to make the most meaningful interpretations and predictions from the test data. Unfortunately, this advice is usually not highlighted and can be easily lost in the mass of documentation that touts the precision of prediction of the *scores* the instrument renders.

Many of the problems associated with standardized tests stem from the fact that probably the majority of users of test results lack sufficient knowledge and background in testing to use them in what Sternberg (1984) describes as a "prudent" and "judicious" way. Many users of test data do not fully recognize that while tests scores can, in many instances, provide some nontrivial incremental validity over that associated with other predictors, they are far from infallible in their prediction of criterion performance. As Sternberg (1984) has observed, however, often the unsophisticated user of test results is so positively disposed to the apparent precision of test scores (for example, the 45th percentile in reading, or a verbal score of 440 on the SAT) that the accuracy of the score for prediction of the performance of individuals is not questioned, despite the existence of other data that may logically call into question the meaning of the score (for example, previous superior academic performance). Clearly, one reform that might be implemented in the system of test use is the requirement that all individuals who use test scores must demonstrate basic training and knowledge in the logic and theory underlying the development and use of norm-referenced tests. While most training programs in counseling, for example, require course work in psychological testing, the extent to which such courses actually train students in the logic and theory of standardized testing may vary considerably. Many such courses may emphasize how to interpret scores on various tests: for example, what a percentile score of 60 in a given area predicts about performance in some larger context, rather than emphasizing the significance of a test's psychometric properties, such as its reliability estimate and the associated standard error of measurement, in making meaningful judgments about the examinee's skill development from a particular test score. Test users could also benefit from broad training in behavioral science because, as Anastasi has noted, "Test scores can be properly interpreted only in the light of all available knowledge regarding the behavior that tests are designed to measure" (1982, 47). In other words, technical knowledge of tests and testing is not sufficient for meaningful use of test results, but must be accompanied by a breadth of knowledge about the constructs the tests are designed to measure. The extent to which most test users meet both the technical and conceptual competence requirements for making appropriate use of test data is questionable. Even if a professional has developed sufficient competence to make appropriate judgments based on a particular individual's test results, often the context in which he or she works may specify the use of test scores in a rather arbitrary fashion. For example, some high schools require a minimum score on a mathematics aptitude or achievement test for pupils to participate in higher level mathematics and science courses. In most instances, if parents intervene and request the higher mathematics placement for their child in spite of his/her not meeting the minimum cutoff score, the child will be so placed, but the parent must be willing to go against the advice of the authorities in making such requests. Unfortunately, pupils most likely to be adversely affected by such policies are also more likely to come from homes where parents are less inclined to question the recommendations of school officials.

V. CONCLUSIONS

As test scores are currently used in our society, large, clearly identified segments of the population are excluded from desired educational and employment placements because they tend to score low on tests used for selection and classification purposes. The populations that are currently disadvantaged in the competition for such placements are those who have been excluded historically from the opportunity structure of our country— black youth and Hispanic youth. How we can break this cycle of intergenerational disadvantage for these populations has been an issue for social-policy analysts for over two decades, yet the problem persists. Throughout this time, it has been recognized that the use of tests for selection and classification purposes has excluded the majority of black youth and Hispanic youth from opportunities that could enhance their quality of life and personal development, and that of their children. However, alternatives to testing that could also serve the meritocratic ideal have not yet been identified. Whether we need alternatives to testing, or whether our society would be better served by testing reform remain open questions. What is not questioned is that under current policies, test scores function to undermine the educational and employment options available to blacks and Hispanics.

If concerns about the extent to which current test use undermines the opportunities available to certain populations of ethnic minority youth are not sufficient to bring about systematic examination of *why* certain populations score higher than others on cognitive tests, and *how* score variations are related to subsequent educational and employment performance, then perhaps less altruistic concerns will motivate such analyses. Current demographic projections indicate that all employers, including the military services, must prepare to face the challenge of a shrinking labor force. There will be fewer potential employees available from which to select for the jobs to be filled. Under this less favorable selection ratio, the utility of any test, no matter how strong its predictive validity, will be greatly diminished in the search for the best fit between available workers and the jobs to be filled. Under these conditions, a fuller understanding of how and why test scores and criterion performance (for example, job performance) are related will be necessary to identify the best fit between potential employees and job requirements.

REFERENCES

Anastasi, A. 1982. *Psychological testing*. New York: MacMillan.

Anastasi, A. 1981. Coaching, test sophistication, and developed abilities. *American Psychologist* 36 (10): 1086–93.

Bennett, G. K., H. G. Seashore, and A. G. Wesman. 1974. *The fifth edition manual for the Differential Aptitude Tests, Form S and T*. New York: The Psychological Corporation, 1974.

Berlak, H. 1985. Testing in a democracy. *Educational Leadership* 43 (2): 17.

Binkin, M., M. J. Eitelberg, A. Schexnider, and M. M. Smith. 1982. *Blacks and the military*. Washington, DC: Brookings Institution.

Bock, R. D., and R. J. Mislevy. 1983. *Profile of American youth: Data quality and analysis of the Armed Services Vocational Aptitude Battery*. Chicago: National Opinion Research Center.

Bock, R. D., and E. G. J. Moore. 1986. *Advantage and disadvantage*. Lawrence Erlbaum Associates.

Bray, D. W., and J. L. Moses. 1972. Personnel selection. In *Annual Review of Psychology* 23, ed. P. H. Mussen and M. R. Rosenzweig, 545–76.

Doering, Z. D., M. J. Eitelberg, and W. S. Sellman. 1982. Uniforms and jeans: A comparison of 1981 military recruits with the 1980 youth population. Paper presented at the annual meeting of the American Psychological Association, Washington, DC, 24 August.

Eitelberg, M. J., and Z. D. Doering. 1982. Profile in perspective: The policy and research implications of the "Profile of American Youth." Paper presented at the annual meeting of the American Psychological Association, Washington, DC, 24 August.

Employment and training report of the President. 1981. U.S. Dept. of Labor, Washington, DC: U.S. Government Printing Office.

Frankel, M. R., and H. McWilliams. 1981. *The profile of American youth: Technical sampling report*. Chicago: National Opinion Research Center.

Friedman, T., and E. B. Williams. 1982. Current uses of tests for employment. In *Ability testing: uses, consequences and controversies*, Part 2, ed. A. K. Wigdor and W. R. Garner, 99–169. Washington, DC: National Academy Press.

Gordon, E. W., and M. D. Terrell. 1981. The changed social context of testing. *American Psychologist* 36 (10): 1167–71.

Goslin, D. 1963. *The search for ability*. New York: Russell Sage.

Hargadon, F. 1981. Tests and college admissions. *American Psychologist* 36 (10): 1112–19

Laurence, J. H., M. J. Eitelberg, and B. K. Waters. 1982. Subpopulation analyses of the 1980 youth population aptitudes. Paper presented at the annual meeting of the American Psychological Association, Washington, DC, 24 August.

Lerner, B. 1981. The minimum competence testing movement: Social, scientific, and legal implications. *American Psychologist* 36 (10): 1057–66.

Office of the Assistant Secretary of Defense (Manpower, Reserve Affairs, and Logistics). 1982. *Profile of American youth.* Washington, DC: Department of Defense.

Savas, E. S., and S. C. Ginsburg. 1978. The civil service: a meritless system? In *Current issues in public administration,* ed. F. S. Lane. New York: St. Martin's Press.

Scarr, S. 1981. Testing for children: Assessment and the many determinants of intellectual competence. *American Psychologist* 36 (10): 1159–66.

Schmidt, F. L., and J. E. Hunter. 1981. Employment testing: Old theories and new research findings. *American Psychologist* 36 (10): 1128–37.

Sternberg, R. J. 1984. What should intelligence tests test? Implications of a triarchic theory of intelligence for intelligence testing. *Educational Researcher* 13 (1): 5–15.

Tenopyr, M. L. 1981. The realities of employment testing. *American Psychologist* 36 (10): 1120–27.

Valentine, L. D. 1977. *Prediction of Air Force technical training success from ASVAB and educational background.* (AFHRL-TR-77-18). Brooks Air Force Base, TX: Air Force Human Resources Laboratory.

Testing Bilingual Proficiency for Specialized Occupations: Issues and Implications

Guadalupe Valdés

I. INTRODUCTION

In 1978 a news item appeared in the *Albuquerque Journal* that read in part:

BILINGUAL TEACHING EFFORTS UNDER FIRE

SANTA FE (AP) – None of 136 teachers and aides in bilingual programs in New Mexico's schools who were tested could pass a Spanish reading and writing exam at the fourth grade level, the director of bilingual education for the state Department of Education said.

Henry Pascual concluded that colleges of education are spending a lot of federal money turning out Spanish-English bilingual teachers who don't know much Spanish. (3 October 1978)

The article also went on to report that Henry Pascual had observed that even in "bilingual" classrooms, all instruction was taking place in English. Spanish monolingual children placed in such "bilingual" classrooms had thus gained nothing from the implementation of bilingual education in New Mexico. They were still being totally immersed in the English language and continued to fall behind conceptually just as their older siblings had done in the days before bilingual education.

The problem was indeed disturbing not only to Pascual, the coordinator who had fought hard to implement bilingual education at the state level, but also to numerous other individuals who were concerned about Spanish-speaking New Mexican children and their need for initial instruction in their first language.

Upon further investigation, it became apparent that the situation was both serious and complex. Native New Mexican Chicano teachers who had grown up speaking Spanish at home understood the spoken language easily, but varied in their ability to express themselves in Spanish. Because they had self-identified as "bilingual," college Spanish requirements had in most cases been waived for them. As products of a totally English educational system, however, they felt uneasy teaching in Spanish. Having never formally learned to read or write in their first language, many could not comprehend second- or third-grade texts written in Spanish. Most could not write in this language, and when they did so, they transferred English spelling conventions to Spanish writing. Thus, the Spanish signs these teachers wrote for their classrooms were frequently incomprehensible to literate monolingual Spanish-speaking adults. On the other hand, Anglo teachers who had taken Spanish in college in order to fulfill basic requirements presented a contrasting profile. These teachers could read well (since that was primarily what college-level instruction had covered), but could not compose comprehensible prose in Spanish, understand the language when it was spoken by native-speaking children or adults, nor express themselves well enough to teach in Spanish. Yet all of these individuals were graduates of state teacher-training institutions. They had taken required courses and had received the state bilingual endorsement. Needless to say, this situation received much publicity, and controversy inevitably followed. New endorsement requirements were instituted, and a vaguely described "proposed examination of a Spanish language proficiency" became a central concern for educators whose jobs were suddenly in jeopardy.

A different but parallel situation took place in a magistrate court in Las Cruces, New Mexico. At a preliminary hearing it was discovered that one of the key witnesses did not speak English. Hurriedly, an individual was summoned who was an employee of the court and was known to be bilingual. He was asked to interpret the testimony of the witness.

The individual summoned was a man of good will. He was a competent juvenile probation officer, and he was indeed bilingual; that is, he spoke both Spanish and English. But he was not bilingual enough to serve as an interpreter. So faulty was his interpretation of the testimony that both the Spanish-speaking magistrate judge and the defense attorney, who was also Spanish-speaking, objected vigorously to the interpreter's version of the testimony and requested another hearing at a later date using another interpreter. A linguist was hired to transcribe and analyze the interpreted testimony so that its errors could be examined by the monolingual assistant district attorney. Within a year of that incident, the legislature introduced House Bill 343, which was subsequently enacted as the Court Interpreters Act of 1985. Once again, individuals who up to that time had worked in the state courts as bilingual interpreters were suddenly threatened. They learned that of as of July 1, 1986, persons wishing to interpret in the state courts would be required to pass an examination that was to be developed and designed by a special advisory committee to the New Mexico supreme court.

These situations, although different in many particulars, had underlying similarities. They both spurred statewide movements that strongly advocated testing of language skills. They both resulted in the development of bilingual proficiency examinations; and they both threatened the jobs of a large number of individuals.

The purpose of this paper is to provide an overview of the key issues involved in responding to public demands for the testing of employees whose jobs require high-level linguistic skills in one or several languages. This discussion will focus on the process of developing and implementing statewide examinations in highly charged political contexts in which employers, employees, and other concerned individuals disagree about proposed solutions.

The position taken in this paper is that while formal testing is not always the best approach to the assessment of abilities, it is effective in the case of bilinguals working in specialized occupations. In these cases, direct or indirect measurement is an effective strategy for reassuring the public about employees' competence, for influencing the training of employees, and for protecting the rights of those individuals who depend on the language abilities of others.

It is expected that in the coming years the demand for bilingual personnel in both industry and public services will increase significantly. It is therefore especially important that policymakers be informed about how to ensure that persons hired for their bilingual skills can indeed function in two languages. Former President Jimmy Carter's embarrassing episode with a Polish-American interpreter could have been prevented if those who hired this interpreter had been informed of the need to assess the proficiency of interpreters before allowing them to interpret.

Specifically, then, this paper will describe New Mexico's development of the Spanish proficiency examination required for its bilingual teachers and the state's ongoing process of developing both oral and written examinations for English/Spanish court interpreters. The discussion will focus on the decisions made at each step of the development process.

II. THE ASSESSMENT OF LANGUAGE PROFICIENCY

Although it might seem that testing people's ability to speak, understand, read, or write a given language would be relatively straightforward, the history of language assessment reveals that it has been just as controversial and plagued with uncertainties and contradictions as other areas of ability testing. This section contains a brief discussion of current language testing practices and shows that these practices have not been directed at measuring the proficiency of individuals in bilingual occupations.

Language Learners and Bilingual Speakers: Some Definitions

The concern for testing language proficiencies or abilities has traditionally involved two different populations: foreign- or second-language learners, and natural bilinguals or multilinguals. Foreign-language or second-language learners are those who formally study another language in an academic context. Foreign-language learners are those who study a language that is not spoken in the context in which they live. High school and college students in the United States who study German, French, Spanish, or Russian, for example, are foreign-language learners. Second-language learners are those who study a language that is normally spoken in the context in which they live. It is expected that this language will become their "second" language; they will use it for normal interaction in their everyday lives after they acquire acceptable fluency in a classroom setting.

Natural bilinguals or multilinguals are those who acquire abilities in two or more languages in the course of their everyday lives. They are not products of formal language instructional programs. Natural bilinguals spontaneously acquire the language spoken around them in the course of interacting with the speakers of this language. Most frequently, natural bilinguals are members of linguistic minorities who reside in multinational states.

Language Testing and Foreign-Language/Second-Language Learners

Most of the efforts to measure language abilities have been directed at foreign- or second-language learners. Indeed, the major language tests in existence today (for example, the Test of English as a Foreign Language (TOEFL), the Oral Interview of the Foreign Service Institute, the International Association for the Evaluation of Educational Achievement (IEA) Tests of Proficiency in English as a Foreign Language) are intended for persons who have studied language formally and who have conscious knowledge about a given language's structure, vocabulary, sound system, and the like. According to Spolsky (1975), foreign-language/second-language testing has passed through three stages of development during this century: the pre-scientific stage, the psychometric-structuralist stage, and the psycholinguistic-socio-linguistic stage.

At the pre-scientific stage, tests were primarily of the translation, composition, and sentence completion type. They were intended exclusively for foreign- and second-language learners and closely followed existing beliefs about how language should be taught and what it meant to "know" a language. At that time, most language courses followed a grammar-translation approach and students were said to "know" a language if they could translate in both directions using the target language and the native language. Oral skills (both productive and receptive) were not taught and consequently were not tested.

During the second stage in the development of language testing, attempts were made to achieve validity by relating tests to existing theories about language. Since it was assumed that problems experienced by learners in the language under study were due to the transfer of elements from the first language, the first language and the target language were normally subjected to contrastive analyses, and classroom activities, particularly pattern drills, concentrated students' attention on these elements. During this period, to "know" a language meant that students could recite previously practiced and memorized dialogues with good pronunciation, that they could respond orally to drills that asked them to transform sentences in order to change verb tense, subject pronouns, and so on, and that they could use traditional grammatical terminology to *talk about* the language. Few expected learners to actually speak the language.

As a result of these approaches to language teaching, tests were produced which sought to measure students' mastery of particular points of difficulty. This contrastivist/structuralist view of language resulted in the development of *discrete point* tests. Oller (1979) defines these tests as those that attempt to focus attention on one point of grammar at a time and in which each test item is aimed at one and only one element at a time. As Davies (1982) recalls, the structural testing school, which gave rise to analytical, discrete point tests, assumed that language is learned by successive progression through skills and that to test those skills, language had to be broken down into its linguistic components (for example, phonology, morphology, syntax, and vocabulary). Typical discrete point tests purported to measure one such component at time and were subdivided into sections that focused on only one subskill. Individual items in a phonology section of an English as a foreign language test, for example, might ask that examinees distinguish between two similar words heard out of context (for example, *watch* and *wash*, *pill* and *peel*). Interestingly enough, many students who scored well on such discrete point tests were not able to use the language on which they had been tested in real-life communication. On the other hand, individuals who had traveled abroad and had learned a foreign language in a context other than the classroom generally did poorly on such tests. These individuals lacked the ability to analyze language that students learn in foreign-language classes, and consequently experienced much difficulty in dealing with language elements out of context.

More recent approaches to language teaching have argued that the focus of language instruction should be functional competence—the ability to communicate with real speakers in the target language. While the methodology and classroom practices that result in such functional development or acquisition of proficiency are still in a state of flux, dissatisfaction with testing practices as well as new advances in theory have led to the third stage of language testing—the psycholinguistic/sociolinguistic stage. The emphasis during this stage, which is still going on, is on *integrative* or *global* tests; that is, on instruments or procedures which Davies (1982, 131) has described as attempting "to assess proficiency (both in production and comprehension) of the total communicative effect of a message." Basic to this approach to testing is the assumption that speakers of a language never actually process language elements one at a time, and that language involves actual communication of meanings.

Within this tradition of integrative or global testing, two principal types of approaches to test development have emerged. One approach (the purely integrative) is the opposite of discrete point testing in that it attempts to assess the learners' ability to use many linguistic elements simultaneously. This assessment is carried out by using test items that are not isolated elements, but "texts" of connected discourse to which the learner must respond or manipulate in some fashion. Test items are considered to be integrative if they require the examinee to process a segment of language as a whole. They need not be actual tests of oral production or comprehension.

The other approach (the integrative and pragmatic) attempts to measure learners' production directly by examining their performance on tasks which involve real listening, speaking, writing, and reading. An example of one integrative and pragmatic measure of proficiency is the OPI (the Oral Proficiency Interview), which involves the use of oral interview examinations modeled after the Foreign Service Institute's (FSI) Oral Interview Process. According to Lowe (1980), the OPI "is a face-to-face test of foreign language speaking competence, lasting 10–30 minutes." Through a conversational interview, the examiners rate the examinees' ability to function in the target language on a scale of 0–5 (from novice-low to superior) according to a set of proficiency definitions. The three areas of focus during each interview are function, content/context, and accuracy. Each of these areas is further subdivided. For example, the accuracy dimension includes such elements as pronunciation, vocabulary, fluency, and grammar; each element contributes in different amounts to the overall production depending on the examinee's level of proficiency. While a great advance over previous types of language tests, the OPI and other similar procedures have provoked strong criticisms from many language-teaching professionals.

Summarizing briefly, then, in developing language tests, the foreign-language/second-language teaching profession has primarily addressed the needs of persons involved in the process of *learning* language; and in all cases, theories about language testing have mirrored theories about language teaching. As a whole, test developers have sought to develop what Clark (1980, 15) refers to as a *common measure*; that is, a "uniform testing procedure that can be used with diverse groups of examinees in a variety of language-learning and language-use situations, with testing results reported on a single uniform scale." Clark (1980, 15) describes the relationship of such measures to highly specialized examinations of bilingual proficiency for specific purposes as follows:

> The "common measure" approach can be contrasted to the rationale and the development procedure underlying the preparation of speaking tests for specialized and closely predefined purposes, as, for example, the job-specific testing protocols recently developed for the Ottawa civil service

(Mareschal 1980) and the generally similar testing approaches being followed by the English Language Consultancy Department of the British Council (Carroll 1978). In the latter two instances and in other comparable projects, considerable attention is focused on analyzing, in greatest possible detail, the specific linguistic demands of a particular employment situation or other predefined language use context; following this detailed analysis, a highly individualized speaking test is developed, in which are featured the particular lexical items, structural elements, and modes of discourse most functionally related to the specific language-use situation in question.

It will be seen that the foreign-language/second-language teaching and testing profession has little to offer to individuals concerned about testing job-specific linguistic abilities. At its best, even the Foreign Service Institute's interview procedure (the FSI Examination), which is used to decide whether individuals speak a language well enough to serve in the foreign service, is not concerned about particular language skills required for specific tasks. Once again, the interview, although intended as a screening instrument for future employees of one particular agency, is designed to be a common measure. It seeks to determine how close a prospective member of the foreign service comes to speaking the target language like an "educated native speaker." The range of abilities such an educated native speaker possesses is generally left undefined, however, and is not limited to a particular set of functions. To date, the questions of what exactly a native speaker can and cannot do with language and how accurate he/she is in real life are the subject of much controversy.

Language Testing and Natural Bilinguals

Because natural or spontaneous bilinguals are not the products of academic programs, the foreign-language/second-language testing profession has not directed much attention to measuring their linguistic abilities. Indeed the measuring of the abilities or language skills of bilingual populations has only been of interest in two cases: school-age children whose language dominance or knowledge of English must be evaluated for program placement; and adult bilinguals through whom linguists, psycholinguists, and sociolinguists have sought to develop measures of language dominance in order to further understand the nature of bilingualism itself.

The language assessment of school-age children is perhaps the best known of these efforts. School districts in many parts of the country have been required to assess the English language abilities of children entering school, at whatever level, if there is reason to believe that English is not their first language. While a full discussion of this area of language assessment is beyond the scope of this chapter, the objective of such assessment is to determine whether or not a specific child "knows" enough English to profit from all-English instruction. Because of the large number of examinees involved, these language-assessment instruments have been designed to measure language abilities indirectly; that is, by viewing a child's performance on a task thought to correlate highly with his/her actual abilities to communicate in real-life settings. For example, the Bilingual Syntax Measure assesses language proficiency by asking that young children answer questions about cartoonlike pictures. Very few assessment procedures measure children's abilities directly; that is, by examining whether children can actually understand classroom language, participate in normal classroom activities, or read class materials.

The measurement of natural bilingual abilities in adult speakers, on the other hand, has received much less attention. According to Baetens Beardsmore (1982), one area of measurement has focused on identifying the mere presence of bilingual speakers in a given society and has thus concentrated on the development of language censuses and linguistic background questionnaires. The other area has sought to measure the linguistic dominance of bilinguals using procedures such as speed of reaction to stimuli presented in two languages (Lambert 1955) and timed continuous free associations to stimulus words in two languages (Lambert, Havelka, and Gardner 1959). While of some use to researchers interested in the study of natural bilingualism, these measures have little applicability to speakers' actual ability to function in specific domains.

In the area of the language assessment of natural bilinguals, then, there are few models of instruments designed to measure bilingual speakers' actual performance in their two languages. Efforts have been directed at developing instruments that will assess school-age children's proficiency primarily in the majority language, but there has been little interest in measuring the functional skills adult bilinguals have in their two languages. While it is clear that there are many different types of natural bilinguals, the differences between various types of speakers of the same two languages have not been assessed. Instruments do not exist that can identify the extent of an individual's bilingualism; that is, the limits of his/her range of skills in each language. Thus, when an individual self-identifies as bilingual (here defined as capable of functioning in more than one language to some extent), it is difficult to determine whether the strengths in each language are similar, whether the range of expression is the same, and especially what the limitations of specific abilities are under different circumstances.

The preceding discussion indicates that activities carried out to date in the field of language assessment have little to offer to those concerned with developing instruments to measure how well a given bilingual speaker can carry out specific tasks in one or both of his/her two languages. Most discussions and controversies that arise in the course of developing examinations for such special purposes arise, however, because individuals who have a stake in the issue often misunderstand the limitations of existing instruments and the effort involved in actually designing and developing an assessment instrument. As will be seen in the following discussion of a specific instrument design, one of the most important steps in arriving at a consensus about how to measure bilingual proficiency is to provide the relevant background information to all concerned individuals so that it can be understood and used in the decision-making process.

III. THE DEVELOPMENT OF NEW MEXICO'S SPANISH PROFICIENCY EXAMINATION FOR BILINGUAL TEACHERS

As was mentioned previously, the publicity generated by the director of bilingual education for the New Mexico Department of Education, Henry Pascual, about the limitations of Spanish language bilingual teachers, caused much controversy throughout the state. Bilingual teachers suddenly felt threatened. Schools of education did not like the implication that they were failing to prepare teachers well; and a small group of "true believers" in bilingual education (including the state director) moved quickly to pass new endorsement requirements. In one version, the proposed requirements stated that applicants for the bilingual endorsement must demonstrate proficiency in the Spanish language at the eighth-grade level or at the "good" level on the Modern Language Association Test. In another version, it was stated that applicants must demonstrate "literacy in Spanish language basic skills as determined by the preparatory institution through tests and/or successfully completed courses."

Confusion and controversy followed. Various groups lobbied aggressively either for or against changing endorsement requirements. Among these groups were:

1. The New Mexico State Department of Education: Because the director of bilingual education had publicly criticized bilingual teachers, the department had a big stake in requiring a test of Spanish language proficiency.

2. Local school-district administrators: Because proposed testing would affect the number of bilingual teachers in the state, local administrators were concerned that a test might be produced that few teachers could pass. Many argued for a locally made vocabulary examination that most teachers could easily pass.

3. Schools of education: The faculty and the deans of the state's five teacher-training institutions wanted to ensure that testing would not result in failure for their students. They opposed new requirements that would result in students having to take several Spanish courses instead of education courses, and therefore

favored each school's implementation of a separate examination. Having little knowledge about language examinations, they proposed using a test prepared to measure the proficiency of high school Spanish teachers.

4. Incumbent teachers: Current teachers resented proposed requirements that expected them to demonstrate Spanish language proficiency by 1982. Many were aware of their weaknesses in the language but felt this weakness did not interfere with their teaching.

5. Departments of Spanish: Faculty in the state's five Spanish language departments resented the implication that their courses in literature and grammar were not preparing teachers to use the Spanish language as a medium of instruction. They favored a grammar-based examination, if an examination was used at all.

6. True believers: This group included members of all of the above groups who disagreed with their colleagues and supported the state director of bilingual education. This group saw itself as the champion of Spanish-speaking children in the state and of their educational needs, and argued for a test that would actually measure teachers' ability to function in Spanish.

As controversy raged in the state, it became clear that information about language testing was needed before decisions could be made. A linguist from one of the state universities was contacted and asked to attend a meeting of all interested parties. She was asked to analyze and critique the examinations suggested by the different groups and to propose an alternative means of assessing the Spanish language proficiency of bilingual teachers.

At the meeting, to which the state director of bilingual education had invited all key decision makers, the linguist discussed several of the existing examinations proposed, selecting specific items to demonstrate how they related or failed to relate to the needs of the particular target population. Since existing examinations in Spanish were primarily based on instructional programs that emphasized traditional grammar, she was able to select items that most native speakers of Spanish would fail even though they were, in fact, quite fluent in the language. After the presentation, it was agreed that bilingual teachers had no need to know details about Spanish syntax since they would not be called upon to teach grammar in the first three grades. It was also agreed that the exact demands that bilingual classrooms made on the Spanish of bilingual teachers needed to be looked at carefully *before* decisions were made about how such linguistic proficiency should be measured.

The development of a specialized examination for New Mexico's specific needs depended on information presented by an individual who was seen as a neutral party. The research solution was acceptable to all parties because they were invited to participate in the data-gathering process.

The state director moved quickly to form a statewide committee in which all concerned groups were represented. A special test-development subcommittee was formed, which included the linguist, a statistician, a bilingual educator, and a Spanish professor. It was agreed that initial work would involve extensive research to identify what bilingual teachers needed to be able to do with language in order to work successfully with monolingual Spanish-speaking children and their parents.

The Design of the Examination

Work on test design and development began in the fall of 1978. Funding for test development (which included research on required language skills) came from a Title VII grant made to the University of New Mexico. Total funding for development during a three-year period (1978–1981) was $103,543.

Research on the Use of Spanish in Bilingual Classrooms

Before beginning work on test design, the development team carried out the following research activities:

- Review and study of existing standardized Spanish language examinations.
- Interviews with local school-district administrators, incumbent bilingual teachers, incumbent bilingual aides, schools of education faculty, parents, and other interested parties about the linguistic demands of the bilingual classroom.
- Observation of instruction in bilingual classrooms at the invitation of teachers.
- Observation of instruction in Mexican schools in the neighboring state of Chihuahua.
- Synthesis of information obtained.
- Identifcation of test objectives.
- Circulation to interested parties of information obtained and proposed test objectives.
- Revision of test objectives in response to feedback.

Summarizing briefly, this research revealed that practicing bilingual teachers should be able to carry out the following functions in Spanish: (1) communicate with young children and their parents; (2) use the language to carry out instruction in the classroom; (3) read and comprehend Spanish language text materials used in bilingual programs; (4) write in Spanish with enough accuracy to teach the writing system to young learners and to be able to write letters and notes to parents.

Once the kinds of functions that teachers should be able to perform had been established, it was then necessary to develop descriptions of activities that teachers would be able to perform if indeed they could function at the desired levels. Using the four areas identified, the groups of individuals listed above were interviewed about *how* such functional levels might be manifested. A combination of strategies was used in eliciting such information. When adequate descriptions of teacher activities were formulated, a survey was sent out to fifty persons in the state identified as "experts" on bilingual education. Questions on the survey were of the following form:

Circle all answers that apply:

A teacher who has good oral Spanish skills should be able to:
1. Understand both rural and local varieties of Spanish.
2. Use both rural and local varieties of Spanish.
3. Understand "baby talk" in Spanish.
4. Explain school rules to young children.
5. Explain school rules to parents.
6. Present information to children in Spanish after preparation.
7. Speak spontaneously in Spanish about "common" classroom subjects (for example, the human body, prehistoric animals).

Individuals surveyed agreed that teachers could communicate with young children and their parents if they were able to understand child language and both rural and standard varieties of Spanish, and if they could explain normal school requirements and activities (for example, school-yard policies, pull-out programs) to persons not familiar with those concepts. Teachers were described as able to teach in Spanish if they could present material in this language easily and comfortably, without undue pauses and hesitations and without revealing large vocabulary gaps. They were able to read in Spanish if they could draw meaning from texts normally used in third-grade classrooms. These texts included math, social studies, and reading materials. Finally, individuals interviewed agreed that in order to teach the Spanish writing system to young children, teachers should be able to spell correctly, use the written accent correctly, proofread material, and find mistakes in children's writing. Moreover, a teacher should be able to write notes and letters home to parents containing few orthographical errors.

Target Populations

As a result of the research, the following target populations of bilingual teachers who would take the state examination were identified:

Population I: Hispanic bilinguals native to New Mexico who had acquired Spanish at home and used English exclusively in the school setting. These persons had good oral skills in Spanish but had difficulty with the written language.

Population II: Hispanic bilinguals from Latin America who had used Spanish in school and had acquired English as adults in the U.S. These persons had both good oral skills and good skills in the written language.

Population III: Anglo bilinguals who had learned Spanish or used Spanish in a natural context (had spent time in a Latin American country). These persons usually had a good oral command of the language and could read and write well.

Population IV: Anglo academic bilinguals who had studied Spanish as a foreign language and who normally did not interact with the Spanish-speaking population. These individuals had marginal oral skills, limited writing skills, but could read well.

From the standpoint of test design, the identification of these populations had implications for the levels of proficiency that the test would be built to measure. It was felt that the test should be designed so that it could discriminate between the limited populations (I and IV) and the fully competent populations (II and III). Given the fact that these populations differed in their control of oral and reading and writing skills, it was decided to divide the test into the following subsections on a preliminary basis:

a. Oral language proficiency

b. Auditory comprehension

c. Reading skills

d. Orthography
   i. difference between oral and written language
   ii. use of written language
   iii. ability to correct common spelling errors

e. Composition skills

f. Knowledge of local dialect forms

It was hypothesized that population I would do well on sections *a, b* and *f;* that populations II and III would do well on all sections, with the possible exception of section *f;* and that population IV would do well on section *c* and possibly *d.*

Preliminary informal pilot testing of test items indicated that, if well designed, populations II and III would pass the examination easily.

Other Considerations

Despite pressure, the instrument was not designed to measure knowledge of Hispanic culture, knowledge about cultural attitudes, subject matter knowledge in general, or formal, explicit rules of Spanish grammar.

In choosing topics for oral and written production, it was evident that without consensus from bilingual educators and administrators about exactly which subjects were to be considered basic, the authors of the test would not be able to determine if poor performance was related to poor language skills or to deficient knowledge in the subject matter area. It was decided, therefore, to test in essentially common areas where poor performance could be separated from poor language skills. A list of such common topics was developed using practitioners' input.

At the start of test construction a large number of provisional test items were assembled for each subsection. Sample tests were circulated to the selected parties in the state identified by the test authors and interested parties as "experts" in bilingual education. These persons were asked to judge the relationship of test items to real-life demands and to comment on the level and difficulty of test items. Responses were compiled and tabulated by the team's statistician and used to modify or exclude text items.

Over a two-year period, different test versions were pilot tested around the state with groups of incumbent teachers, student teachers, and Spanish language majors. In each case, examinees were given an opportunity to rate the test and to comment on particular sections. Item analyses were carried out at each step by the team's statistician and results used to modify the examination.

Once the pilot testing of the examination was completed, attention was given to the establishment of performance standards. It was evident to the test development team that a cutoff point imposes a false dichotomy on a continuum of proficiency, and that excellence and incompetence cannot be unambiguously separated at the cutoff; it was equally clear that standards and cutoff points for passing each of the test's subsections needed to be established. The procedure followed in setting such standards involved three steps: (1) tabulating the scores of incumbent teachers who were known to be members of populations II and III (fully proficient teachers); (2) tabulating the scores of incumbent teachers who were known to be members of populations I and IV (limited proficient teachers); (3) submitting the final version of the examination to a group of judges who were asked to take the test themselves, examine the scores made by proficient and limited proficient teachers, and make recommendations about cutoff scores for each test subsection. Based on this information, standards and cutoff scores were tentatively established so that the impact of these scores on the number of examinees who actually passed the examination could be studied. It was felt that in order to ensure statewide support for the examination, a sufficiently large number of persons needed to succeed in passing the examination.

A compromise solution was also reached concerning reporting scores for separate subsections of the examination. Most examinees could then succeed in passing some sections of the examination. It was decided that all passed sections need not be retaken. Retakes would involve failed sections only.

Table 1 presents an overview of the final plan of the examination, known in its final form as the Four Skills Examination (FSE): A Spanish Language Proficiency Examination for Certification of Bilingual Teachers Grades K through 8, as it is currently being administered. Each section of the examination is discussed briefly.

Oral Production. This section measures examinees' ability to perform three different tasks orally. The test is designed to be administered in a language laboratory where a certain amount of privacy is available to examinees because of the partitions between recording stations; examinees are allowed to read the directions for each task, to prepare their remarks, and then to record. They are given explicit information about how they will be graded on the task and reassured that pauses, repetitions, and self-corrections are normal. They are encouraged to "show off" their command of the language.

A typical task included in this section has the following form:

Preparation time: 4 minutes
Recording time: 2 minutes

Your class is going to take a trip to one of the Indian pueblos. You are sending out permission slips to parents. There is a monolingual Spanish-speaking child in your class. Explain to the child where the class is going and why. Tell the child to take the permission slip home and have it signed by a parent or guardian if s/he is going to make the trip. The slip must be returned to you within three days.

This portion of the examination is graded on a pass/fail basis by three judges, who rate each response on a scale of 1 to 5 based on topic focus, fluency, vocabulary, and appropriateness. An average score of 3 on two of three tasks is required in order to pass this section.

TABLE 1.
Overview of the Four Skills Examination

Section	Skill Measured	Design/Administration
I.	Oral production	Examinees record themselves speaking. They are asked to carry out three different tasks.
II.	Auditory	Examinees hear four comprehension passages about which they must make judgments as to mood, relationships between speakers, attitudes, etc.
III.	Reading skills	Examinees read passages taken from materials used in bilingual classrooms in grades 1-3, and demonstrate ability to assign meaning to familiar words in context; read for main ideas; and reach conclusions about materials read.
IV.	Writing skills	*Orthography*: 1. Examinees write words left blank in 25 sentences. 2. Examinees correct spelling errors in high frequency words. 3. Choose correctly accented forms of high-frequency words. *Composition*: Examinees write a letter to parents about a school-related matter. Choice of two topics is given.
V.	Knowledge of local dialect	Examinees are asked to choose best standard equivalent for dialect forms.

Auditory Comprehension. This section measures how well examinees understand rapid conversational interaction, and how well they are able to comprehend subtle meanings conveyed in such conversations. Since research carried out in the state with teachers, administrators, and parents revealed that such understanding was crucial to establishing good relationships with both students and the Spanish-speaking community, these items were designed to be quite demanding. A typical conversation included in this section might involve an interaction between a child and her father in which the child is wailing for a toy. One of the multiple-choice questions heard after the conversation would require that examinees describe the tone of the father's response as either impatient, angry, resigned, or playful. Responses in this section require that examinees' comprehension of Spanish go beyond mere literal comprehension. Sixteen out of twenty correct answers are required in order to pass.

Reading Skills. Items included in these sections are typical of those found in other reading examinations. In this case, however, only Spanish language materials used in bilingual classrooms in New Mexico were used as reading passages.

Writing Skills. The writing section of the examination is divided into two parts: an orthography section, which focuses on examinees knowledge of the Spanish spelling system; and a composition section, which tests examinees' ability to actually write connected prose in Spanish. Items in the orthography section of the examination require that examinees demonstrate their ability to spell high-frequency words known to be typical of children's vocabulary and/or text materials. Spelling ability is measured using dictation items, multiple-choice items in which correctly accented forms are chosen, and items in which examinees are asked to find and correct spelling errors. Out of forty total items, thirty-two correct responses are required to pass.

The composition section of the examination focuses on examinees' ability to write a letter home to parents. They are required to write a letter of at least 150 words on one of two school-related topics.

The composition section is graded in three steps. If one of the steps is not passed, the grader stops and the examinee fails this section of the examination. In the first step, the grader determines whether the composition contains at least 150 words and whether it has been written on one of the assigned topics. In the second step, the grader carries out a holistic evaluation of the composition and rates each of three factors (communication, appropriateness, and expression) on a scale of 1 to 5. An average rating of 3 is required on this step in order to pass. Finally, on the third step, each error in the composition is underlined. Total number of errors must number less than twenty. Each error is rated on a scale of 1 to 3 depending on the severity of the error. Compositions receiving an error score of 16 or less are rated "very good"; those with a score of 17–30 are rated "good"; those with a score of 23–30 are rated "fair," those with a score of 31–38 are rated "weak," and those with a score of 39 or more are rated "poor." A rating of "fair" or above is required for passing.

Knowledge of Local Dialect. This section was added to the examination as a response to pressure from native New Mexicans. Since a growing number of natives of Latin America were entering the bilingual teaching profession, it was felt that they should become familiar with the variety of Spanish spoken in the state of New Mexico. A section on the proposed state test requiring all prospective bilingual teachers to demonstrate such familiarity would result in the acquisition of knowledge about these important language differences by all persons teaching in New Mexico. Items in these sections are of two types. One type requires examinees to read a sentence in the standard language and select one of four possible equivalents heard on tape, choosing the most frequent New Mexican form. The other type requires examinees to write the standard equivalent of each regional form heard. Out of twenty total items, sixteen correct responses are required to pass.

The State Testing Program

In 1981, the New Mexico State Superintendent of Education officially endorsed the Four Skills Examination as acceptable to the Department of Education as proof of acceptable Spanish language proficiency for bilingual teachers. Since the test development team comprised all interested parties that had originally opposed the establishment of one state test, there was no opposition to the superintendent's endorsement.

The Testing Division of the University of New Mexico took responsibility for administering the test and agreed to supervise its administration twice a year on the campuses of all five institutions of higher education. Cost to examinees is $25.00. Fees are used to cover administrative costs and the correction of subjective items. Correction of these sections is carried out by a team of raters supervised by one of the test's coauthors.

The Spanish Proficiency Examination and Its Success

New Mexico's Spanish language proficiency examination for bilingual educators is an example of an examination developed in a context which, at the outset, was controversial. Five years after it was first developed, it is firmly established as the test that bilingual educators must pass in order to be certified. It is seen as an examination that is fair and actually relevant to teachers as they prepare to work with Spanish monolingual children. Because the test was produced in the state, it is viewed as a product of persons who know about New Mexican children and teachers. As a result, it has had an important impact on the training of bilingual teachers, on the design of courses offered by departments of Spanish, and on bilingual instruction throughout the state.

The process by which the test was developed contributed directly to its acceptance. An important first step was that individuals in key positions were able to bring together members of different factions and to provide them with information about the nature of language testing. Equally important was the provision to these groups of a concrete plan for test development that was firmly based on an investigation of actual language use.

IV. THE DEVELOPMENT OF ORAL AND WRITTEN TESTS
FOR COURT INTERPRETERS

Not all examinations start from square one. Although assessing language proficiency for special purposes is complex, the development of assessment instruments has already been carried out in a number of fields. In the field of court interpreting, for example, there is already an oral examination measuring the ability of Spanish/English bilinguals to interpret in the legal setting. This examination was developed under the auspices of the Administrative Office of the U.S. Courts as a result of the passage of the Federal Court Interpreters Act of 1978. It was produced by a team of individuals who carried out research on the court process, including linguists, psychologists, United Nations interpreters, practicing court interpreters, federal court judges, and interpreter trainers. The original examination is revised yearly.

Additionally, extensive information about the specific linguistic demands that interpreting makes on bilingual individuals is available from numerous sources. The investigation carried out in California courts by Arthur Young and Company (1976–1977) is particularly useful.

In some ways, then, the task of setting up an examination program for court interpreters in New Mexico was less difficult than the development of the examination for bilingual teachers. In other ways, however, the process was more difficult. The political context surrounding the passage of the Court Interpreters Act was highly charged. The New Mexico administrative office of the courts opposed the move and lobbied against it actively. Warring factions in both the House and the Senate opposed all bills introduced by Democrats; and dwindling state revenues made requesting funding for test development impossible. Worst of all, the act mandated both testing and certification of interpreters by July 1, 1986, a mere fifteen months after its passage.

In this case, however, the legislator who had introduced the bill had provided for the establishment of a Court Interpreters Advisory Committee, which was to include a linguist, a state district judge, a court clerk, a supreme court justice, and a representative from the administrative office of the courts. Advised of the difficulties of setting up a language testing program even when specific models were available, he provided a mechanism whereby "true believers" who also had professional expertise in the development of statewide examinations could be appointed to the committee (in addition to the core group). Three such individuals were appointed: one worked professionally in the training of interpreters for the hearing impaired; another was a retired attorney who was also a certified federal court interpreter; and finally, the chair of the committee was a linguist who was also a certified federal court interpreter.

Working without funding but with clerical support from the administrative office of the courts, the committee developed the following:

1. A court interpreters manual, which included an introduction to the legal system and a presentation of the standards of conduct to be followed by interpreters in New Mexico.

2. A written test assessing examinees' knowledge of the legal system and standards of conduct for both English/Spanish interpreters and interpreters for the hearing impaired.

3. A written vocabulary screening examination for English/Spanish interpreters.

4. An oral examination (modeled after the federal examination) assessing individuals' abilities to sight translate legal documents, interpret testimony into both languages using the consecutive mode, and interpret both testimony and legal arguments into Spanish using the simultaneous mode.

Items for the written examination, including the vocabulary segment, were field tested with students enrolled in a university course for court interpreters. The oral procedure was piloted with three practicing interpreters and cutoff scores were tentatively established. Both exams were administered for the first time in the summer of 1986.

Since that date, analysis of test results continues and revisions have been made to both the written and oral examinations. It is expected that revision and analysis will continue.

The ongoing development of the New Mexico court interpreters oral and written examinations is an example of a situation in which work is carried out by individuals personally committed to providing a means by which bilingual proficiency can be assessed. In this chapter, these individuals are labeled "true believers." It is not uncommon for such individuals to volunteer their time to work on such projects. The key element in this case, however, is that a policymaker recognized the need to place these individuals in positions of authority that would permit them to carry out needed work. Had these same individuals not been a part of the committee charged with advising the supreme court about test development and certification, the examination might not have been developed at all. Without funding and without expertise, July 1, 1986, would have come and gone and incompetent interpreters would still be in the courts. This expertise—the familiarity of three individuals with research findings about courtroom behavior, court interpreters, and the federal examination—saved many months of gathering such information. In this particular case, an informed legislator provided the means to get a job done.

V. DEVELOPING BILINGUAL PROFICIENCY EXAMINATIONS FOR SPECIAL PURPOSES: RECOMMENDATIONS

New Mexico's experience with developing one successful examination and beginning the development of another has important implications for others. Specifically, this experience has made clear that the following questions must be addressed:

1. Who are the interested parties in the move for or against test development?

2. Who are the true believers? How much expertise do they have in language test development?

3. What information is available to interested parties about the nature of language testing?

4. Are existing tests appropriate for assessing the linguistic demands of the occupation in question?

5. Should a specialized test be developed?

6. Is funding available to carry out the task, or are true believers with expertise available?

7. Are models of such tests already available in the field?

If the development of a specialized test is considered necessary, the following activities must be carried out:

Dissemination of information about language testing. If there appears to be little knowledge about the testing of bilingual proficiency and the nature of language testing, a means must be provided for disseminating this information to interested parties.

Impaneling of test development committee. The test development committee should include individuals who have expertise in linguistics and psychometrics. Other members may be selected from the most important groups of concerned individuals.

Evaluation of existing tests. As its first task, the committee should carry out a detailed study of all existing related tests that could possibly be adapted for use or used as models for test development.

Investigation of linguistic demands made by occupations. As its second task, the committee should carry out an investigation and analysis of the kinds of activities bilingual workers must carry out in their two languages. This investigation should include interviews with employees, employers, the public served, and other interested parties. When this information is already available from other sources, it should be disseminated to others involved or concerned about the project.

Drafting of survey of language skills needed to meet job demands. Information gathered should be compiled and analyzed and a questionnaire prepared that asks "experts" to rate the importance of different skills in carrying out specific job-required tasks. If this information is already available, it should be made available to other concerned individuals.

Identification of target populations. Characteristics of potential test takers should be identified. Information about possible performance of different groups on an examination derived from observation of job contexts should be used in test design.

Drafting of test objectives. Based on the information gathered, a list of the abilities the test proposes to measure should be drawn up and circulated to interested parties. If the information is available, it should be disseminated widely.

Construction of test items. Test items should be constructed so that they relate directly to the test objectives. Feedback about test items and their relationship to test objectives should be sought from a panel of experts.

Construction of preliminary test versions and pilot testing. A preliminary version of the test should be constructed and pilot tested with appropriate samples of individuals from the target populations.

Validation and standard setting. Once all item revisions are complete, procedures for conducting a final validation of the objectives and test items for suitability, accuracy, job-relatedness, and so on, will be set in motion. The method(s) to be used for setting standards must be determined, applied, and tested for possible bias.

Establishment of testing procedure. The procedure to be followed in test administration should be designed and set in motion.

Monitoring of test impact/effectiveness. Periodically, the impact of the examination both on the employment of certain target populations, on training programs, and on the quality of service offered should be carried out.

VI. CONCLUSION

The assessment of bilingual proficiency for specialized occupations is a complex activity. It is expected that in the coming years, in different areas of the country and in different occupations, the need will frequently arise to determine whether a given employee is bilingual enough to carry out certain tasks. The experience of agencies and states that have already carried out such work can be of value to others who will face the same challenge in the future.

REFERENCES

Arthur Young and Company. 1976–1977. *A report to the judicial council on the language needs of non-English speaking persons in relation to the state's justice system.* 3 vols. Sacramento, CA: Arthur Young and Company.

Baetens Beardsmore, H. 1982. *Bilingualism: Basic principles.* Clevedon, Avon: Tieto Ltd.

Carroll, B. J. 1978. *Specifications for an English language testing service.* London: The British Council.

Clark, J. L. D. 1980. Toward a common measure of speaking proficiency. In *Measuring spoken language proficiency,* ed. J. R. Frith, 15. Washington, DC: Georgetown University Press.

Davies, A. 1982. Language testing. In *Surveys 1: Eight state-of-the-art articles on key areas in language teaching,* ed. V. Kinsella. Cambridge: Cambridge University Press.

Lambert, W. E. 1955. Measurement of the linguistic dominance of bilinguals. *Journal of Abnormal and Social Psychology* 50:197–200.

Lambert, W. E., J. Havelka, and R. C. Gardner. 1959. Linguistic manifestations of bilingualism. *American Journal of Psychology* 72:77–82.

Lowe, P. Jr. 1980. *Handbook on question types and their use in LS oral proficiency tests.* Washington DC: CIA Language School, Mimeo.

Mareschal, R. 1980. Evaluating second language oral proficiency in the Canadian government. In *Measuring spoken language proficiency,* ed. J. R. Frith. Washington, DC: Georgetown University Press.

Oller, J. W. 1979. *Language tests at school.* London: Longman.

Spolsky, B. 1975. Language testing: Art or science? Keynote paper presented at the Fourth International Congress of Applied Linguistics. In *Proceedings of the Fourth International Congress of Applied Linguistics,* 9–28, Stuttgart, Germany: Sonderdruck.

Informal Assessment of Asian Americans: A Cultural and Linguistic Mismatch?

Chui Lim Tsang

Asian Americans have been touted as the "model minority" in the United States. They are believed to be "smarter and better educated and (to) make more money" (Ramirez 1986) than other ethnic minorities and whites. Yet despite their outstanding academic achievements, Asian Americans still face major barriers in achieving high-level positions in business and industry. Their income, when adjusted for hours of work and level of education, is still less than that of whites. Colleges and universities admit a lower percentage of Asian Americans than whites even when Asian Americans score the same or higher on standardized tests. Racism no doubt contributes to some of the inequities Asian Americans face in gaining access to educational and economic opportunities, but linguistic and cultural differences are also major factors. This paper discusses how these linguistic and cultural differences can subtly influence the ways in which native English speakers evaluate the abilities, intentions, and attitudes of Asian Americans. These informal evaluations often prevent Asian Americans from gaining equal access to educational and economic opportunities.

This paper is divided into four sections. In the first section, the demographic profile and the academic and economic achievements of Asian Americans are discussed. In the second section, the barriers Asian Americans face in accessing educational and economic opportunities are presented. It is posited that a major factor contributing to inequality is the widespread use of culturally based informal evaluations. The third section discusses research findings on culturally specific linguistic conventions and how native English speakers interpret these conventions, often resulting in unfavorable judgments of the abilities, intentions, and attitudes of Asian Americans. The paper concludes by suggesting research that must be conducted to increase our understanding of the impact of these cultural and linguistic differences. Questions are raised about policies and strategies adopted by those in power and by Asian Americans to address this inequity.

I. ASIAN AMERICANS: AN OVERVIEW

Demographic Profile

Asian Americans are a heterogeneous group comprised of people of different ethnic descent, language, culture, and geographic origin. The term "Asian American" is commonly used to include those who came to the U.S. from China, Japan, India, Korea, the Philippines, Vietnam, Cambodia, Laos, and Thailand. The Census Bureau uses the racial designation of Asian and Pacific Islander (API), which includes, in addition to these groups, those who trace their ancestry to the Hawaiian Islands, Samoa, and Guam. In this paper, which deals primarily with Americans of Asian descent, the more limited term "Asian American" is used.

According to the 1980 census, the total population of Asian Americans was 3.7 million, or about 2% of the U.S. population. Of this number, 1.5 million are concentrated in four major metropolitan areas: Los Angeles, San Francisco, New York, and Honolulu.

Asian Americans are the fastest-growing minority group in the U.S. The Asian-American population increased by 142% in the decade between 1970 and 1980. According to Lean Bouvier, vice president of the Population Reference Bureau in Washington, the number will jump to 6.5 million by 1990 and to almost 10 million by the turn of the century (Butterfield 1986).

The ethnic makeup of the Asian-American population is changing. In 1980, Chinese surpassed Japanese as the largest group. In addition, since 1975 over eight hundred thousand refugees have been admitted to the U.S. from East Asia (Refugee Report, Feb. 20, 1987). By 1990, Filipinos are projected to become the largest Asian group, and the number of Koreans will increase significantly. Indians and Pakistanis have also been predicted to increase by a half-million by 1990 (Butterfield 1986).

Two important features of the Asian-American population are central to the issues discussed in this paper—the high percentage of immigrants and the large proportion of the population who lack proficiency in English. Approximately 59% of Asian Americans in the U.S. are foreign-born immigrants. Two-thirds of the Asian-American population speaks an Asian language at home, and in this group, it is estimated about 20% of those age five or older may be of limited English proficiency (U.S. Bureau of the Census 1984).

This diverse group's changing demographics and steady population increase due to immigration must be recognized in order for us to understand clearly how language differences between Asian Americans and whites, the dominant social group in the U.S., can have far-reaching consequences.

Academic Achievement of Asian Americans

Even though the academic success of Asian Americans reported in the media is somewhat exaggerated, the group in general is doing better than the norm and in some cases has outscored whites. According to the Bureau of the Census (1983), in 1980 the percentage of Asian Americans with college degrees was almost twice that of whites—39.8% versus 21.3%. The dropout rate for Asian Americans is less than that of whites (Tsang and Wing 1985). The *High School and Beyond* test data show that the average Asian-American student scored slightly higher than the average white student in mathematics (Peng, et al. 1984). Forty-six percent of all 18-year-old Asian Americans take the SAT, while only 24% of 18-year-old whites take the test. The mean SAT mathematics score for Asian Americans is 514, compared with 484 for whites (Tsang and Wing 1985). (However, appraisal of the SAT score report for Asian Americans is complicated by the fact that the College Entrance Examination Board does not differentiate Asian foreign students from U.S. citizens and permanent residents of Asian descent. Comparisons therefore must be viewed with caution. In 1982–83, foreign students accounted for 10% of the total number labeled Asian Americans by the College Board.) In the 1985 Westinghouse Science Talent Search, one of the country's most prestigious high school academic contests, all five top scholarships were awarded to Asian Americans (Ramirez 1986). Nationally, the percentage of Asian Americans enrolled in programs for the gifted was almost twice as high as the percentage of whites, 5.25% versus 2.88% (DBS Corporation 1982).

More strikingly, however, many articles and news releases failed to mention low verbal scores of Asian Americans revealed in similar test or data sets. These less-publicized statistics are perhaps even more important for us because they reveal a pattern of lower achievement associated with the immigrant status of a large proportion of the Asian Americans now residing in the U.S.

According to a study done by Tsang and Wing (1985), 18.7% of all Asian-American students surveyed by the federal government in 1980 were categorized as limited English proficient (LEP). However, only 14.8% were enrolled in special programs. Tsang and Wing also noted that the lack of proficiency in English is revealed in the test scores of Asian-American students who were included in another 1980 survey conducted by the federal government. Of the Asian-American students who have lived in the U.S. for five years or less, scores on both verbal skills and science are substantially lower than those of white students. More disturbing, though, is the lack of progress in verbal skills of these immigrant students reported in a follow-up survey conducted in 1982—their English skills have lagged further and they show far less progress in English than other Asian Americans and whites.

Moreover, the mean verbal score of Asian Americans on the SAT is lower than the mean verbal score of all students and is substantially lower than that of whites (395 versus 443). Surprisingly, even among Asian-American SAT candidates whose best language is English, the verbal score was lower than that of white candidates, 427 versus 439 (Tsang and Wing 1985). The implications of this last point are discussed in Section IV of this paper.

The consequences of the lower verbal scores of Asian Americans demand further attention. In addition, the large influx of Asian-American immigrants in the next two decades will force us to focus more on their English verbal skills.

Economic Achievement of Asian Americans

As the "model minority," Asian Americans are believed to have achieved parity through their hard work and intelligence. Nationally, the income of Asian Americans is higher than the norm and even higher than whites on a household basis. The 1980 census shows that the annual median family income of Asian and Pacific Americans was $22,075 as compared to $20,840 for white families (U.S. Bureau of the Census 1981). Asian Americans are also well represented in white-collar professions. An analysis of the educational level and occupations of Asian Americans shows that the group as a whole has fared relatively well (Kan and Liu 1986). Even when Asian Americans have less than four years of college, the percentage holding administrative and managerial positions is comparable to that of whites.

TABLE 1
Education and Occupation by Race, 1980

With 4 or more years of college education

White	Black	Hispanic	Chinese	Japanese	Korean	Filipino	Asian Indian	Viet-namese
Professional, administrative, and managerial occupations								
67.9%	67.8%	59.8%	61.6%	63.7%	48.4%	49.5%	67.5%	50.6%
Other occupations								
32.1%	32.2%	40.2%	38.4%	36.3%	51.6%	50.5%	32.5%	49.4%
Number								
16,743	973	443	8,183	5,658	2,701	7,650	5,545	589

With less than 4 years of college education

White	Black	Hispanic	Chinese	Japanese	Korean	Filipino	Asian Indian	Viet-namese
Professional, administrative, and managerial occupations								
14.6%	7.9%	7.6%	14.8%	15.1%	11.7%	19.5%	19.0%	8.8%
Other occupations								
85.4%	92.1%	92.4%	85.2%	84.9%	88.3%	80.5%	81.0%	91.2%
Number								
62,793	8,414	4,502	11,620	12,988	4,590	9,973	3,624	3,285

Source: Kan and Liu (1986).

Upon closer scrutiny, however, there is another side to the success of Asian Americans. Data show that the high earnings of Asian Americans may result from more education and longer hours of work (U.S. Commission on Civil Rights 1980; Kan and Liu 1986). Their high income does not mean that they have the same access to the economic system as whites. For Asian Americans to earn the same amount as whites, they generally have to be better educated and to hold higher positions (Kim and Hurh 1986). When factors contributing to high median family income are further analyzed, the data show that a high percentage of Asian Americans reside in large metropolitan areas where the cost of living is relatively high. Multiple wage earners in a single family also contribute significantly to higher family income, as children in Asian families tend to reside with their parents even when they are financially independent.

II. DIFFERENTIAL ACCESS TO OPPORTUNITY

Competence vs. Racism

High academic scores and high median income notwithstanding, compared to whites, Asian Americans do not have equitable access to educational and business opportunities. Inundated with academically qualified applicants, univeristies are placing more emphasis on subjective evaluation of factors other than a student's academic record and SAT scores. This type of evaluation process is believed by many in the Asian-American community to lead to rejection by major U.S. universities of an increasing number of Asian Americans with high academic records.

In the business sector, especially at the upper management levels of large corporations, Asian Americans are conspicuously underrepresented. While many in the Asian-American community claim that low representation in the corporate world results from lingering racist attitudes that white Americans harbor about ethnic minorities, many whites, especially those in the corporate world, argue that there is truth in the stereotypes used to discount Asian Americans' executive aptitude. Defenders of the admissions policies of universities assert that the subjective assessments of assertiveness, leadership quality, and the ability to communicate are valid screening devices to ensure that their entering freshmen are well-rounded students.

In the following sections, the conflicting claims of racism and lack of competence are examined in more detail. Particular attention will be focused on the cultural and linguistic factors that may have fostered such arguments.

Asian Americans and Access to Higher Education

Private universities and colleges in the U.S. have long relied on factors other than academic records and test scores to determine their admissions policies. However, as more Asian Americans qualify for admission because of their outstanding academic records, the issue is becoming more sensitive. Asian Americans, who represent roughly 2% of the population of the U.S., constituted 11% of the freshman class at Harvard, 21% of the freshman class at MIT (Biemiller 1986), and 16% of the freshman class at Stanford (Philip 1986). Faced with too many qualified Asian-American applicants, many believe that universities, overtly or covertly, are limiting the number of Asian Americans they admit.

In recent years, the University of California at Berkeley, the flagship of the University of California system, has placed more emphasis on nonacademic criteria for admission. The percentage of Asian-American freshmen enrolled at Berkeley has declined from a high nearing 27% of the freshman class in 1983 to barely 20% in 1986. (For other relevant statistics see tables 2, 3, 4, and 5.)

TABLE 2
Asian Freshman Enrollment 1983-86
University of California at Berkeley

1983	1,196	26.9%
1984	1,008	24.1
1985	843	21.0
1986	691	20.6

Source: Lye (1986).

TABLE 3
Percentage of Applicants
Application/Admission Ratio 1979-1986

	Asians	Whites
1979	76.7%	72.7%
1980	57.7	56.8
1981	47.6	49.0
1982	43.4	56.9
1983	47.7	61.1
1984	34.3	48.1
1985	42.0	48.0
1986	29.0	32.0

Source: Lye (1986).

TABLE 4
National SAT Averages in 1984

	Verbal	Math
Asians	398	519
Whites	445	487

Source: Lye (1986).

TABLE 5
Estimated Eligibility Rates for 1983 Graduates of California's Public High Schools

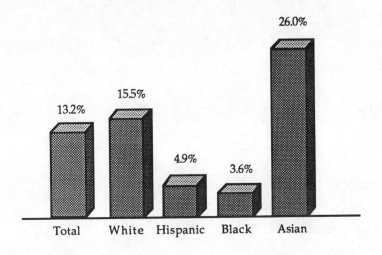

Source: Lye (1986).

Many believe that this decline in Asian-American enrollment can be traced to new admissions policies that stress nonacademic factors. These nonacademic factors now considered by U.C. Berkeley include a variety of subjective qualities such as leadership, character, motivation, accomplishment in extracurricular activities, and economic hardship, as judged by essays the applicants submit to the Admissions Office (Asian American Task Force 1985; Lye 1986).

What factors contribute to this declining enrollment? Do admissions officials apply subtle cultural and linguistic standards, either consciously or subconsciously, that serve to exclude Asian Americans?

Statistically, admissions records of all the universities discussed show that Asian-American freshmen generally score higher in their aggregate test scores than white freshmen (Butterfield 1986; Biemiller 1986; Asian American

Task Force 1985). Private universities stress that the lower number of Asian Americans enrolled, compared to the number of qualified candidates, results from the universities' attempts to maintain ethnic diversity, alumni community, and equal representation. It has been suggested, however, that if all other factors are held constant, the new nonacademic factors stressed by the top universities do limit the number of Asian-American students admitted.

How the universities rate the students' "other" qualities is crucial. A common stereotype is that Asian-American students spend most of their time on academic learning and relatively little time on extracurricular activities, but according to data reported by Tsang and Wing (1985), Asian-American high school students' participation rates in selected extracurricular activities, from varsity sports to community involvement, is comparable to that of white students.

TABLE 6
Student Participation in Selected Extracurricular Activities

Extracurricular activities	Asian-Pacific	White
Athletics:		
Varsity athletic teams	30%	34%
Other athletic teams	37	40
Artistic:		
Debating or drama	9	13
Band or orchestra	13	14
Chorus or dance	15	18
Intellectual:		
Honorary club	28	17
School newspaper, yearbook	18	19
Subject-matter clubs	26	20
Student council, government	21	16
Community:		
Vocational education clubs	7	22
Community youth organizations	10	16
Church youth group activities	27	35
Junior achievement	9	4

Source: Tsang and Wing (1985).

Assuming that Asian-American applicants to U.C. Berkeley are similar to those represented in table 6, what are the reasons for their disproportionately high rejection rate? While racism may be a contributing factor, I posit that subconscious, culturally-based procedures used to evaluate the applicants' written essays may play an important role. For students admitted under special consideration, half of the freshman class in 1987, essays counted more heavily than SAT scores. Admissions officers may be applying culturally-based evaluative criteria in judging the subjective qualifications of the students. For Asian-American applicants to these universities, personal qualities, character, motivation, and intention are judged according to how the applicants present this information in their essays. Because of the large number of immigrants in this group for whom English is a second language, lack of English proficiency has likely been a factor in some rejections.

Important cultural and linguistic differences, however, are frequently conveyed not in the use of correct grammar and pronunciation, but in the discourse and narrative of spoken or written texts. Although officials at U.C. Berkeley and other universities have stated that grammatical mistakes will not be a criterion in their evaluation of students' qualifications (Lye 1986), other subtle cultural nuances, attitudes, and values can be miscommunicated and therefore negatively evaluated because of a student's lack of command of the discourse and writing conventions of the language. Asian Americans face similar subjective evaluative gatekeeping situations in the job market.

Asian Americans and Access to the Job Market

As was discussed earlier, the high median family income of Asian Americans represents a higher level of education and more hours worked than whites and does not reflect parity in the job market. Two indicators of economic parity are discussed here: advancement/level of position and choice of profession.

Occupationally, the majority of the Asian Americans who hold managerial or professional positions are at the lower end of the field. Asian Americans in general have not attained positions of power and control (Kim and Hurh 1986). In the corporate world, only half of one percent, a scant 159 out of 29,000, of the officers and directors of the nation's largest companies listed under the Fortune 500 have Asian surnames (Ramirez 1986).

The choice of professions is limited for Asians as well. They are generally limited to professions that are technical in nature. A relatively large percentage of Asian Americans have achieved professional employment in areas such as architecture, engineering, dentistry, and accounting (Vernon 1982). The reasons given for Asian Americans' preference for (and ability to excel in) professions that require abstract and mathematical skills rather than verbal skills have invariably been related to the group's unfamiliarity with the English language. Harry Kitano of UCLA (Ramirez 1986) believes that the stereotype of an American corporate officer as a white male has discouraged Asian Americans from pursuing corporate careers. Instead Asian Americans choose professions where they believe performance is judged objectively.

In this paper, however, I will argue that familiarity with culturally specific communicative conventions, rather than knowledge of language per se, is the most important factor in creating the perception of competence. A recent, concrete example of how cultural and linguistic differences have influenced the employment opportunities of Asian Americans can be seen in the case of the licensing of foreign nurses in California.

In response to the severe nursing shortage nationwide, foreign nurses were recruited to work in the U.S. on temporary visas. As a condition of their recruitment, these nurses had to pass a licensing examination within six months. Of the more than ten thousand foreign nurses recruited, approximately 60% were Filipinos (Tamayo 1981). The passing rate for the Filipino nurses in the California licensing examination was a dismal 12.6%. It was far lower than the 84.4% passing rate for whites. Other minorities' passing rates were 53.6% for Native Americans, 52% for Hispanics, 36.8% for blacks, and 22.8% for Asian and Pacific Islanders.

The validity of the nurses' licensing examination was challenged on the grounds of job-relatedness, that is, it was claimed the test did not reflect the actual content of the job. As a result, the State Board of Registered Nursing held a public hearing and proposed that interim permits be issued for two years to allow the foreign nurses to acculturate before taking the test. In the meantime, foreign nurses were to practice under the supervision of registered nurses. This proposal brought immediate protest from nursing advocates. Among the complaints were some questions about the competence and attitude of the Filipino nurses. The low examination scores were supported by personal anecdotes of incompetence (Campbell 1981).

Interviews with those on both sides of the dispute revealed that many of the charges of incompetence and poor communication could be traced to cultural differences. Campbell (1981) compiled a list of charges and countercharges. Many complaints about the competence and "bad attitudes" of Filipino nurses reflect the differences in culture and what is considered acceptable behavior in each culture. For example, the Filipino nurses were accused of not working hard enough. The Filipino nurses claimed that they did not know how to appear to be working hard as U.S. nurses do. The Filipino nurses were charged with being unprofessional because they generally did not question orders or take initiative, yet cultural constraints discourage Filipino nurses from challenging authority directly. Cultural differences in displaying cues that indicate acknowledgment (feedback or "back-channeling") also contributed to the perception that Filipino nurses do not acknowledge others when addressed. As a result, the nurses were also accused of not acknowledging instruction. Another strong indicator of cultural misunderstanding can be seen in complaints that the Filipino nurses did not understand and follow instructions. When they did call for clarification, however, they were accused of calling doctors too much.

As a result of the controversy, the legislature proposed new guidelines, which added an oral test to the licensing procedure. This case illustrates how communicative differences can substantially affect employment opportunities. Little has been written in the testing literature about subjective evaluations such as oral tests, even though subjective evaluations are widely used to determine individual access to economic and educational opportunities. The importance of these culturally-based evaluations, however, has not gone unnoticed in the fields of linguistics and anthropology.

Cultural/Linguistic Mismatch and Competence Assessments

It is well established (Gumperz 1982a, 1982b; Halliday and Hasan 1976) that native speakers subconsciously evaluate and interpret abilities and intentions of others through language behavior, both verbally and in writing. Speakers are evaluated according to their ability to employ the proper speech conventions in various situations in ways acceptable to the dominant social group.

While the full extent of the problem caused by mismatches in speech conventions is not fully understood, the literature reviewed here supports the position that negative judgments frequently result from impressionistic assessments like those mentioned about the Filipino nurses. The more commonly discussed problems of grammar, sentence construction, or pronunciation are not at issue. Even in fields such as the teaching of English as a second language, where professionals are considered more "enlightened" because of their experience with individuals of other cultures, Chinese speakers are often characterized as "excessively deferential, evasive, and lacking in assertiveness" (Wong 1986).

Speech conventions carry with them subtle, culturally-based meanings and attitudes. Often proper or improper usage of these speech conventions is used by native speakers to evaluate work-related abilities and attitudes (Gumperz 1982a, 1982b). These culturally specific speech conventions, most often displayed subconsciously, can convey the wrong signals when persons of different cultural backgrounds attempt to interpret the linguistic behaviors of others according to their own cultural and linguistic norms. Violation of the native speaker's expectation can result in negative evaluation of the speech partner's intent. The subtle features can be speech prosody, turn allocation, politeness markers, and word order (Gumperz 1982a, 1982b). Investigation into the evaluative process used by native English speakers is important to members of the Asian-American community because informal assessments of this nature can hamper the access of qualified Asian Americans to academic, social, and economic opportunities.

We will introduce some pertinent research findings to explicate the possible effects of cultural mismatches in both content and style. The examples to be introduced involve settings where English speakers are evaluating non-native English speakers with respect to their abilities, intentions, and attitudes.

III. RESEARCH ON CULTURALLY SPECIFIC LINGUISTIC CONVENTIONS

Cultural influences on language are manifested in many ways. Anthropologists and linguists have studied ways in which cultural knowledge is encoded in aspects of the grammar, for example, in the organization of sets of related words such as those denoting kinship or color. However, we will deal only with the less frequently discussed area of interactions between content, form, and discourse structure that produce culturally specific patterns.

The first part of this section establishes that discourse strategies specific to one language can cross over to another language when speakers of the first language begin to acquire the grammar and vocabulary of the second language. Consequently, native speakers of the second language, who possess their own culturally specific patterns of discourse, may misinterpret the intent of the non-native speaker who is displaying different communicative norms even while using the grammar and vocabulary of the second language. The impact of such a mismatch in language conventions is discussed in the second part of this section. The third part focuses on the manifestation of this cultural/linguistic mismatch in written discourse, while the fourth part relates cross-cultural linguistic behavior to real-life gatekeeping situations such as job interviews.

Culturally Specific Discourse Strategies

A possible explanation for the persistent stereotype that Asian Americans are humble, nonassertive, and lacking in leadership skills may lie in the different discourse strategies used by native speakers of Asian languages. For example, native Chinese speakers favor a discourse style that appears to Westerners to be indirect (Kaplan 1966). To native Chinese speakers, however, that same style is believed to be appropriate and effective (Young 1982). This style carries over even when Chinese speak English. In business meetings where discussion is conducted in English by native Chinese speakers, the participants employ a discourse strategy whereby a buildup precedes the topic summary statement. The summary statement is italicized in the following example.

> Chairman: So by purchasing this new machine, do you think we need to recruit additional workers or will our existing workforce cope with our requirement?

> Alpha: I think that with this new machine, the production time will be shortened or will become more efficient. And the number of staff required, I think, we can utilize the existing staff for the time being. And no more new staff is necessary. *So that we can solve the problem in recruiting the new staff.*

This discourse style has been attributed to the basic topic/comment sentence structure of Chinese (as opposed to the subject/predicate structure of English). The topic in the topic/comment sentence sets a framework for the predication (Li and Thompson 1976). It also sets the spatial, temporal, or perceptual framework for the following assertion (Chafe 1976). It is also believed that in languages like Chinese, old information is usually at the start of the sentence (Chao 1968). The order of the information in the discourse also conforms to the unmarked word order under the following clause types in Chinese.

Because_____therefore_____(Causal)

If_____then_____(Conditional)

Although_____but_____(Concessive)

Following the sequencing of information within the sentence boundary, Chinese speakers systematically favor steadily unraveling and building up information before arriving at the important message. The listener is presented with all of the old information and rationale before the punchline is delivered. In the following example, which illustrates this point, the speaker is making a request to increase the budget on magazine advertising:

> Theta: One thing I would like to ask. Because most of our raw materials are coming from Japan and . . . this year is going up and up and, uh, it's not really I think an increase in price but, uh, we lose a lot in exchange rate. And, secondly, I understand we've spent a lot in exchange rate and. . . secondly I understand we've spent of money in TV ads last year. *So, in that case I would like to suggest here: chop half of the budget in TV ads and spend a little money on Mad magazines.*

The Chinese discourse style differs markedly from the one favored by English speakers, who prefer to state the summary before the rationale or information is given. The English speaker's preference for this discourse order is also carried over to written discourse. Remember how persistently your English teacher urged you to state the thesis of the narrative (which interestingly is sometimes called the topic sentence) at the beginning of each paragraph?

English speakers, when asked to listen to the same discussion, commented on the lack of clarity, precision, and forcefulness of the discourse.

The style led some to be suspicious of the intent of the speakers, who were believed to be "beating around the bush." Discourse styles are culturally specific. No matter how carefully non-native speakers attend to English grammar and pronounciation, an inadvertent use of different discourse style can cause the speakers to be judged negatively. Conversely, native English speakers evaluate the attitudes and intentions of others according to their correct use of appropriate speech style.

Face-to-Face Job Interviews

A common, but critical speech situation is a face-to-face job interview. In a job interview, an applicant has to impress the interviewer, who most often is ignorant of his/her skills, interests, and other positive attributes. As Akinnaso and Ajirotutu (1982) have outlined, a formal job interview is distinguished from other natural speech situations by the following characteristics:

- It normally arises out of a scheduled appointment.

- Its purpose is explicit by nature.

- A deliberate recording of the proceeding is kept.

- An agenda or some form of program is used.

- It follows a fixed organizational structure and the strict allocation of rights and duties.

At a prearranged time, a candidate is interviewed by one or more representatives of the employer. The purpose of the interview is well understood by all who are involved. Typically, the interviewer attempts in a short period of time to elicit the responses he or she desires. The candidates attempt to impress the interviewer with their verbal answers or comments based on what they think the interviewer wants to know. An account of the job interview is kept because the activity is supposed to lead to some kind of decision. The written record serves to document the outcome of this activity.

A job interview typically follows a certain format, including an opening that consists of a greeting and introduction. Experienced interviewers generally try to put candidates at ease by engaging them in small talk before the formal interview begins and the interviewer tries to elicit the information he or she wants. The closing of an interview is signaled with explicit markers such as "I have no more questions" or " Do you have any questions?" During this time a role reversal takes place and the candidate can ask the interviewer questions.

A job interview follows strict communicative rules mainly because of the difference in power between the interviewer and the candidate. By agreeing to participate in the interview, the candidate has agreed to follow the rules set by the interviewer, who has the power to commence, interrupt, terminate, or change the topic. The candidate is compelled by his or her desire to be hired to provide the answers the interviewer needs to evaluate his or her ability to perform the work.

TABLE 7

A Sample Job Interview Activity Sequence

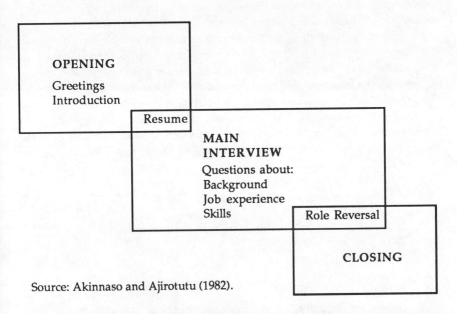

OPENING

Greetings
Introduction

Resume

**MAIN
INTERVIEW**

Questions about:
Background
Job experience
Skills

Role Reversal

CLOSING

Source: Akinnaso and Ajirotutu (1982).

According to Akinnaso and Ajirotutu, the special evaluative nature of a job interview requires that verbal exchanges be structured in such a way that the interviewer can elicit the responses he or she needs to evaluate the candidate. Often, information is elicited indirectly, so that the candidate must infer the information wanted. To successfully negotiate a job interview and to interpret correctly the subtle intent of the questions posed, a candidate must have a clear understanding of the value system of the interviewer. In addition, he or she must be able to convey responses in a culturally appropriate style with proper nonverbal cues. The interviewer evaluates the candidate's abilities through these culturally determined conventions of use. Since the ability to negotiate such linguistic conventions may or may not be relevant to the abilities required on the job, the candidate who scores highest in an interview may not be the person with the best job qualifications. In these cases, "What counts is the ability to conform to the principles of rhetoric by which performance is judged in bureaucratic systems" (Gumperz and Cook-Gumperz 1982).

In a typical job interview, the interviewer is most likely a member of the socially dominant group. He or she will therefore employ the values of the dominant social group in evaluating candidates. Those candidates unfamiliar with the culturally specific linguistic rules can expect to be judged negatively if their responses do not fall within the expected range. The use of the wrong culturally specific form or content in a response can be perceived negatively and may reflect upon the candidate's ability. Furthermore, the more often an interviewer hears incompatible speech conventions, the more negative cultural stereotypes about attitudes, values, and abilities will be reinforced.

Unfamiliar with the speech conventions and the underlying structure of the interview process, immigrant Asian Americans frequently fail to negotiate the complexity of the speech conventions required in a job interview. They fail to convince the interviewer of their abilities and are thus barred from jobs even though their qualifications for the job may not be in question.

In a study conducted by the author (Tsang 1985) using a videotaped sequence of mock job interviews of three Chinese-American females, the candidates committed many errors that violated the accepted speech conventions of the job interview. A common error committed by the candidates, all in their thirties and all residents of the U.S. for an average of five years, was responding in culturally inappropriate ways.

> Interviewer: If you were the manager, were there cases you would have dealt with differently?
> Candidate: Uh, meaning?
> Interviewer: You would have handled the customer differently than the manager did?
> Candidate: Usually I agree with the manager 'cause they got more experience than I. That's why I always agree with them.
> Interviewer: Was there a case you didn't agree with them?
> Candidate: No, I don't think so. No.

In this case, the interviewer, a white woman in her forties who was a personnel officer from a national corporation, was seeking to clarify how the candidate dealt with troublesome customers in her previous job as a cocktail hostess. According to the candidate, her manager usually asked someone else to wait on the troublesome customers. The interviewer was probing for the candidate's true feelings about a stressful situation where conflict was obvious. She wanted to know about the candidate's ability to negotiate with her superior in instances where different ideas prevail. Instead of interpreting the question that way, the candidate thought the interviewer was asking whether she always agreed with her supervisor, a culturally acceptable behavior for Chinese. The candidate did not change her culturally inappropriate response, even when the interviewer cued her again by asking a followup question, "Was there a case you didn't agree with them?"

Another common mistake committed by the Asian-American candidates was their tendency toward self-deprecation (another normal behavior in Chinese culture) when asked to evaluate themselves.

> Interviewer: What kinds of grades did you get in your computer classes?
> Candidate: Cs and Bs, but never an A.

> Interviewer: What kind of courses did you take at the city college?
> Candidate: English, ESL.
> Interviewer: How did you do?
> Candidate: That was a couple of years ago.

In both examples, the candidates failed to make use of the opportunity to display and to convince others of their abilities. In the first instance, the candidate could have said, "I would have gotten an A had my English been better at that time." In the second example, the candidate totally avoided the question even though it was known that she did very well in that class.

Significantly, all of the candidates failed to understand the underlying nature of an interview. Every question asked and every response in the interview is an opportunity for the candidates to display their skills and abilities. The interviewer expects certain responses with each question that she asks, and each response is evaluated according to her expectation, resulting in an impression of the candidate's abilities that the interviewer employs in determining who is to be hired. Too often the Asian-American candidates answered the questions at the superficial level.

> Interviewer: Do they keep you busy?
> Candidate: Yes, all of the time. (By not elaborating on the answer, the candidate fails to convey to the interviewer her ability to handle a large workload, the exact information the interviewer was expecting. The result left the interviewer questioning the candidate's efficiency and her ability to stand up under pressure.)

> Interviewer: How do you like completing our application? Was it hard?
> Candidate: It's OK.

> Interviewer: How do you like your job at Dean Witter?
> Candidate: Good, I love it a lot.

Interviewer: What was your job at the hair-styling salon like?
Candidate: Like, uh.
Interviewer: What kind of things did you do?
Candidate: I answer the phone.

In all instances, the interviewer was asking for more than what appears on the surface of the question. The candidates, however, because of their unfamiliarity with the underlying structure and inherent purpose of the interview, responded only to the surface question. Their lack of understanding of the conventions used in a job interview led the candidates to be negatively evaluated.

Written Discourse Accent

Outside of pronunciation accent and grammatical error, one area that has received attention recently is the difference between writing styles of Asian Americans and white Americans. As Wong describes (1986), "Experienced teachers have repeatedly attested to the existence of something noticeably unnative-like in the written discourse" of non-native English speakers. The phrase "written discourse accent" has been used to describe these elusive qualities that are not triggered by surface grammatical errors. This working phrase is used here to cover features ranging from the deviation from expected content because of cultural differences to the organization of "narrative" due to linguistic differences both in sentence and discourse level of any written materials. Native speakers tend to form impressions of the character, intention, and abilities of others based on discourse material and the form in which it is presented. Such written discourse accent may color the judgment of native speakers in gatekeeping situations and result in negative evaluations of non-native speakers.

Wong (1986), in her review of literature concerning the acquisition of English for Chinese speakers, discussed several levels of research that relate to this topic. As was discussed earlier, at the sentence level, she found that the topic-comment nature of the Chinese sentence (proposed by Li and Thompson) may contribute to differences in organization of units larger than sentences. The topic in Chinese exerts significant discourse influence over the boundary of sentences, while in English the subject exerts less influence. For this reason, Chinese speakers "may end up with correct individual sentences which nonetheless create an impression of foreignness when read in succession."

Research studies have also pointed out Chinese speakers' preference for certain English sentence types, and their use of conjunctions based on the influence of the native language and familiarity with the language (Hu, Brown, and Brown 1982; Johns 1984).

Kaplan's claim (1972) of native-language discourse style as a chief factor in deviation from the expected organization of English written discourse (a claim also suggested by Young 1982) was criticized by other researchers in this area. Both Wong (1986) and Mohan and Lo (1985) question Kaplan's characterization of the Chinese indirect discourse style versus the linear and direct discourse style favored by native English speakers.

Mohan and Lo pointed out that the different instructional emphasis in language writing skills, such as correct sentence structure versus proper organization, may contribute to the difference in written English discourse styles of non-native English speakers. Wong, on the other hand, asserts that "digression, lack of paragraph unity, incoherence in thought, etc., are hardly the monopoly of foreign learners of English but are common problems among 'basic writers' who are native English-speaking but unfamiliar with the convention of written exposition." However, the persisting difference in discourse style between writings of those of advanced academic levels merits further research.

Cultural orientation and values play an important role in the perceived accent in the written discourse of non-native English speakers. Since cultural values can be retained over generations, second- or third-generation Asian Americans in the U.S. may still express such cultural values in their written discourse. This topic has also been studied outside of the U.S. For example, studies have found (Hu, Brown, and Brown 1982) that Chinese-speaking students display certain culturally specific tendencies in the contents of their writings that are consistently different from those of Australian students. "In short, the Chinese and Australian students approached the topic with a different set of cultural assumptions and role expectations." While this study conducted by Hu, Brown, and Brown uses Australian students as a comparison group, the point about the different writing style of the Chinese students demonstrates a consistent cultural pattern

For example, Chinese and Australian students were asked, "Pretend that you have a brother who does not work hard at school, what would you say that might persuade him to work hard?" The Chinese students frequently emphasized the importance of education to the nation, while the Australian students rarely mentioned this point. Chinese students wrote as if they were directly addressing a younger brother, using imperatives such as "Try to make sense of your life and study hard at school." The Australian students employed a more objective approach, using suggestions such as "If he works hard, he may one day be as brainy as his big brother" (McKay 1984).

In a separate study of topic predictability and its relation to the cultural background of the students, McKay shows that writing topic is highly influenced by the writer's cultural background, even if the topic is written in a foreign language. McKay (1984) found widespread similarities in essays written by Chinese students in response to the open question, "You were standing in a long queue at a bus stop one evening. First, describe the scene, and then go on to say what happened when it began to rain heavily." Many common themes and episodes can be found in the 113 essays analyzed. Most described the reason for the bus trip, with 41 indicating that they were going to visit a friend or relative, while 31 stated that they were going to or returning from work. Fifty-one of the 113 students mentioned that the rain started suddenly and 55 referred to women, children, or old people in the crowd. And most striking is the drawing of a moral lesson, atypical in personal narrative essays in English, whereas 47 of the Chinese students ended their essay with a moral lesson. The following is a typical example:

> There were several old persons, they must have been ill because of the heavy rain. I hesitated for a moment, but I didn't move. "Why shall I give up my seat and the others don't do? Just then, the young people all came out and gave up their seats. They asked the old to stand in their places. After these, they stood in front of the old to prevent the rain.

> All the waiting persons were moved by their deeds. The old persons' hearts were very warm though they only could say "Thank you. Thanks very much." My face became red and I felt very shy. So I gave up my seat to a pale middle-aged woman.

> The thing happened in 1984. Does everyone only take care of himself? Is everyone selfish? The answer is "No." In today's society, people know it's important to warm each other. (McKay 1984)

While all the participants in these studies are students in a foreign country, the principal findings in these research projects still have important implications for Asian Americans. Because of their recent immigration and the predominant practice of their native languages and cultures in their homes, a large number of Asian Americans can be expected to exhibit cultural values specific to their backgrounds that may not be compatible with those of dominant white society in the U.S. The question remains to be answered whether second- and third-generation Asian Americans growing up with English as their best language still exhibit in their English any such cultural traits in the content or use of linguistic conventions.

Job Application Letters of Asian Americans

Written discourse accent can be interpreted in different ways in various communicative situations in the U.S. It has been argued that middle-class whites in the U.S. share a particular cultural style in writing persuasive job application letters. Those who do not produce the expected style are quickly passed over in favor of those whose style is compatible (Murray 1981). Asian Americans, for various reasons, deviate from this norm in their writing styles more often than middle-class whites do, and are thus negatively evaluated and consequently rejected for jobs for which they are qualified.

A good letter of application should include information that is recent, positive, and most importantly, relevant. In a good letter, the information about the applicant's skills must relate directly to the need or the potential need of the employer. A successful job seeker must draw the correct inferences from the information available in order to construct a pertinent application letter of effective persuasive power and proper style. Murray argues "the life experience of middle class whites seems to include practice in recognizing unstated expectations of evaluators and in appropriately tailoring self-presentations." Asian Americans are at a disadvantage because they lack such practice and experience.

A related issue is the gatekeeper (interviewer or evaluator) who employs screening strategies that quickly reject applicants who seem odd, irrational, or incompetent. These strategies are adopted for specific reasons. First, employers must use their time as efficiently as possible. Their task is therefore not to consider the largest number of applicants, but to screen the number of applicants to a select few who are well qualified for the job. Second, accepting someone who appears "odd" or has "a negative attitude" exposes the gatekeeper to criticism if the candidate fails to live up to expectations. Third, the tolerance for error in screening out a qualified candidate is much greater than the tolerance for letting in the wrong person, since those who are rejected have either "odd" or other "unqualifying" characteristics. In short, the prevailing practice is—when in doubt, reject!

In view of this information, it is no surprise that Asian-American job applicants fare much worse than their white counterparts. In a study of fifty-seven application files for engineering positions with the evaluation carried out by three whites, Asian Americans were three times more likely to be rejected than whites. There were twelve rejections out of sixteen Asian Americans and five out of fifteen for whites. All letters containing grammatical errors were automatically rejected. However, examination of other letters rejected show the function of the three maxims: recency, positivity, and relevancy.

A Filipino American was rejected because the gatekeeper considered the applicant to lack knowledge of "what's expected of him" and that "he doesn't know the score." This applicant had included in his letter that he was "Mr. Mathematics of 6th grade" in a Manila school. The gatekeeper deemed the inclusion of such information ridiculous, particularly since the applicant had not listed comparable information about his college education. Furthermore, the information was not judged relevant even though mathematical skills are essential for an engineering position.

In another letter furnished by a Chinese-American, the applicant stated, "I am very unsatisfy (sic) with my current employment. I believe I am qualified for the work described and am interested in hearing more about the opportunity at your company." The fact that the applicant shows dissatisfaction with his current employer implied to the gatekeeper that this person would be difficult to get along with. The honest feeling of the applicant is thus interpreted as a bad attitude and the applicant is seen as a potential troublemaker.

A Jordanian engineer's statement that he is "deeply interested in various civil engineering tasks" was judged an illogical use of the word "deeply" in a letter of this nature. Similarly, an Indian applicant's characterization of himself as possessing qualities of "cheerfulness" was considered incongruous with the norm for the task for which he was applying.

In an engineering position, the ability to write standard English narrative is job-related. The applicants, however, were being selected according to their ability to write English using subtle, culturally specific forms, structure, and content to relate what is considered to be relevant information. The applicants discussed were therefore rejected because they violated social norms of which they were unaware. Once again, the evaluator's cultural values and linguistic conventions interacted to produce a negative judgment of the applicants' abilities, attitudes, and intentions.

IV. CONCLUSION

In the last section I have shown that the values specific to a culture can be conveyed in both spoken and written forms of languages other than that of the host culture's. Yet native speakers of English often interpret the intention, abilities, and attitudes of non-native speakers based on their expression of culturally incompatible values and language-use conventions. These interpretations are often not correlated to the real abilities of the speakers. Since these casual judgments are often used in job interviews, college admissions applications, and other such gatekeeping encounters, Asian Americans who do not possess the same linguistic background as those judging are at a disadvantage. Uninformed evaluators may make decisions that are culturally based without even being aware of how their backgrounds determine their judgments.

Many questions remain unanswered. First, research must be conducted to determine the extent to which cultural aspects of communication influence evaluative processes. Basic research in this area has netted good data, and educators, armed with this basic knowledge, have obtained useful results in educational settings such as classroom interaction. But systematic research in situations where linguistic behavior is the basis for informal evaluation has not been undertaken. Extensive research must be done to further verify how culture shapes such informal judgments. Researchers should also study the correlation between these judgments and actual qualifications, including on-the-job performance. Since many Asian Americans who have been denied access to educational and economic opportunities were born in this country and speak English as their best language, it would be revealing to study the extent to which home culture and home language have affected their use of American English linguistic conventions. Finally, item analysis of the standardized tests, particularly the verbal section, should be conducted to help understand the low verbal scores Asian Americans consistently obtain.

For the policymaker concerned with unbiased assessment of candidates, the studies reported here clearly indicate the important role these informal assessments play in the gatekeeping process. Of particular concern is when proposals have been made to allow for more extensive use of such informal assessment, as in the case of the University of California admissions policy. While such flexibilities can sometimes be beneficial, the lack of rigor in the judgment process renders them unsound. There is, in general, too much room for abuse, whether conscious or not.

In fact, evaluators may search for linguistic behaviors in the candidates they judge that fit into the stereotype of the candidates' ethnic group. Low verbal test scores and culturally specific behaviors not only serve to explain why Asians have not gained access to certain employment and academic opportunities, but also are now used as reasons for excluding Asians from these opportunities. The issue is now whether there is a true question of competence or whether these factors are an excuse for discrimination.

To settle this issue, cultural and linguistic differences must be demonstrated to directly affect the quality of work, whether academic or professional. On the other hand, the dominant group may intentionally or unintentionally impose entry requirements for abilities not necessary for the tasks involved. If these subjective evaluations must be used, policy guidelines must be set up to ensure that evaluators receive proper training so they do not make decisions based on irrelevant criteria.

The Asian-American community must become aware of the factors that may affect the outcome of any evaluation. Educational achievement, based on formal testing and evaluation, is not the only basis on which economic or even educational opportunities are awarded. Should the community continue the passive and tacit strategy of "tell us what is required and we will show you what we can do?" Or should it actively discover how access to opportunities is determined? Another question is whether or not the group should be treated as a social minority. Should Asian Americans be treated as individuals and compete with other ethnic groups with no special treatment accorded? All of these are important questions with far-reaching implications. Asian Americans will play an increasingly important role in our society. Can white Americans accept a pluralistic society? At the heart of our nation's history is the ideal of equal opportunity for all. Asian Americans may test how strongly we believe in that ideal.

REFERENCES

Akinnaso, F. N., and C. S. Ajirotutu. 1982. Performance and ethnic style in job interviews. In *Language and social identity*, ed. J. Gumperz. Cambridge: Cambridge University Press.

Asian American Task Force on University Admissions. 1985. *Task force report*. San Francisco.

Biemiller, L. 1986. Asian students fear top colleges use quota system. *The Chronicle of Higher Education* 33(12).

Butterfield, F. 1986. Why Asians are going to the head of the class. *New York Times*, Section 12, 3 Aug., 18–23.

Campbell, D. R. 1981. Interactional sources of incompetence allegations in the dispute over licensing Filipino nurses in California. Paper presented at the 80th annual meeting of the American Anthropological Association, Los Angeles.

Chafe, W. 1976. Giveness, contrastiveness, definiteness, subjects, topics and point of view. In *Subject and topic*, ed. C. Li. New York: Academic Press.

Chao, Y. R. 1968. *A grammar of spoken Chinese*. Berkeley and Los Angeles: University of California Press.

DBS Corporation. 1982. *1980 elementary and secondary schools civil rights survey: National summaries*. Washington, DC: Office of Civil Rights, U.S. Department of Education.

Gumperz, J. J. 1982a. *Discourse strategies*. Cambridge: Cambridge University Press.

Gumperz, J. J., ed. 1982b. *Language and social identity*. Cambridge: Cambridge University Press.

Gumperz, J. J. and J. Cook-Gumperz. 1982. Introduction: Language and the communication of social identity. In *Language and social identity*, ed. J. J. Gumperz. Cambridge: Cambridge University Press.

Halliday, M. A. K., and R. Hasan. 1976. *Cohesion in English*. London: Longman.

Hu, Z., D. F. Brown, and L. B. Brown. 1982. Some linguistic differences in the written English of Chinese and Australian students. *Language Learning and Communication* 1:39–49.

Johns, A. M. 1984. Textual comprehension and the Chinese speaker of English. *Language Learning and Communication* 3:69–74.

Kan, S. H., and W. T. Liu. 1986. The education status of Asian Americans: An update from the 1980 census. *Pacific/Asian American Mental Health Research Center* 5, nos. 3/4.

Kaplan, R. B. 1966. Cultural thought patterns in intercultural education. *Language Learning* 16:1–20.

———. 1972. *The anatomy of rhetoric: Prolegomena to a functional theory of rhetoric*. Concord, MA: Heinle and Heinle.

Karabal, J., and A. H. Halsey. 1977. *Power and ideology in education.* New York: Oxford University Press.

Kim, K. C., and W. M. Hurh. 1986. Asian Americans and the "success" image: A critique. *Pacific/Asian American Mental Health Research Center* 5, nos. 1/2.

Li, C., and S. Thompson. 1976. Subject and topic: A new typology of language. In *Subject and topic,* ed. C. Li. New York: Academic Press.

Lye, C. 1986. Is there a "ceiling" under the table? *Berkeley Graduate* 1 (3).

McKay, S. L. 1984. Topic development and written discourse accent. Paper presented at the 1984 TESOL Convention.

Mohan, B., and W. A. Lo. 1985. Academic writing and Chinese students: Transfer and developmental factors. *TESOL Quarterly* 19:515–534.

Murray, S. 1981. "Gatekeepers" shared procedures and the disproportionate elimination of Asian-American applicants. Paper presented at the 80th annual meeting of the American Anthropological Association. Los Angeles.

Peng, S. S., O. A. Jeffrey, and W. B. Fetters. 1984. *School experiences and performance of Asian American high school students.* Washington, DC: U.S. Department of Education, Office of Educational Research and Improvement (April).

Philip, T. 1986. Stanford studies possible Asian bias in admissions. *San Jose Mercury News* (November 12).

Ramirez, A. 1986. America's super minority. *Fortune,* 27 Nov., 148–61.

Refugee Reports. 1987. Indochinese Refugee Program as of June 30, 1986. Vol. 7, no. 8.

Tamayo, W. R. 1981. Foreign nurses and the U.S. nursing crisis. *Immigration Newsletter* 10, no. 4.

Tsang, C. L. 1985. Job talk. Paper presented at the seventh annual meeting of the National Association for Asian Pacific American Education. New York.

Tsang, S., and L. C. Wing. 1985. *Beyond Angel Island: The education of Asian Americans.* ERIC/CUE Urban Diversity Series #90.

U.S. Bureau of the Census. 1981. *1980 Census of population, Volume I, Characteristics of the population, Chapter D, Detailed population characteristics, Part I, United States summary, Section A: United States.* Report no. PC-80-1-D1-A. Washington, DC: Bureau of the Census, U.S. Department of Commerce, December.

————. 1983. *1980 Census of population, Volume I, Characteristics of the population, Chapter C, General social and economic characteristics, Part I, United States summary.* Report no. PC80-1-Cl. Washington, DC: Bureau of the Census, U.S. Department of Commerce, December.

————. 1984. *1980 Census of population, Volume I, Characteristics of the population, Chapter D, Detailed population characteristics, Part I,*

United States summary, Section A: United States. Report no. PC-80-1-Dl-A. Washington, DC: Bureau of the Census, U.S. Department of Commerce, December.

U. S. Commission on Civil Rights. 1980. *Success of Asian Americans: Fact or fiction?* Clearinghouse Publication 64. Washington, DC: U.S. Commission on Civil Rights (September).

Vernon, P. 1982. *The abilities and achievements of Orientals in North America.* New York: Academic Press.

Wong, S. C. 1986. What we do and don't know about Chinese learners of English: Suggestions for needed research. Eighth annual meeting of the National Association for Asian Pacific American Education. Los Angeles.

Young, L. W. L. 1982. Inscrutability revisited. In *Language and social identity,* ed. J. Gumperz. Cambridge: Cambridge Univ. Press.

Black and White Cultural Styles in Pluralistic Perspective

Thomas Kochman

I. INTRODUCTION

American society is presently in a period of social transition from a structurally pluralistic society to a culturally pluralistic one. The difference between the two kinds of pluralism is in the political arrangement of their culturally heterogeneous parts. Within structural pluralism the socially subordinate cultural person or group unilaterally accommodates the dominant (Anglo-American male) cultural group on the latter's terms. This pattern of accommodation can be said to have constituted an American policy orientation regarding the integration of immigrants and (with further important qualification) indigenous and other minorities into the larger American society. As Theodore Roosevelt said in 1919: "If the immigrant who comes here in good faith becomes an American and assimilates himself to us he shall be treated on an exact equality with everyone else." (*El Grito* 1968, 1).

The "us" or "American" in Roosevelt's statement represents the socially dominant Anglo-American male, only recently (within the framework of cultural pluralism) identified as a "hyphenated" American too, alongside Afro-American, Irish-American, Polish-American, Italian-American, Jewish-American, et al., but having (within the framework of structural pluralism) effectively pre-empted the unhyphenated term "American" for themselves, with others being less "American" to the extent that they were "hyphenated." As Roosevelt said in the same speech: "But this [equality] is predicated on the man's becoming in very fact an American and nothing but an American. . . . There can be no divided allegiance here. Any man who says he is an American but something else also, isn't an American at all."

Presumably to the extent that other groups regarded themselves (or were made to regard themselves by others) as "something else also," they were also less entitled to social equality. Thus we have the condition established here of "cultural assimilation (to the dominant Anglo male group) as a prerequisite to social incorporation," or perhaps, more accurately, as a first step, cultural dissimilation with regard to one's original non-Anglo ethnic group (and, especially, repudiation of it in terms of political allegiance). Of course, to the extent that non-white racial groups were generally regarded as "unassimilable"—a view that kept them from participating in and benefiting from the white ethnic labor movement (Hill 1973)—they could not achieve the racial/cultural identity that, within the dominant group's integrationist policy, was theoretically prerequisite to achieving social equality.

Practically speaking, structural pluralism exerted its political influence within the public sector through the schools and other official Americanizing agencies, such as for Native Americans, the Bureau of Indian Affairs (Fisher 1969). But except for the neighborhood public school there were few other Americanizing forces working directly at the local community level to overcome the competing influence of non-Anglo ethnoculturalism operating through and within the local religious institution and family. In this pattern, the dominant group controls the process of social incorporation into and the patterns of behavior within the public sector, but leaves the local community sector relatively free to culturally define itself. In effect, this pattern constitutes the definition of and limits to the "melting pot," the dominant metaphor used to characterize the "Americanization" process (and one fitting within a structurally pluralistic conception of "integration"). As Roosevelt again put it:

> We have room for but one language here, and that is the English language, for we want to see that the crucible turns our people out as Americans, of American nationality, and not as dwellers in a polyglot boarding house.

Equity within structural pluralism is seen as treating everyone the same. This serves both the social interest of cultural assimilation to Anglo-American male norms—to benefit equally from the same treatment one has to become like the (Anglo-American male) person for whom that treatment was designed—and the social interest of economy and efficiency: officials need only to choose the one "best" way, with individuals held responsible for adapting themselves as best they can to that same "best" treatment. The fact that the same treatment might produce unequal effects, a point emphasized in the Bilingual Education Act of 1968 (*United States Statutes at Large*, Vol. 81, 817, taken from Hakuta 1986, 198), was indifferently accepted as the unavoidable "fallout" of this form of equity:

> There is no equality of treatment merely by providing students with the same facilities, textbooks, teachers, and curriculum; for students who do not understand English are effectively foreclosed from any meaningful education.

The structural arrangement within cultural pluralism reflects greater political equality among the culturally heterogeneous units. "Anglo-Americans" are one group among other "hyphenated" Americans, and the accommodation process among different culturally distinctive groups is reciprocal rather than unilateral. As with structural pluralism, the public arena again provides the stage within which culturally pluralist issues are developed and negotiated (as for example, with regard to what would constitute intergroup "reciprocity"). The dominant metaphor within cultural pluralism is the "salad bowl," not the "melting pot," in which the identity and integrity of the culturally distinctive units remain intact while contributing to the overall quality, effect, and purpose of the whole.

Equity within cultural pluralism moves from treating everyone the same—an equality of input (comparable to giving every flower in a garden the same amount of sunshine, fertilizer, and water, which guarantees that only certain flowers will fully grow)—to an equality of effect. Following the agricultural metaphor and model this would amount to allowing variable treatments so long as they were or could be demonstrated to be equivalent.

The golden rule of "doing unto others what you would have done unto you," which the news columnist Sidney Harris (*Chicago Sun-Times*, 20 June 1983) has pointed out may conceal a cultural bias—it assumes that others want what you want for yourself—also needs to be refashioned within cultural pluralism to become "do unto others as they would want done unto them."

In fact, our present etiquette rule that gives individuals (self-determining) choices as to what they want for themselves within the context of an informal party gathering, and defines what mainstream Americans presently regard as being "considerate of others," might be usefully extended to define the pattern of social interaction between culturally diverse groups within more formal contexts at the larger societal level, too. (Japanese "consideration" of others, by way of contrast, as Lebra [1976, 38–43] points out, is based on empathy and identification: putting oneself in someone else's shoes. This works insofar as there is a sufficient sharing of basic cultural patterns and values. But even in a culturally homogenous society such as Japan, this can go awry, as when empathy becomes inaccurate and doing for others becomes transformed into "meddlesomeness").

The civil rights movement did for "people of color" what the labor movement did for white ethnics with one important difference. Blacks, Hispanics, and women have come to reject the condition of racial/cultural assimilation (or perhaps more accurately, ethnic cultural dissimilation) as a prerequisite to social incorporation. This view was not immediately expressed within the original "affirmative action" guidelines that initially put pressure upon white, male–dominated mainstream institutions to incorporate previously excluded social minorities and women based simply upon considerations of race, gender, and ethnic background. But the rejection of the above condition began to emerge when members of minority groups started looking for cultural role models within the upper echelons of the organization (Blacks, Hispanics, and women were asking whether they must, respectively, become culturally transformed into "white," "Anglo," "males," to become promoted within the white, male–dominated mainstream organization). This question brought forth issues relating to cultural equity and has presently forced the dominant white male target group to address the fundamental question of reciprocity: how to incorporate the cultural patterns and value orientations of previously excluded ethnic minorities and women within a heretofore white, male–dominated "corporate culture" without undermining corporate "bottom-line" issues, such as productivity and profits.

The motivation that has caused the white male to search for some kind of culturally reciprocal response to pressures emanating from previously disenfranchised minorities is based upon pragmatic expediency rather than a commitment to the value of cultural pluralism itself. Nonetheless, I think it is also necessary to make the case that cultural (more so than structural) pluralism provides the organization (as well as the larger society) with a richer cultural mix from which to draw, thereby also providing it with a greater flexibility of adaptive response to changing circumstances: a kind of maximization of its "evolutionary potential" (Sahlins and Service 1960; Castile 1975).

Structural pluralism does not take advantage of cultural heterogeneity because political accommodation to the dominant social group's norms forces the socially weaker party to suppress its cultural distinctiveness. In so doing it keeps the dominant group and the society as a whole from readily availing themselves of the cultural diversity within their midst. It is no social accident that the dominant social groups in societies around the world know essentially only their own language and culture and that it is the subordinate group members in those societies who are bilingual and bicultural.

Essentially then, within either the old or the new pluralism, there is the need to consider not only the existence of cultural diversity, but also matters relating to the social status or legitimacy of the different cultural patterns and perspectives (which ultimately derive from the social status of the different groups who own them) and, fundamentally, the political question of representation and voice. For it is a combination of these factors that will determine the relative capacity of these different perspectives to influence public policy and the larger societal interpretation of behavior and events.

There are also more specific ways to demonstrate the advantages of cultural pluralism. One way is to consider that any culture's greatest strength can at times also become its greatest weakness. Two recent publications (Weisz, Rothbaum, and Blackburn 1984; Gilligan 1982) illustrate this point well.

In the first mentioned piece (Weisz, et al.), the title "Standing Out vs. Standing In" reflects, respectively, the different cultural attitudes in the United States and Japan towards the relationship of the individual to the group. In the United States, there are cultural pressures to "stand out" as an individual, even if it is at the expense of the will or interests of the group. In Japan, there are cultural pressures to "stand in"—the Japanese have a saying that 'the nail that stands out is hammered back down'—Japanese individuals are expected to comply with the will or interests of the group against their own will (Lebra 1976, 158). The psychologies of control in the United States and Japan, respectively, are directly linked to the above "self" or "group" orientations. The American psychology aims at "primary" control: the belief that one can enhance reward or reduce punishment by influencing realities to fit the self, and, more generally, that one can (and should) act to influence existing realities. The Japanese psychology aims at achieving what the authors call "secondary" control, which aims to enhance reward (or reduce punishment) by influencing the psychological impact of realities upon the self, and is more generally, a process of accommodation to existing realities. Thus, Americans who are anxious seek out psychotherapy *to get rid of* the symptoms of anxiety, whereas Japanese (in Morita therapy) seek to *accept themselves* as anxious persons (Weisz, 964; Reynolds 1980).

Insofar as American and Japanese societies would, respectively, consider each of these different forms of control as reflecting their culture's greatest strength, one might ask how the cultural predisposition to one or the other form of control might, under certain circumstances, become a weakness. For Americans, the weakness becomes transparent in those situations where failure occurs despite their best efforts at exercising primary control, as for doctors, when the patient dies. The argument here is that the commitment to the belief that things can (and should) be controlled sets Americans up to experience deep frustration and disappointment, and considerable loss of self-esteem when faced with situations beyond their control. For Japanese, the weaknesses inherent in being committed to accommodating existing realities may surface when individuals do not take advantage of opportunities to change existing realities when that requires "challenging the unknown."

In considering the maxim of Alcoholics Anonymous (AA): "God grant me the serenity to accept what I cannot change, the courage to change what I can, and the wisdom to know the difference," it becomes clear that Americans, by virtue of their commitment to primary control, are going to have difficulty gaining the serenity to accept the things they cannot change. Japanese individuals, in turn, seeking how best to gain and maintain security through the maximization of predictive control, may have problems with finding the "courage to change what they can." Each society's greatest cultural strength can, under certain circumstances, become its greatest weakness.

But the weakness manifests itself precisely because social pressures within each society force individuals to commit to one cultural orientation *at the expense of* the other. Thus for Americans, the failure to exercise primary control (as when withdrawing from certain competitive skill situations) is seen as "relinquishing" control rather than, for example, practicing a form of secondary control (such as allying oneself with the forces of chance or fate) (Weisz, 956–57). But, as the AA slogan implies, the individual who holds both value orientations and is comfortable going either way, and can see when one or the other pattern is called for, can deal more effectively with changing circumstances than individuals who are essentially committed to only one *or* the other cultural orientation. Put in mathematical terms, for any organization or society, A *plus* B is a better choice than A *or* B. And while it may be difficult for those individuals who have been socialized their whole life toward one cultural pattern and value orientation to go against the grain, and adopt what, for them, essentially amounts to an alien cultural style, a larger social unit consisting of culturally heterogeneous individuals or groups can retain such flexibility of response by maintaining and promoting the culturally distinct perspectives and practices found therein. This would also entail providing social opportunities for their articulation and expression.

Gilligan puts forth a similar argument in her assessment of the strengths and weaknesses of the socialization of mainstream American males and females. Males from the mainstream American culture, and perhaps generally, define masculine identity in terms of a process of separation from the mother and identification with the father. The problem area for men is in getting close: what Gilligan calls the "explosive connection," for it is here that the reversal of the male socialization process of separation and individuation occurs and places masculine identity at risk. Females on the other hand are more comfortable with getting close, because socialization into the female identity builds upon continuous connectedness and identification with the mother figure. As Gilligan says (p. 12):

> While for men, identity preceded intimacy and generativity in the optimal cycle of human separation and attachment, for women these tasks seem instead to be fused. Intimacy goes along with identity, as the female comes to know herself as she is known, through her relationships with others.

As women are comfortable in the area of intimacy that threatens men, men are comfortable in the area of separation that threatens women: what Gilligan calls "dangerous separation," and which becomes manifest when women engage in competitive achievement, as in the workplace. However, the mature individual, as Gilligan argues (pp. 151ff.), is one capable of integrating both masculine and feminine cultural styles comfortably. Again, A *plus* B is a better choice than A *or* B, both for the individual and for the society as a whole, especially when the climate is set in the organization or society for culturally different people to become cultural resources for each other.

II. CULTURAL PLURALISM AND BLACK AND WHITE CULTURAL DIFFERENCES

Insofar as present mainstream American attitudes towards cultural diversity by and large have been those generated by structural pluralism, differences in Black and White mainstream linguistic and cultural patterns, perspectives, and values are likely to be seen through a mindset that attaches greater social respectability, if not conceptual validity, to the White mainstream cultural style. The ubiquity of such a mindset becomes obvious when we realize that

Black and White cultural and linguistic differences are manifested in approaches to assessing others and being assessed oneself in terms of ability and performance in school, college, and the workplace (for example, consider judgments and inferences which follow emotionally heated confrontation as an instance of Black functional "truth-seeking" style, described below). Indeed, through its school system and other social agencies, the dominant social group still insists upon "linguistic and cultural assimilation as a prerequisite to social incorporation," thereby instituting a policy and program whereby pressures are brought to bear upon Blacks and members of other minority groups to accommodate the dominant social group exclusively on the latter's terms. And in fact, when interest has been shown in American minority languages and cultures in the past it has generally been geared to understanding them *for the purpose of easing their social and cultural transition into the American mainstream* (Zintz 1963; Aarons, Gordon, and Stewart 1969; Cazden, John, and Hymes 1972), an attitudinal stance consistent with the "melting pot" concept within structural pluralism.

What disturbs me about this accommodation process is its unidirectional and nonreciprocal character. Those members of minority cultures who wish to become socially incorporated into the American mainstream do need to learn about mainstream American linguistic and cultural patterns. In some instances, it might even benefit them to use and embrace such patterns as necessity or desire might dictate.

But what about the needs of the American mainstream? The nonreciprocal nature of the process of cultural assimilation of minorities does not permit the mainstream American culture to learn about minority cultural traditions nor benefit from their official social incorporation. It also suggests an unwarranted social arrogance: that mainstream American society has already reached a state of perfection and cannot benefit from being exposed to and learning from other (minority) cultural traditions. I reject that assumption, and I demonstrate that in the stance I take here by promoting a view of the culturally different patterns and perspectives of Blacks and mainstream Whites from a social standpoint that regards them as equally respectable and valid (of course, therefore, also equally accountable to criticism, as on functional grounds, when such may be warranted) (Kochman 1981, 34–35, 151).

Styles of Work and Play

The following sections will detail the contents of some of the culturally different patterns as they appear in the domains of work and play. An overview is presented in figure 1 below.

FIGURE 1
Styles of Work and Play

Black	White
Patterns	
Mental "Reflex"	Mental "Set"
Spontaneous	Methodical
Improvisational	Systematic
Exaggerated	Understated
Expressive	Restrained
Personalized	Role-Oriented

Issues
Being/Doing: Individuality
Team Work/Play: Individuality; Functionality

Being and Doing

In American mainstream culture Whites (especially males) are taught to see themselves as individuals rather than as members of a group. Yet when they become members of an organization or team they are frequently called upon to subordinate their individuality to fit the hierarchy and role-requirements established by the group. The nature of the subordination process takes the form of seeing the group as more important than oneself ("There is no letter 'I' in the word 'team'"). This process often leads to a fused self or identity (organized around what mainstream individuals do professionally) such as when White males talk about themselves in terms of a corporate "we" rather than as an individual "I."

Organizational culture also qualifies individuality in other respects. White mainstream American cultural style in the areas of organized work and play is serious, methodical, and systematic, characterized by what Harrison (1972, 35–37) has called "mental set": a stance or attitude in which action or activity (doing) is seen to evolve out of a tightly structured plan, schedule, or procedure. The conception and implementation of the plan is comprehensive (attempts are made beforehand to take all relevant variables into account and control for them), prescribed (from top management on down), and systematized (through standard operating procedures). The purpose of mental set is to render processes and outcomes orderly and predictable.

Within this role-oriented structure, individuals operating within and through mental set are taught to see themselves in essentially instrumental terms ("You are what you do!"). Those parts of the self that are drawn upon are those mental and physical skills that functionally contribute (in some direct way) to organizational objectives. Aspects of the self that cannot be justified as directly contributing to the established task are disallowed as not only non-functional but as subversive. They are seen to promote and sustain individual allegiance to non-work-related values which, among other things, White mainstreamers believe, threaten the undivided attention to task necessary to do work well. Individuals with similar skills, roles, and tasks are seen within the team or organizational framework as "interchangeable" parts. As a result of these social pressures within the organization, the more distinctive aspects of White male individuality (self and identity) within mainstream American culture are more often realized in isolation: outside the context of a work group, rather than within it.

The relationship between the individual and the plan within the framework of "mental set" is analagous to that between the performer and the text within the "compositional" tradition in the performing arts. The principal interaction there is between the performer and the text or composition (Keil 1972, 83ff). The role and responsibility of the performer is with regard to the text: the revelation of its "embodied meaning," and consequently, with a sense of fidelity to the author's or composer's original conception. Thus, performers are constrained in their interpretation and rendition of the text so as not to take "undue liberties." Chicago symphony oboist Ray Still makes this point in the context of objecting to the tradition (apparently as a result of his having been influenced by jazz music values):

> It's almost an unwritten law that we're not supposed to glissando—sliding from one note to another, as jazz musicians do so often—on a wind instrument. Only string instruments and the voice are supposed to do it. When I do it—I like my glisses— some eyebrows are raised. They say, "Oh, Ray is bending his instrument, now, trying to show his jazz technique." But that tradition burns me up. Why shouldn't we do it? (Levinsohn 1986, 20).

Black cultural style in work and play evolves out of a conception that sees "change" rather than "set" as the constant aspect of cosmic and social order. Consequently, the Black cultural psyche operates out of "mental reflex" (Harrison 1972, 35), one oriented to "move through changes" as changing modes or circumstances determine. In conjunction with the Black penchant for generating powerful imagery, change becomes that aspect of order that "revitalizes an event," (Harrison, 7). The cultural style that Blacks have developed that serves "going through changes" is improvisation. And the force within the individual that motivates and complements improvisation is spontaneity ("I'm not a prize fighter, I'm a *surprise* fighter").

Consistent with this view of cosmic and social order, Black cultural style evolves out of a performance (as opposed to compositional) tradition (Keil, 84–85); consequently, the principal interaction is between the performer and the audience (the goal there being "engendered feeling" [Keil, 86]). Within this tradition, performers are granted great license to improvise with regard to the text—in effect to generate new "text" as they go along—and, through the simultaneous and direct demonstration of the individual performer's virtuoso ability and powers of evocation, to produce "engendered feeling" in the audience (Keil, 86).

There is, of course, a performance dimension within the Western compositional tradition, too, that aims at "engendered feeling," but, as Keil argues, with "music composed for repetition, 'engendered feeling' has less chance" than when "music is left in the hands of the performer (improvised)" (p. 86, n. 6).

Critical differences between the compositional and performance traditions, then, are those of substance, principal focus, and direction. As Keil says, "a good composer gives some spontaneity to his form and, conversely, a good improviser tries to give some form to his spontaneity" (pp. 85–86). Likewise, as Harrison (1972) notes, actors in the White American theater aim at generating *affective memory*, which allows them to repeat the same emotion night after night. In the Black theater, on the other hand, actors try to generate *effective memory*, which allows them to produce real, spontaneously conceived emotions, so as to produce (as the *context* rather than the *text* demands) the truest emotional response capable of galvanizing the (audience's) collective unconscious (Harrison, 157). Thus, where White mainstream cultural style is oriented to shape the context to fit the text, Black cultural style is oriented, rather, to shape the text to fit the context.

Black individuality is realized within the framework of strong interpersonal connectedness, but, as Young states (1970, 255) "not with absorption or acceptance of group identity as higher than individual identity" (see also Lewis 1975, 225). Moreover, while there is emphasis on instrumental forms of doing, focus is also on individual character and style ("doing one's *own* thing"), leading to more personalized and idiosyncratic expressions of doing (as opposed to the more routine, uniform, and impersonal [role-oriented] forms of doing characteristic of self-presentation within White mainstream organizational culture).

Stylistic Self-Expression

Stylistic self-expression within White mainstream culture is minimalist in character: "a style of no style" (Abrahams, personal communication, but see also Abrahams 1976, 8–9, 90–91); thus, characterized by economy and efficiency ("the shortest distance between two points," "no wasted moves"), and modest (self-effacing) understatement and restraint ("If you've got it, you don't need to flaunt it").

Stylistic self-expression within Black culture is characterized by dramatic self-conscious flair. A nice descriptive example comes from Milhomme's portrait of Felix Toya, Ghana's dancing traffic policeman (*LA Extra*, May 1986, 16–22):

Dubbed "Toyota" or "Life Boy" by the city's taxi drivers, Constable Toya attracts as much pedestrian traffic as he directs vehicles. Lookers applaud and cheer, drivers toot their horns, and sometimes take an extra turn on the roundabout as Felix oscillates and gyrates, lifts, bends and pirouettes, making an art form out of his assigned task, never missing a step or a signal-change. Few Ghanians own Walkmans, but in the privacy of his own mind, Constable Toya creates a symphony of sounds and rhythms to which he moves with grace and precision. He is the ultimate street performer, taking cues from his environment and entertaining a diverse audience of fleeting yet appreciative fans.

Black stylistic self-expression is also characterized by inventive (humorously ironic) exaggeration as in the self-promotion of demonstrably capable aspects of self ("If you've got it, flaunt it") or even by less demonstrably positive capabilities ("If you don't have it, flaunt it, anyway"), which is all part of Afro-American boasting: the "making of one's noise," (Reisman 1974, 60; Kochman 1981, 65). As "Hollywood" Henderson said, "I put a lot of pressure on myself to see if I can play up to my mouth" (Atkin 1979, 16). But exaggeration also serves to characterize (and neutralize the impact of) negative situations, such as poverty ("The soles on my shoes are so thin, I can step on a dime and tell you whether it's heads or tails").

Conflict and Confluence

Individuality/Functionality

The functional rule for getting things done follows the norms for appropriate stylistic self-presentation and expression within the two cultures. The White mainstream cultural rule is governed by the principles of economy and efficiency, which serve to promote the uniform, impersonal, minimalist, and instrumental (role-oriented) style considered standard within mainstream White organized work and play. Thus the rule here is "make only moves that are necessary to getting the job done."

The Black cultural rule serves to promote the standards within the Black performance tradition, which is, as Abrahams has said (1976, 9) for individual performers to bring about an experience in which their creative energies and the vitality of others may find expression. Blacks accomplish this by executing tasks with bold originality and dramatic flair. Insofar as it is in "how" things get done that the energetic involvement of others and stylistic self-expression occur, rather than in "what" gets done, Blacks say (to protect the individual right of original self-expression), "Tell me what to do but not how to do it." Consonant with this purpose, the functional rule for Blacks is "so long as the moves that are made do not interfere with getting the job done, they should be allowed."

These two different cultural rules clash in the workplace and in the playground with great regularity (see Kochman 1981, 145–52). One example of this clash is in the restrictions set forth in the professional football rules governing "spiking" the football (throwing it forcefully to the ground): a self-celebrating expression of personal accomplishment (resembling an exclamation point [!]) by which Black players punctuate their achievement. Were a player to "spike" the football after scoring an important first down, he would be penalized. The official reason given for assessing the penalty is "delay of game." In actuality there is no real "delay of game" because after a team scores a first down the line markers have to be moved, and a new football is thrown in from the sidelines; there may even be a TV commercial. At issue is the different aesthetic standard governing stylistic self-expression within Black and White mainstream culture. "Spiking" the football is permitted in the end zone after a touchdown, but only by the player who actually scores the touchdown. So when the White quarterback of the Chicago Bears, Jim McMahon, scored a touchdown and gave the football to one of the linemen to spike (in recognition of his cooperative and instrumental role in the touchdown) the officials assessed a penalty on the ensuing kickoff. As a measure of the acceptance of the Black cultural view on such matters in professional sports, it is significant that the reaction of both White announcers at the time of its occurrence, and of Bear quarterback Jim McMahon, when interviewed afterward, was to regard the penalty assessment as "stupid."

Other aspects of cultural conflict center around the issue of individual entitlement for stylistic self-expression and authorization for making changes in how a task is to be done. In White mainstream organizational culture, stylistic self-expression, when it occurs at all, tends to be a function of rank. Consequently, it is often the chief executive male officer in the organization who in manner or dress, "shows-off," or otherwise demonstrates a more individually expressive (non-instrumental?!) style (for example, Lee Iacocca, Ray Kroc, Douglas MacArthur, and so forth).

In Black culture, however, stylistic self-expression is an individual entitlement. Consequently, one does not have to be the president of the company to drive an expensive top-of-the-line car or wear fashionable clothes. However, this cultural pattern often gets Blacks into trouble in White mainstream organizations since the latter interpret such individual stylistic self-expression as a presumption: a laying claim to a greater rank or title in the organization than the Black person actually holds.

As to authorization for how a task is to be accomplished, the Black dictum "Tell me what to do, but not how to do it," while establishing a protection for the individual right to self-expression, also asserts that the final authority for the implementation of a task rests with the doer/performer. However, White mainstream organizational culture, through the framework of "mental set," sees the authorization of a standard protocol or procedure to rest with the designer of the plan: the manager/composer. This difference also gets Blacks into trouble in the organization because they get accused here once again either of arrogating to themselves authority to which their rank or role in the organization does not entitle them, or of being insubordinate or uncooperative, even when they do the task differently in the interests of getting the job done, when doing it in the way it was officially prescribed would have failed.

The Role and Function of Competition

In organized work and play within White mainstream culture, the role and function of competition is to provide a climate and context to determine which pair of adversaries (individual or group) can dominate the other. The role and function of competition in organized work and play within Black culture is twofold. It is not only to set the stage for determining which opponent can dominate the other, though it is also that (and intensely so), but also for each individual or group to use their opponent (as a foil is used in theater), to show off their skill in the process of doing so. The cultural difference is one of focus and emphasis. For Blacks, as Abrahams has said (1970, 42), competition provides the atmosphere in which performers can best perform. The Black goal therefore is divided between winning (dominating one's opponent), and showboating (displaying one's ability vis-à-vis one's opposition so as to show it off at its highest level of accomplishment). This display function sets competition within Black culture apart from its counterpart in White mainstream culture. As basketball player Lloyd Free said (Elderkin 1979, 17):

> The fans have the right idea about pro basketball's regular season. . . . They know there are too many games and it's silly to play all that time to eliminate so few teams from the playoffs.

> So why do they even come to our games? . . . They come to see a show and that's why guys like myself and Dr. J and David Thompson are so popular. We make the fun and the excitement. Man, you just don't get serious in this business until the playoffs.

This divided function of competition (winning and showboating) together with another cultural pattern, that of individual identity not being subordinate to group identity (the individual can succeed even if the team does not) leads to a more diffuse focus in competitive play. This diminishes somewhat the singular importance attached to team winning that exists within White mainstream culture, represented by the assertion attributed to Vince Lombardi: "Winning may not be everything. But losing isn't anything." It especially takes the hard edge off losing. (As Blacks say, "The best you can do is the best you can do.") In the following passage, Red Holzman responds to a question about frequent reports that today's players don't take defeat as hard as yesterday's heroes. Without attributing this different attitude directly to Black cultural influence, he nonetheless supports the culturally dichotomous view presented here (albeit within the framework of differences in "older" and "newer" player attitudes towards losing [Elderkin 1981, 16]):

> When I first started to coach in the pros, guys would come into the locker room after a tough loss and break up the furniture or brood or act like there was no tomorrow. It was like they had committed a crime by losing.

> Now as a coach, I certainly don't want my players to take any defeat lightly. But when you're part of an 82 game schedule, you're playing five times in the next six nights, and you're rushing to catch an airplane. I don't think it's too smart to carry those kinds of feelings with you. In that respect, I think today's players handle things a lot better emotionally.

Also, Blacks attach some importance to "having fun" in organized play, which also translates into winning and losing not being taken as seriously as in White mainstream culture, as Lloyd Free's comments above also suggest. The different Black cultural view on the nature and function of competition, combined with attitudes towards individual display and showmanship, and losing and "having fun" in organized play, have no doubt helped shape the more general public attitude often expressed today that tends to regard baseball and basketball as being as much "entertainment" as "sport."

The element of "fun" and "showboating" that Blacks bring into organized competitive play is negatively valued by Whites, except perhaps where it has commercial value (cf. the "Harlem Globetrotters"), especially insofar as Whites tends to see organized or competitive play as more like work: serious (even somber) and important, and therefore, prescriptive, patient, methodical, systematic, role-oriented, and so on. It is as though Whites are bringing work-related values into organized competitive play, thereby making "play" resemble "work," while Blacks are bringing play-related values (such as spontaneity, improvisation, and fun) into organized competitive play, thereby making "work" resemble "play." Also, insofar as Blacks introduce these values alongside stylistic self-expression—also regarded as "extra-curricular" within the strictly functional White cultural mind-set—Blacks would be regarded by Whites as not sufficiently "serious" or "interested" in getting the job or task accomplished.

Concentration

This interpretation is reinforced by the different meaning that Blacks and Whites give to "concentration to task." For White mainstreamers "concentration" means undivided attention: focusing upon one thing and one thing only. For Blacks, "concentration" means divided attention: attending to task accomplishment while simultaneously concentrating on doing it with flair or expressive style. Because Black attention is divided here, Whites believe that the focus on style is *at the expense of* focus on task to the ultimate detriment of task accomplishment. But this view misrepresents the Black cultural pattern which inherently protects against that happenstance by giving no credit for stylistic self-expression *if the person does not succeed in accomplishing the task.* Thus, in the above description of the "dancing policeman" Felix Toya, it was very important that he never missed a signal change even as he never missed a step. As Holt said with regard to Black (functionally) expressive performance, "everything must come together" (1972, 60; see also Kochman 1981, 138ff.).

Of course, the White view that sees Black divided attention to task as dysfunctional with regard to task accomplishment may in some instances simply be a pretext for discrediting Black preoccupation with stylistic self-expression. This view is based upon the value-orientation within White mainstream culture that sees allegiance to non-work-related values (as it defines "work") as corrosive of the American commitment to the work ethic. There is no question that Black preoccupation with stylistic self-expression does express an allegiance to values other than those promoted by and within White mainstream American culture. But so far, that allegiance has not sacrificed task accomplishment, nor is there any indication to lead one to suppose that it will. Moreover, the Black introduction of these other "play" values (such as "fun") into the workplace may ultimately have a revitalizing effect and in the end constitute a real contribution to mainstream American organized work and play culture.

Expenditure of Energy

Another difference in work style within Black and White mainstream culture centers around expenditure of energy. The White mainstream concept of "hustle" describes a work or play pattern of high energy expenditure often greater than is actually needed to perform a given task. The message being communicated with this "energy to spare" approach is, directly, worker zeal for the task at hand, and, more generally, from the organizational standpoint, a cooperative "ready, willing, and able" worker attitude. The Black approach is based upon a "conservation of energy" principle: to expend only as much (or little) energy as it takes to accomplish effectively the task at hand. One Black woman said that that pattern came about as a result of Blacks "picking cotton" all day long where the goal was to make only those moves that were absolutely necessary. But whether the "conservation of energy" principle originated with cotton picking or simply was applied to that and/or other oppressive and exploitative "colonial" work situations is not clear. [1]

Regardless of the origin of the pattern—the application of the conservation of energy principle to work and play situations—expenditure of excess energy is seen by Blacks as "wasteful," and "stupid" ("definitely 'uncool'") and, when directed by others, still carries with it strong connotations of "being exploited." Yet to Whites, the conservation of energy principle, as the antithesis of "hustling", often communicates lack of dedication to task or of motivation or interest in the job.[2] This is so even when Blacks actually accomplish the same amount of work with their "energy-efficient" method that White workers accomplish with and through "hustling" (see Kochman 1981, 157–59).

Examples

The following two descriptive accounts are especially illustrative of conflict and confluence in Black and White mainstream cultural styles, especially so in showing the interaction of several of the cultural themes listed and discussed above. They are taken from Koogler's (1980) description of two events involving

---

[1] Sithole (1972, 71ff.) points out that the amount of work that is done, as for example, by Zulus on a road gang in Durham, South Africa, is determined by the pace of the work song.

> In the past Roads Department personnel tried to hurry the workers by suggesting fast-moving songs, whereupon cooperation between the workers and the leader disintegrated and the entire work output decreased. Today, however, it is accepted that the work songs will be slower, and, therefore, allow the workers to dance as they slowly raise their pick-axes, rest a little as they make two or three jabs in the air, and then finally allow their pick-axes to strike the ground. Of course, with all the energy that the song and dance generates, strenuous work becomes lighter and easier.

[2] This attitude seemed to be part of the TV announcers disappointment at Carl Lewis not using all of his attempts to try to "break the world record" in the broad jump during the 1984 Summer Olympics, after having, in effect, "won" the event on his first try. (The pattern for athletes [perhaps indicative of White cultural attitudes towards energy expenditure] is to use all of their attempts even if they have already won.) Of course, Lewis's attitude and strategy might also have been dictated by the situation of his being entered in four different events with his goal being to win the gold medal in each event rather than to set a world record, and he therefore needed to conserve his energy for other events yet to follow. Yet, if he had not won the broad jump in his first attempt he had to be prepared to try again up to the limit. Thus, I would argue that the "conservation of energy" vs. "hustling" principles did in fact apply here and, respectively, enter into both Lewis's decision not to make any further attempts and the White TV announcers reaction to that decision.

the same kindergarten class consisting of twenty-one white children (twelve females and nine males) and eight Black children (three females and five males). The first event, a "Valentine Dance" was led by the class's regular White female teacher. The second event, a music room activity was led by a Black female teacher, whose contact with children occurred in the music room where she provided special music activities for all of the elementary classes. The accounts of the two events as observed and reported by Koogler (127ff.) are as follows:

Event I – "The Valentine Dance"

The teacher gathered all of the children on the rug as she started a record of valentine dance music. She directed the children to form two parallel lines, boys in one, girls in the other. Boys were then asked to face the girls. The person one was facing was considered one's partner.

The teacher demonstrated the patterned group dance using the following order of action: boys would walk to the midpoint between the parallel lines, facing their respective partners, each bowing. They would return to their starting position and repeat. This time the girls would meet their respective partners at the midpoint. Partners would then join hands, dance around in a circle, singing, "I want you to be my valentine."

Following the demonstration, class members tried to imitate the dance. The black children (with the exception of one female) left their positions, ran to one end of the parallel lines and clustered together, giggling. Soon after, they began "hand-slapping" and "finger-snapping" in time with the music.

While the white children attempted to dance, one black boy left the cluster, ran between the lines of children singing, "Be mine, be mine, you sweetie valentine." With this, he threw kisses, clapped his hands, and stopped periodically to engage in rhythmic body movements of the hips and shoulders. Then he ran around several of the white boys, stopping periodically to rearrange their positions, thus pairing them with different girls. When he approached his closest friend, he said: "Man, you don't want her. Let's move you around." With this his friend (a white boy) left the dance and joined the cluster of black children.

The teacher, angered by the behavior of the black boy, escorted him to the principal's office. He tried to physically resist, then pleaded with her to allow him to stay. The teacher continued to remove him. Meanwhile, the student teacher tried to coax the remainder of the nonparticipating children to join in the dance. Finally, two black girls reluctantly decided to join as partners, only to be ridiculed by the black males.

The student teacher reprimanded the males, who were trying desperately to stop giggling. She sent one of the boys behind a partition as punishment. He became angered and threw objects into the dance area. The dance began to break up as children began hitting each other and running around the room.

The teacher reentered the classroom and began separating fighting children.

Event II – Music Room Activity

The music teacher started the musical activity by playing a song on the piano. The children clustered on the floor as the teacher sang and played the familiar song. Soon the children joined in the singing.

Shortly, the same black male who had been escorted to the principal's office during the Valentine Dance ran to the front of the group and began rhythmic body movements, snapping his fingers as he slowly changed the tempo of the tune. A black girl responded, "cool man, you're cool," as she joined him, snapping her fingers. The teacher, still playing the piano, changed her timing to coincide with the finger snapping.

As the music continued, some of the white children stopped singing to listen and watch the performance. A few whites joined in, stamping their feet in a marching movement. (Some matched the tempo: others were unable to do so; nevertheless, they kept stamping their feet.) Black children then began clapping their hands and engaging in body movements as they followed the leader around the classroom. White children who had been watching gradually began singing and clapping. Several attempted rhythmic hip movements.

During the second part of the music period, the teacher asked the children to group themselves into four groups in order to sing parts of the song separately. The children divided into five groups [according to their friendship groupings, largely by sex and race], so she divided the song into five parts. As the teacher played the piano, she signaled each of the groups at the appropriate time. When she signaled a group of three black boys, they were standing in front of the class with a set of drums. They acted out their portion of the song using percussion and shoulder movement.

Analysis

One of the clear issues leading to a conflict of cultural styles in Event I was the mainstream cultural orientation of "mental set," which sees activity evolving out of set patterns. This is exemplified by the Valentine Dance's predetermined, random pairing using sex as the pairing criterion, and a highly patterned group dance which individual participants were not allowed to modify (Koogler, 129). Attempts by the Black students to establish their own culturally expressive style pattern in gesture and dance were rejected insofar as they did not fit the "White" dance pattern. What is relevant here is not only the stylistic differences in the expressive patterns themselves but the inflexibility of the authority person (what Koogler calls interference stemming from too strong leadership). This inflexibility did not allow for either 1) variation with regard to the prescribed pattern, or 2) (a matter of authorization and entitlement) the right of students to initiate changes in a set plan (Koogler, 129, notes that the black boy who ran between the lines was, consistent with Black cultural norms, "asserting leadership and soliciting audience participation").

In the first instance, the "variation" amounted to the introduction of a wholly different "Black" stylistic pattern, in part, as Koogler argues, because the Black students were unfamiliar with the kind of pattern they were required to perform. My own view, however, would be to see it as culturally consistent for the teacher to have been inflexible also in allowing individual students (while staying basically within the "White" cultural pattern) to try to shape it to their personal taste, were that to have happened. I say that based upon the impersonal and role-oriented nature of the predetermined pairing, which suggests support of the mainstream cultural view of individuals as (except for sex) "interchangeable parts," and, going along with that orientation, a tendency to regard uniform processing through standard operating procedures to be the appropriate way to execute the set arrangement laid out in the original composition of the dance structure. The teacher (as part of the White mainstream compositional tradition herself) might even see her own authority and role to be subordinate and restricted here: one bound to represent literally the set plan as conceived by the composer, rather than (more flexibly) as a basis for improvisation.

Event II was free of cultural conflict because the Black music teacher was responsive both to the right of students to initiate changes in a set plan (for example, changing the number of parts from four to five, organizing themselves according to race as well as sex, allowing spontaneous student leadership to emerge) and more generally to allow for individual variation by letting students define for themselves the stylistic character of their respective individual contributions. (For other examples of conflict and confluence between Black and White cultural styles, including patterns of self-presentation, performance, and value orientation, see Houston 1973; Kochman 1981, 153ff.).

Styles of Discourse

Truth-creating processes

Argument versus discussion. Black and White "truth-creating processes" are those protocols and procedures that each cultural group has established as appropriate for the working through of disagreements and disputes or for otherwise "getting at the truth." For Blacks, the appropriate truth-creating process is "sincere" argument (as opposed to the form of argument that is quarreling, which Blacks also have). For White mainstream people, discussion rather than argument is the idealized (if not always realized) truth-creating process. Thus, a White middle-class couple will say that they had a "discussion that 'deteriorated' into an argument," therein showing that argument is more like quarreling than a sincere attempt at truth-seeking. Notwithstanding the occasional failures by those in the American mainstream to realize discussion norms, the cultural standards are there nonetheless to structure attitudes and otherwise serve as a social barometer for evaluating verbal behavior or discourse style, either that of oneself or others. The same holds true for Blacks in those social contexts where sincere argument rather than discussion is the cultural standard for expressing disagreement and resolving disputes.

Black argument as a cultural style is (as for other ethnic groups), confronting, personal, advocating, and issue-oriented. White discussion style is non-confronting, impersonal, representing, and peace- or process-oriented, the latter expressed by such concepts as "compromise," and "agreeing to disagree." An overview of these differences is shown in figure 2.

The issues that divide Blacks and Whites culturally and account for how they assess each other's behavior—Blacks regard Whites here as "insincere" and "devious"; Whites see Blacks as "argumentative" and "threatening"—revolve around the value of contentiousness or struggle, the separation (or fusion) of reason and emotion, the separation (or fusion) of truth and belief, and finally, self-control. I will briefly consider each of these in turn. (For a more complete discussion see Kochman 1981, 16–42).

Struggle. In the context of truth-seeking, struggle or contentiousness is unifying for Blacks, polarizing for Whites. Blacks view struggle or contentiousness as positive, while Whites view it as negative. A metaphor to describe the difference would be individuals holding opposite ends of a rope while pulling against each other. Whites essentially see only the opposition: individuals pulling in opposite directions. Blacks see individuals pulling in

FIGURE 2
Truth-Creating Processes

Black   White

Argument   Discussion
Patterns
Confronting   Non-confronting
Personal   Impersonal
Advocating   Representing
Truth- or issue-oriented   Peace- or process-oriented

Issues
Struggle
Reason/Emotion
Truth/Belief
Self-control

Behavioral Meanings
Black   White
"Whites are insincere   "Blacks are argumentative
and devious"   and threatening"

opposite directions, to be sure, but more tellingly, also being held together by
the same rope (that is, the individuals are cooperating in their opposition, and
cooperating more than they are opposing).

Black and White attitudes towards the value of struggle stem from
these different positions. Thus, if disagreement at a meeting were likely to
generate heat and strong emotions, Whites would say it was better not to
contend than to contend ("I can't talk to you now. You're too emotional!"); on
the other hand, Blacks would say it was better to contend than not to contend.
This is because Whites see the prevention of potential damage to the harmony
of social relationships as taking precedence over the expression of their
individual views. If they were to threaten such harmony (however contrived or
artificial), Whites would see this as "selfish," "self-indulgent," or "impolite."
For Blacks, on the other hand, the powerful expression of one's personal views
takes precedence over sustaining a surface harmony that may have no real
(sincere) foundation, which Blacks would see as "hypocritical" or a "charade."

The attitudes of Whites and Blacks are also based in part on their
respectively different (culturally determined) capacities to manage
emotionally charged disagreements. Both attitudes and capacities are directly

linked in turn to systems of etiquette within the two cultures (See Kochman 1981, 106–129; 1984).

For example, the etiquette system governing social interaction in the public arena within White mainstream culture declares that (except under certain socially "marked" occasions, like a "talk" or "lecture") the social rights of the receiver deserve greater consideration than the rights of the assertor. As a consequence, mainstream Americans are socialized to regard the protection of their own and other people's sensibilities (when they are in the receiver role) as deserving principal consideration, even when that may be at the expense of their own or others' feelings (emotions) when they or others are in the assertor role. This pattern within the mainstream American etiquette system generates (relative to Black culture) a low offense/low defense pattern of public social interaction. This is because protecting the sensibilities of themselves and others requires mainstreamers to moderate the intensity level of their self-assertion to the level that "others" (that is, receivers) can comfortably manage. And insofar as the intensity level that mainstream receivers can comfortably manage is culturally programmed to be low ("sensitive"), the level of self-assertion must also be commensurately low. Thus, low defense generates low offense. In turn, low offense (under the rubric of *protecting* sensibilities) maintains low defense because it withholds from mainstreamers regular exposure to the more potent stimuli that would enable them to learn how to manage intense interactions more effectively (at least so as not to be overwhelmed by them).

By way of contrast, Black culture generates a (relatively) high offense/high defense pattern of public social interaction. This comes about as a result of the culture granting the assertor rights that are at least equal to, and often greater than (especially when aroused), the rights of the receiver. As Harrison said (1972, 150):

> Blacks are not known . . . to ever be totally desensitized, defused, or repressed in their emotions when dealing with definable antagonisms. A black person would not pussyfoot with an insult from a white—or a black—if rendered with the slightest edge of an acerbity that might threaten one's security: the response would be fully acted out, regardless of the name of the game which deems it necessary to be sensitive to the other feller.

Thus, where the process of accommodation in White mainstream culture is for assertors to consider the sensibilities of receivers first, even at the expense of their own feelings (emotions), the process of accommodation in Black culture is the reverse: for receivers to accommodate assertors' feelings (emotions) especially when they are charged (as when following the "impulse towards truth" in sincere argument).

And it is the greater priority given to feelings (emotions) over sensibilities within Black culture that produces the high offense/high defense pattern. The receivers' orientation to accommodate self-presentations of high emotional intensity exposes them to such presentations on a regular basis, which, in turn, improves their capacity to manage them effectively. In such a way does high offense generate high defense. Reciprocally, the greater capacity of receivers to manage emotionally charged self-presentations allows individuals to assert their feelings (emotions) more freely with the confidence that others can receive them without becoming overwhelmed by them. In such a way does high defense sustain and promote high offense.

Comparatively, then, the psychological consequences of these different sociocultural orientations is that for Whites it hurts them more to hear something unfavorable than it hurts them not to express their feelings (as in abandoning themselves to the "impulse towards truth"). For Blacks, it hurts them more not to express their feelings than to hear something unfavorable.

These different attitudes and capacities generate different levels of comfort and tolerance among Blacks and Whites when meetings become emotionally charged and lead to directly opposite evaluations of such proceedings. Thus, at one such meeting among Black and White staff at a local psychological clinic in Chicago, Blacks left saying that was the "best" staff meeting that they had ever had. Whites left saying that it was the "worst" staff meeting that they had ever had.

Another way of characterizing Black and White attitudes towards struggle is that Blacks put truth before peace whereas Whites put peace before truth. In the mainstream American political arena, to be "peace"-oriented ultimately means to accommodate established political arrangements, before which truth is sacrificed in the form of compromise. The Black orientation in the political arena is, as with interpersonal disagreements and disputes, again to put truth before peace, which is to say, to keep the truth intact and politicize on its behalf.

These different cultural orientations account for the way Blacks and Whites assess each other's public self-presentation style, as for example the cultural style of public officials. For example, those who admired Chicago Mayor Harold Washington, (mostly Blacks), did so partly, as the *Chicago Sun-Times* said (21 August 1984, 35) for "sticking to his guns." In Washington's case this meant not compromising his reformist platform despite the fact that politically, for the first three years of his office (and during the time that the above *Sun-Times* editorial was written) he was opposed by a majority bloc of aldermen, who prevented him from getting any of his administrative appointments passed through the city council (to push for his reformist programs). His critics, mostly Whites, such as the culturally mainstream editorial writers of the *Sun-Times* believed he was "too stubborn [prideful?!] to be [politically?!] effective." Thus, the *Chicago Sun-Times* editorial (23 April 1986, 2) said, "We believe an accommodation [between the Mayor's administration and his political opposition] should have been reached, and could have been reached, without terrible violence to principle." The orientation that principle (truth) should be bent to accommodate political realities reflects the White mainstream cultural view. However, the Black cultural view (such as, to change the political realities to accommodate the truth) was the one that prevailed in this instance. Washington refused to compromise his reformist agenda by seeking an accommodation with the leader of the political opposition, Ed Vrdolyak, whom he viewed as the "incarnation of corruption." Instead, he pushed for a redistricting of the city ward map which forced new aldermanic elections that gave Washington the majority voice in the city council and enabled him for the first time since his election to put his own administrative team in office to push forward his reformist program.

It is also possible to look at the White mainstream and Black cultural styles as situationally (as well as ethnoculturally) determined. In this view, the priorities within the White mainstream cultural pattern (that sacrifices truth to accommodate political realities) are consistent with an establishment ("in-power") social orientation. Similarly, the priorities within the Black cultural pattern (that keeps the truth intact and seeks to politicize on its behalf), are consistent with a non-establishment (out-of-power) social orientation. Thus, when the Equal Rights Amendment became an issue for White middle-class women, they reversed their usual socially mainstream priorities of placing peace before truth by putting truth before peace, and also by replacing their customary discussion mode with sincere argument.

Reason and Emotion/Truth and Belief. Mainstream American culture believes that truth is objective, which is to say, external to the self; consequently, it is something to be discovered rather than possessed. This assumption has led mainstream Americans to view themselves instrumentally as objective truth seekers following the model and method of cognitive science in getting at (scientific) truth. In that instrumental view the means must be consistent with the end: one needs a rational means to produce a rational (reliable) result, one that also would be replicable from person to person insofar as individuals applied the same (rational/scientific) method to the truth-seeking process. Replicability of method would also ensure a standard or uniform mental process leading to a predictable outcome (see the discussion under "mental set" above).

The emphasis on replication and standardization of method produces a generalized focus and concern with process, also leading individuals to come to see themselves in processual terms and to regard as intrusive those aspects of self that would interfere with the instrumentalization of themselves as neutrally objective (rational) truth seekers. Emotion and belief are especially suspect: those elements of self that were part of an earlier traditional view that saw truth as subjective, as something internal, to be possessed, as in belief (and defended through argument [Ong 1982]), as opposed to something objective, external, and discoverable. This has led mainstream Americans to see emotion and belief as contaminants, that undermine their neutrally objective self/stance that defines and regulates rational (scientific) engagement and inquiry. The effort to free reason and truth from the contaminating influence of emotion and belief has led people to define reason and objective truth seeking *in terms of* the other category: not by virtue of what rationality is (a mental process characterized by a clear, accurate, and logical progression of thought), but by what it is not. So practically speaking, people now consider themselves and others "rational" to the extent that they are *not* emotional. And insofar as "rationality" is promoted at the expense of emotionality, people socialized to realize "rational" self-presentations are often, in reality, becoming socialized to realize unemotional self-presentations instead.

The above mainstream American cultural attitude and practice ultimately lead to the separation of reason and emotion. Likewise, the following line of reasoning on the relationship of objective truth seeking and belief leads to the cultural separation of truth and belief. Mainstream Americans say "no one person has a monopoly on the truth," and "the more strongly individuals believe that they do own the truth, the less likely it is to be the truth." The first of these statements asserts that individuals vary in their points of view, that the best that individuals can have is a point of view, and that any individual point of view can only be part of the truth (the more complete or "whole" truth theoretically constituting a sum of all of the different points of view that are or can be brought to bear upon the overall topic or situation). Expressed in mathematical terms a truth that contains the perspectives of individuals A and B is more complete (and therefore "better") than a truth that contains only the point of view of individual A or individual B. This view ultimately leads mainstreamers, such as news journalists, to define appropriate truth seeking as a balance of opposing viewpoints.[3]

The second statement ("the more strongly individuals believe that they do own the truth, the less likely it is to be the truth") incorporates the views expressed in the first and also says something about the nature of the self as objective truth seeker. In addition to being rational, individuals are obliged to be sufficiently open-minded to receive and reflect upon points of view other than their own. Implicit in this view is the implication that to the extent that individuals believe that their point of view is *the* truth, they will be less likely to be so receptive or considerate. So strongly held beliefs in themselves have also come to be seen as polarizing and defeating of the kind of interactional cooperation individuals need to realize for the objective truth-seeking process to work. This is in spite of the fact that it may be other attributes—those that

---

[3] The positions are assumed a priori to have an equal claim on the truth regardless of the respective merits of the position. The moral goal is to realize a fair and equitable process rather than to proselytize on behalf of one or another particular position.

accompany the assertion of owned truths (beliefs/convictions)—that more directly account for such "closed-minded" resistance, not the fact of having strong convictions, per se, or expressing them in a certain (as opposed to tentative) manner. Nonetheless, the public presumption that strongly held views disable the objective truth-seeking process has led individuals to view positively those who do not hold or express strong views whether those individuals are actually engaged in objective truth seeking or not—their stance evokes the "open-minded" attitude of the objective ("scientific") truth seeker. So personnel forms test for mental "rigidity" or its converse, "flexibility," by asking recommenders to rate individuals on whether they are "respectful and accepting of others," insofar as they adapt their thinking "to allow for other persons' points of view." Individuals who are less able to adapt their thinking to allow for other points of view are presumably rated as *less* respectful of others. [4]

Some Functions of Neutrality

The equation of the absence of emotion/strong convictions with the neutrality necessary for "rational deliberation" within the framework of objective truth seeking has served to legitimize and promote neutrality (often characterized as impersonal involvement or detachment) as a *general* mainstream cultural style, which is to say, as the preferred manner of public self-presentation even when individuals are not engaged in the process of objective truth seeking. Neutrality that was conceived and employed as a means to an end has thus been taken out of context to become instead a socially authorized end product of mainstream American acculturation. And as such it takes on a new social character and works to serve mainstream American social and political interests in other ways.

For example, neutrality as a generalized public posture easily translates into indifference, thereby enabling mainstream Americans to serve goals and interests that they might be less able or willing to serve were they socialized into another kind of public cultural style, as for example, the more contentious (agonistic) style that defines the Black (or for that matter Jewish) public presentation of self and engagement of others in truth seeking and other forms of social discourse (Kochman 1981; Schiffrin 1984; see also Ong 1982 for a discussion of the agonistic style of learning in "oral" cultures).

Neutrality also does not compel ownership of a point of view. And that allows for the production of *representatives* (as opposed to *advocates*) and

---

[4]   Note that being "objective" is equated here with being open to other people's viewpoints *regardless of how those other viewpoints were arrived at.* The effect of only one individual being "open-minded" and/or "neutrally objective" does not necessarily promote *objective* truth. It may simply weaken the self by allowing for a unilateral *adaptation to another person's* "closed-minded," non-negotiable assertions.

generates the characteristic impersonal public participation style of mainstream Americans. I call it involvement without commitment (that is, conviction). Thus individuals can engage in "discussion" without having a point of view or predisposition to an outcome, but not in sincere "argument."

The process of developing spokespersons rather than advocates—those whose role and function is to represent other people's views rather than their own—begins early in school. Students, by and large, are essentially given "credit" for representing the "authoritative" points of views of others, as on exams and papers, but not for cultivating or developing their own view of things, even when such an explicit formulation might be very helpful and relevant to what they ultimately do for a living (such as a "philosophy of education" for a teacher).

Later on, when individuals are asked to become "team" players in organizations, they are also asked to represent the authorized "official" point of view. To the extent that they have strong personal convictions, they are likely to be less able or willing to represent points of view with which they do not agree, and especially those with which they personally disagree.

The socialization into a neutral (representational!) style may also facilitate disaffiliation with one's original roots/loyalties, thereby setting the stage for subsequent reaffiliation to mainstream organizational norms and values ("One needs to move out [in order] to move up"). Ultimately, it helps to promote an identity in terms of what an individual does (one that commits being to doing) as opposed to one that commits doing to being.

In generating indifference, neutrality also facilitates a greater acceptance of authority (Barnhard [1938] 1954). It allows individuals to sacrifice truth in the interests of truce (peace) and regard "compromise" as the morally sanctioned "solution" to ideological or political conflict (the mainstream American notion of "compromise" requires that individuals accept as the new truth that which is defined within the framework of the new political reality[5])

---

5 Compare Cooper's review and summary of Caplan and Caplan's *Arab and Jew in Jerusalem* (1980, 114):

> One difference is in the concept of compromise. The Arabic term nearest to the English word "compromise" is *Teswiyeh*, which to Jerusalem Arabs means suspending rather than ending an active dispute. "The meaning of Teswiyah seems to be based upon an ethical imperative to continue fighting forever for what is right, although it might be expedient to interrupt the struggle or to hide it for a time because it interferes unduly with practical aspects of life." (quoting Caplan and Caplan, p.114). Western negotiators, in contrast, view a compromise as involving each side's giving up a little of what it regards as a just claim and finding a middle ground which each side can agree is relatively just. They admit that each side's notion of what is right may not be absolute. Thus the settlement implies that each party has modified its original demands *as well as the principle on which it is based* [italics added].

and to rationalize the accommodation to established political interests as simply being "realistic" (Kochman 1971).

Blacks do not separate reason and emotion or truth and belief. The goal of Black presentations is not "rationality," per se, if by "rationality" one means exclusively a linear processing and presentation of information, but "consciousness," which simultaneously attends to what is going on inside one's gut as well as one's head: a mind/body fusion instead of a mind/body dichotomy. Similarly, truth is not separated from belief, but rather, expressed in terms of belief, and processed (in truth seeking) through the crucible of argument.

Evaluations of Behavioral Meanings

The separation of reason and emotion and truth and belief by Whites when they engage in disagreements and disputes produces the more detached and impersonal style of self-presentation characteristic of discussion, which, in conjunction with the avoidance of direct confrontation, Blacks personally characterize as "insincere," and generally consider to be dysfunctional of the truth-creating process. The Black characterization of Whites as "insincere" refers both to their impersonal self-presentation style when engaging in disagreement ("It seems as though Whites do not believe what they are saying themselves"), as well as White unwillingness to engage in direct confrontation, or any kind of dialogue at all, as when things begin to get emotionally charged.

Blacks also have characterized the White discussion style as "devious," perhaps a more severe indictment even than "insincere." This characterization stems from Whites frequently not owning the position they are representing, nor seeing such ownership as a requirement when engaging in disagreement or debate. The basis for the White style and attitude has its roots in the mainstream culture that (as discussed above) gives credit for "authoritative" views, not the individual's own view (often discredited as simply "opinion"). Such "authoritative views" have become established within White mainstream culture as making one's self-presentations more persuasive. From the Black standpoint, however, only those views that an individual takes ownership of are admissible when engaging in disagreement or debate. This is because Blacks believe that all points have to be processed through the crucible of argument, even those of established "authority." Whites often see such authoritative views as above challenge (at least by non-experts). Moreover, in not accepting them as their own, they also do not accept responsibility for the validity of the view that they are representing and whose contents they are being challenged on. (White student: "It wasn't me that said it." Black student: "But you introduced it.") Blacks see the White behavior here as "cheating," as attempting to get credit for a particular view without allowing such a view to be processed through the crucible of argument. Thus, when White students would say, "Well, Marshall McLuhan said . . .," Black students would interrupt, "Wait a minute! Marshall McLuhan's not here. If he were here I'd be arguing with him. Are you willing to accept the view that you are representing as your own [to allow it to be processed through argument]?" The White student is then caught up short, saying, "I haven't thought enough about it to have a personal position on it." Blacks tend to view such comments with great suspicion.

In some instances, Blacks do not believe that Whites do not have a position on what they are (re)presenting, but rather, believe that Whites are trying to avoid the anticipated challenge to the position by claiming not to own the position that they, in fact, do have. And *that*, Blacks would allege, is "cowardly" and "devious."

Finally, the Black characterization of the non-confronting, impersonal, representational, "peace" (process)-oriented White presentation style here as "devious" derives from its similarity to the pattern of self-presentation that Blacks adopt when they are "lying," as one Black woman put it. The White style for Blacks is the opposite of the "for real" style (which for Blacks is confronting, personal, advocating, and truth (issue)-oriented). Thus, the White "discussion" style here is the one that Blacks adopt when "they do not care enough about the person or issue to want to waste the energy on it" or, when "it is too dangerous to say what they truly feel and believe." This often occurs for Blacks in those situations where they cannot be "for real" and have to "front" (that is, hide their true feelings and opinions).

Whites characterize the Black style as "argumentative." This characterization stems from the personal approach that Blacks use when engaging in argument. Blacks do not just debate the idea, as Whites do. They debate the person debating the idea. Thus, in such a context, your idea is only as good as your personal ability to argue it.[6]

The White view of Black style as "argumentative" also stems from the Black view that insists that Whites own and defend the position that they may only be representing, which Whites may be unwilling or unable to do, for reasons given above.

More seriously, Whites also characterize the Black argumentative style as "threatening," as when meetings get emotionally charged. This view has its origin in differences in White and Black cultural views of "self-control" as well as what constitutes "threatening" behavior.

Briefly, emotional *self-control* in White mainstream culture is characterized and practiced as self-restraint: containing or reining in

---

6 This also means that it would be inappropriate for others to jump in to support the person who, because of personal inadequacy, cannot marshall enough support for their own position themselves. Such attempts are rebuffed, usually by the person who is winning the argument, by "Wait a minute. I am arguing with *him* [that person being the one who has been temporarily caught shorthanded in coming back with a reply]. When I'm through arguing with *him*, I'll argue with *you*."

emotional impulses. Consequently, when emotions are "out" they are perceived by Whites (as they function for Whites) as "out of control." For Blacks, self-control is characterized and practiced as control over emotions, not only at the level of containment, but also at the level of emotionally intense self-expression. The Black cultural concept for controlling one's emotions is "being 'cool'." And the caveat "to be cool" is often invoked in situations that are "hot" (Abrahams 1976, 84–85). But "being cool" in such situations does not mean realizing a state of emotional self-denial or restrained emotional expression, but rather being in control of one's emotional heat and intensity (whether laughter, joy, or anger). So in Black culture it is possible for individuals to be "hot" and "cool" at the same time (instigating performers who try to heat up the scene while "proclaiming [their] own cool," Abrahams, 84). So what constitutes a state of "out of control" for Whites constitutes an "in-control" state for Blacks.

The White view of Black emotional behavior as "threatening" also stems from Blacks and Whites having different conceptions of what constitutes a "threat," which is linked in turn to different cultural conceptions about when a "fight" begins. For Whites a "fight" begins when emotional confrontation gets intense (as when opponents raise angry voices, get insulting, and utter threats). For Blacks a "fight" begins, when, in the context of such an angry confrontation, *someone makes a provocative move*. Were neither of the opponents to "make [such] a move," notwithstanding the loud, angry, confrontive, insulting, intimidating talk, from the Black standpoint, they are still only "talking" (See Kochman 1981, 43ff. for a complete discussion). A "threat" for Whites then, begins when a person *says* they are going to do something. A "threat" for Blacks begins when a person actually *makes a move* to do something. Verbal threats, from the Black standpoint, are still "only talk."

III. RATER COGNITIVE CONTRUCTS AND PERFORMANCE ASSESSMENTS

The identification of the different Black and White protocols for managing disagreements and disputes and styles of self-presentation at work and at play has obvious relevance for Black and White social relations. But it also has special application for the present work of the National Commission on Testing and Public Policy. For one, work and play contexts often provide the behavioral "data" from which various official assessments of individual performance are made, whether informally, by supervisors in the workplace, teachers in the classroom, or more formally, by interviewers in interview or counseling type situations (Erickson and Shultz, 1982).

Secondly, the different Black and White cultural perspectives (in the form of theoretical assumptions, patterns of expectation, and value-orientations) underlie and shape the cognitive contructs that Black and White raters, respectively, are likely to bring with them when assessing worker performance. This brings up the fundamental question of the nature and extent of cultural or other influences on these performance evaluations and the larger question of the objectivity or impartiality of rater assessments, generally.

On this last point, one does not have to go far in the literature to find studies that have shown the existence of researcher, reporter, or referee bias despite authorial claims (often implied) that the work is impartial or objective. For example, Greenwald's study (1975) showed general research prejudice against the acceptance of studies for which the null hypothesis is true. In the area of rater assessments, Landy and Farr (1980, 97) cite work which finds that "performance ratings may represent specific instances of implicit personality theories of raters—assumed values on performance dimensions that are independent of actual behavior of the ratee on those dimensions." In her analysis of theories of individual psychological growth and development that were considered to be sexually neutral in their scientific objectivity, Gilligan (1982, 6) has found a "consistent observational and evaluative bias." And while no concept would seem so basic to the idea of science as the "disinterested observer," which would imply that scientists adopt a neutral or uncommitted attitude towards their hypotheses, Mitroff (1976, 53) found that it seemed virtually impossible for the scientists he interviewed to discuss the status of a physical theory and evidence for and against that theory in purely impersonal or so-called "objective" terms (that is, without reference to proponents of one or the other theory). Furthermore, not only did they reject the notion of the "disinterested scientist," as an accurate *descriptive* account of the workings of science, they also rejected it as a desired *prescriptive* ideal or standard.

> Not only was it recognized that in point of actual conduct the good scientist was often highly committed to a point of view—at the very least to his pet theories and hypotheses—but, even more interesting and important, strong reasons were evinced why this situation *ought* to be the case, that *ideally* scientists *ought not* to be without strong prior commitments.

And it is undoubtedly this commitment to a point of view that makes scientists subject to what Erickson calls "Naroll's law," (1976, 143), which stipulates that "the training and temperament of any social scientist is such that he will invariably overlook a variable that confounds his data. This lurking variable will always be identified by some other researcher."

Of course, the existence of problems in the realization of objectivity does not necessarily require that we abandon it as a worthwhile goal, either in scientific inquiry or in performance evaluations. But it may be necessary to be less sanguine about obtaining it, and more skeptical towards authors who claim to have achieved it. It may even be useful to consider alternative strategies to realizing fairness in performance evaluations than through individual bias-free rater assessments.

For example, objectivity or impartiality in performance evaluation would seem to be realized to the extent that raters are successful in factoring personal biases out. But this last accomplishment itself would seem to depend upon raters' awareness of those subjective factors that are likely to have an impact upon their performance assessments and their ability to control for them, either by actually becoming free of their influence or, alternatively, being able to assess the extent of their influence on the performance judgments that they make.

But how conscious are raters of those subjective factors that are likely to affect their perception or evaluation of performance behavior? More to the point, what factors are likely to preclude that awareness and need to be overcome for that awareness to come about? Likewise, once that awareness is there, what kinds of things do raters need to know or do, or be able to do, to control for their effect on the assessment process. It is these last questions that I will deal with briefly here.

First, I start with the premise that raters are not aware of the range and substance of those subjective factors that guide their performance evaluations, such as, among others, those that inform their particular cultural orientation or ethnic style. On the one hand, this may be due in part to raters' assumption that the standards for judging performance are the same for everyone, which would cause them to overlook the role of culture in shaping the cognitive contructs that raters bring with them when assessing performance generally, and specifically, the role that their own culture plays in shaping the character of their own distinctive cultural perspective.

Moreover, even if raters were generally to become aware that their culture does play a role here they would be hard-pressed to discover the exact nature of that influence. This is because cultural learning itself becomes internalized at the level of the subconscious, giving it an essentially implicit character. Thus, to become consciously aware of the distinctive character of their own cultural orientation it would become necessary for raters to make explicit what has essentially become implicit. But this is difficult for members of any culture to do insofar as they have only their own (insider) cultural categories to work with. For example, some aspects of one's culture are too close to be clearly distinguishable. Other patterns are too taken-for-granted even to be noticed. Both of these notions are captured in the anthropological maxim: "One cannot see one's own culture for wearing it," and in the saying: "Fish would be the last to discover water." Other times it becomes a matter of getting the right angle: like trying to obtain an outside-in perspective from looking inside-out, as when one is obliged to use the window one is looking through to discover how one looks through that same window, or trying to see one's profile with only one mirror.

Compounding matters still further is the way individuals habitually view behavior, generally, which is not to respond to behavior, per se, but to *what that behavior means*. And the meaning that individuals regularly assign to such behavior is the meaning coming from their own culture (again, essentially having only their own culture to draw upon). Thus, cross-cultural conflicts between Blacks and Whites arise not only because the meanings that they respectively attribute to the same behavior are different, but also because they narrowly view behavior in terms of the meanings and categories of just their own culture.

The solution to all of the above problems is for observers and raters to have other cultural perspectives than just their own to draw upon. This would enable them to identify the distinctive parameters and character of their own culture—the distinctiveness of one's own culture really becomes apparent only when seen through the perspective provided by some other culture—thereby also increasing their awareness of the role that culture plays in the assessment process.

Insofar as raters do not become aware of their own cultural orientation or bias, they become subject to the influences of ethnocentrism. This can take the form, as discussed above, of raters viewing behavior exclusively in terms of the meanings of their own culture. Or it might take the form of people simply gravitating towards those individuals whose culture or social orientation most closely resembles their own. These two forms of ethnocentrism are among the most problematic for raters who would like to claim objectivity for their ratings, because they tend to enter into performance assessments outside rater awareness, thereby allowing raters to believe that they are being impartial or objective in their performance assessments when they are not.

A nice illustration of this last pattern can be seen in the work of Erickson (1976) and Erickson and Schultz (1982). They showed that counselor/student "co-membership," or patterns of rhythmic synchrony or asynchrony, arising from, respectively, similar or different ethnic backgrounds, produced different amounts of special help offered to students (as in the form of bending or breaking of organizational rules, or extra assistance involving counselor time after working hours). The greater amount of assistance was offered to those students of the same general ethnic background as the counselor or with whom the counselor experienced co-membership.

Insofar as official rater assessments constitute the basis of, and often, the justification for, the promotion of unequal social treatments and entitlements, it becomes important, even critical, to ensure that performance assessments are equitable, reasonable, and fair. This means, at one level, establishing the fairness of rater performance assessments: in effect, by rating the performance assessment of raters making performance assessments. In this regard I have indicated above the basis for my own misgivings about the extent to which raters can claim to have taken their personal biases into account when making performance assessments.

And what does "having taken one's personal biases into account" mean? Is it raters simply becoming aware of the range of subjective factors that are likely to influence their performance assessments? That would certainly seem to be a necessary prerequisite. But is it sufficient for the realization of objectivity? Once awareness is created, is it not also necessary to consider how that awareness might have to be processed to promote or ensure a bias-free assessment? But how does one rid oneself of a prejudice? Is that even possible? And if it is not, then how does one safeguard against its potentially contaminating effect on the realization of fairness in performance assessments?

Maybe there is the need to acknowledge the difficulty, even improbability, of raters becoming entirely free from personal bias. Maybe the only reasonable expectation is to recognize that while objectivity is still something to strive for, all that individuals might really be capable of achieving is honesty about 1) the range of subjective factors that are likely to have a bearing on the assessment process and, 2) the depth of their commitment to a particular point of view, and from that, 3) a sense of their individual limitations in either factoring their personal biases out, or in their ability to properly assess their influence on the performance assessments that they make.

Whether the goal is objectivity or honesty about the nature and extent of personal bias, one thing that is clear is that raters will have to engage in the process of factoring their personal biases in—identifying them so as to become aware of their real or potential contaminating presence—before they can begin to factor them out, and/or claim that they have taken their personal biases into account.

But how then does one hope to realize a fair and equitable assessment process if rater objectivity can no longer be presumed. Or perhaps the real question should be how can an assessment process function fairly and equitably when raters are simply required to become honest about the nature and extent of their personal bias, rather than to become bias-free? [7]

In that case, it would become necessary to take steps to ensure that rater prejudices do not translate into discriminatory judgments. I envision that this would require that raters not only work hard to explore and disclose the nature

---

[7] I would argue, at any rate, that honesty about the nature and extent of one's personal biases would make an individual closer to actually becoming objective, insofar as it would add a measure of control to the assessment process that does not seem to exist at the present time. Now indivuduals seem to be able to claim that they are being "objective" a priori, that is, without having had to engage in any process of self-examination to justify reaching that determination.

and extent of their personal biases, but also become able to assess their probable impact on the performance judgments that they make. And to help raters realize these objectives, I would require that they obtain information about the different ways that members of other cultures might view the same behavior.

In fact, achieving equity and fairness in performance assessments may be better served by a presumption that raters have not been successful in freeing themselves from personal bias. For then, greater efforts might be taken to ensure that the assessment process is fair than are now taken under the perhaps gratuitous assumption that performance judgments by raters are indeed objective and impartial.

I do not know what that new assessment process would ultimately look like. Perhaps a performance assessment can only be considered fair if there is an agreement between rater and ratee on the standards by which the ratee is to be judged. Or, perhaps the process should consist of raters from different social and cultural backgrounds—but including that of the ratee—coming together to identify what they can agree upon with regard to a particular performance: both the performance itself and the standard by which the performance should be judged, with procedures set up to work out some settlement of those differences that remain. Perhaps some assessments would simply reflect a balance of differing viewpoints. It is obviously too early to tell whether such a process would be more fair and equitable than the one in place at the present time. Undoubtedly, there will be new problems to solve, for every new solution generates a whole new set of problems. The ultimate test to determine whether the new process is better then the old one will be whether the problems generated by the new solution are fewer than the problems generated by the old solution. Is the realization of honesty with regard to personal bias easier for raters to achieve than objectivity? Insofar as honesty might be considered a prerequisite to the realization of objectivity, anyway, nothing is really lost by trying.

REFERENCES

Aarons, Alfred A., Barbara Y. Gordon, and William A. Stewart, eds. 1969. Linguistic-Cultural differences and American education. *Florida FL Reporter* 7(1).

Abrahams, Roger D. 1970. *Positively Black*. Englewood Cliffs, N.J.: Prentice-Hall.

———. 1976. *Talking back*. Rowley, MA: Newbury.

Atkin, Ross. 1979. "Hollywood Henderson" at Super Bowl. *Christian Science Monitor*, 18 January, 16.

Barnhard, Chester I. [1938]. 1954. *The functions of the executive*. Cambridge: Harvard University Press.

Castile, George P. 1975. An unethical ethic: Self-Determination and the anthropological conscience. *Human Organization* 34 (1): 35–40.

Cazden, Courtney B., Vera P. John, and Dell Hymes, eds. 1972. *Functions of language in the classroom*. New York: Teachers College Press.

Cooper, Robert L. 1980. Review of *Arab and Jew in Jerusalem: Explorations in community mental health* by Gerald Caplan and Ruth B. Caplan. Cambridge, MA: Harvard University Press. *Language in Society* 15 (1): 111–15.

Elderkin, Phil. 1979. The serious side of a supershowman. *Christian Science Monitor*, 4 April, 17.

———. 1981. Red Holzman—the Marco Polo of pro basketball. *Christian Science Monitor*, 5 March, 16.

Erickson, Frederick. 1976. Gatekeeping encounters: A social selection process. In *Anthropology and the public interest*, ed. Peggy Sanday. New York: Academic Press.

———. 1979. Talking down: Some cultural sources of miscommunication in interracial interviews. In *Non-Verbal communication*, ed. A. Wolfgang. New York: Academic Press.

Erickson, Frederick, and Jeffrey Shultz. 1982. *The counselor as gatekeeper*. New York: Academic Press.

Fisher, A. D. 1969. White rites versus Indian rights. *Transaction* 7 (1): 29–33.

Gilligan, Carol. 1982. *In a different voice*. Cambridge: Harvard University Press.

Greenwald, Anthony G. 1975. Consequences of prejudice against the null hypothesis. *Psychological Bulletin* 82 (1): 1–20.

Hakuta, Kenji. 1986. *The mirror of language: The debate on bilingualism*. New York: Basic Books.

Harris, Sydney J. 1983. We tarnish Golden Rule by inflicting cultural bias. *Chicago Sun-Times*, 20 June.

Harrison, Paul C. 1972. *The drama of nommo*. New York: Grove.

Hill, Herbert. 1973. Anti-Oriental agitation and the rise of working-class racism. *Society* 10 (2): 43–54.

Holt, Grace Sims. 1972. Communication in black culture: The other side of silence. *Language Research Reports* 6:51–84.

Houston, Susan. 1973. Black English. *Psychology Today,* March, 45–48.

Keil, Charles. 1972. Motion and feeling in music. In *Rappin' and stylin' out,* ed. Thomas Kochman. Urbana: University of Illinois Press.

Kochman, Thomas. Crosscultural communication: Contrasting perspectives, conflicting sensibilities. *Florida FL Reporter* 9:53–54.

———. 1981. *Black and White styles in conflict.* Chicago: University of Chicago Press.

———. 1984. The politics of politeness. In *Meaning, form and use in context: Linguistic applications,* ed. Deborah Schiffrin. Georgetown University Roundtable on Languages and Linguistics. 1984. Washington, DC: Georgetown University Press.

Koogler, Carol C. 1980. Behavioral style differences and crisis in an integrated kindergarten classroom." *Contemporary Education* 51 (3): 126–30.

Landy, Frank J. and James L. Farr. 1980. Performance rating. *Psychological Bulletin* 87 (1): 72–107.

Lebra, Takie S. 1976. *Japanese patterns of behavior.* Honolulu: The University of Hawaii Press.

Levinsohn, Florence H. 1986. Still the oboist. *Reader [Chicago's Free Weekly]* 16: (3).

Lewis, Diane K. 1975. The Black family: Socialization and sex roles. *Phylon* 36 (3): 221–37.

Milhomme, Janet. 1986. Brakedancing in Accra. *LA Extra,* 16–22 May, x–37.

Mitroff, Ian I. 1976. Passionate scientists. *Society* 13 (6): 51–57.

Ong, Walter J., S.J. 1982. *Orality and literacy: The technologizing of the word.* New York: Methuen.

Reisman, Karl. 1974. Noise and order. In *Language in its social setting,* ed. William W. Gage. Washington, DC: Anthropological Society of Washington.

Reynolds, David K. 1980. *The quiet therapies: Japanese pathways to personal growth.* Honolulu: The University of Hawaii Press.

Roosevelt, Teddy. (1919). 1968. In *El Grito: A journal of Mexican American Thought.* "Editorial: Keep up the fight for Americanism." Berkeley, CA: Quinto Sol Publications. Vol. 1 (2): 5.

Sahlins, Marshall P., and Elman R. Service. 1960. *Evolution and culture.* Ann Arbor: University of Michigan Press.

Schiffrin, Deborah. 1984. Jewish argument as sociability. *Language in Society.* 13 (3): 311–35.

Sithole, Elkin T. 1972. Black folk music. In *Rappin' and stylin' out,* ed. Thomas Kochman. Urbana: University of Illinois Press.

Weisz, John R., Fred M. Rothbaum, and Thomas C. Blackburn. 1984. "Standing out and standing in: The psychology of control in America and Japan." *American Psychologist* 39 (9): 955–69.

Young, Virginia H. 1970. Family and childhood in a southern Negro community. *American Anthropologist* 72:269–88.

Zintz, Miles V. 1963. *Education across cultures.* Des Moines: Wm. C. Brown.

Index